ECONOMIC HISTORY

THE SCOTTISH BANKS

FINANCE, MONEY AND BANKING

THE SCOTTISH BANKS

A modern survey

MAXWELL GASKIN

Routledge
Taylor & Francis Group

LONDON AND NEW YORK

First published in 1965

Reprinted in 2006 by
Routledge
2 Park Square, Milton Park, Abingdon, Oxon, OX14 4RN

Routledge is an imprint of Taylor & Francis Group

Transferred to Digital Print 2010

© 1965 Routledge

British Library Cataloguing in Publication Data
A CIP catalogue record for this book
is available from the British Library

The Scottish Banks
ISBN 0-415-37851-6 (volume)
ISBN 0-415-37850-8 (subset)
ISBN 0-415-28619-0 (set)

Routledge Library Editions: Economic History

UNIVERSITY OF GLASGOW SOCIAL AND
ECONOMIC STUDIES

General Editor: Professor D. J. Robertson

6

THE SCOTTISH BANKS

UNIVERSITY OF GLASGOW SOCIAL
AND ECONOMIC STUDIES

Old Series

published by Cambridge University Press
General Editor: Professor A. K. Cairncross, C.M.G.

1. The Crofting Problem. ADAM COLLIER
2. The Scottish Economy. Edited by A. K. CAIRNCROSS
3. Adam Smith and the Scotland of his Day. C. R. FAY
4. John Millar of Glasgow. WM. C. LEHMANN
5. Factory Wage Structures and National Agreements.
   D. J. ROBERTSON
6. Economics of Shipbuilding in the United Kingdom.
   J. R. PARKINSON
7. Glasgow Limited: Industrial War and Peace.
   T. T. PATERSON

New Series

published by George Allen & Unwin Ltd
General Editor: Professor D. J. Robertson

1. The Economics of Subsidizing Agriculture.
   GAVIN MCCRONE
2. The Economics of Physiocracy. RONALD L. MEEK
3. Studies in Profit, Business Saving and Investment in
   the United Kingdom, 1920-62. Vol. 1. P. E. HART
4. Scotland's Economic Progress. GAVIN MCCRONE
5. Fringe Benefits, Labour Costs and Social Security.
   Edited by G. L. REID & D. J. ROBERTSON

THE SCOTTISH BANKS

A Modern Survey

BY

MAXWELL GASKIN

Senior Lecturer in Economics
University of Glasgow

London
GEORGE ALLEN & UNWIN LTD
RUSKIN HOUSE · MUSEUM STREET

PREFACE

This book had its origins thirteen years ago in my appointment to teach monetary economics and banking in the economics department of a Scottish university. At that time my knowledge of Scottish banking was such as an economist usually acquires in the course of a training in which British banking, past and present, is more or less equated with English banking. As I began to repair this gap in my education I became aware not only of the long and individual history of banking in Scotland but also of the persistence into the present of features which had not been fully explained. The attempt to clarify these in my own mind led to some studies of particular aspects of Scottish banking. With the publication of the Report, Memoranda, and Minutes of Evidence of the Radcliffe Committee, in 1959 and 1960, the time had clearly come for a more extended survey of modern Scottish banking. In the breadth of scrutiny which it brought to bear on the British financial scene the Committee gave much more attention to the Scottish banks than has been customary in this century; indeed one would have to go back to the great banking inquiries of the last century to find a similar degree of interest in Scottish banking. At the same time the data gathered by the Committee and presented in its Report and in the volumes of Memoranda and Evidence, as well as the vast improvement in the published statistics of Scottish banking which has stemmed directly from the Committee's work, have provided a much more adequate factual basis for examining the subject than has ever existed before.

In this book I have attempted to survey the Scottish banks as they stand in mid-1964. A study of this kind today cannot confine itself to a straight description of the institutions in their domestic setting. The Scottish banks are part of the British banking system, linked to London, and as involved as any other part of that system in British financial policy. At the same time they are major economic institutions of Scotland, deeply involved in the fortunes of the Scottish economy, with their own peculiar problems deriving from their environment and their past. I have tried in this book to give due prominence to all the possible viewpoints from which the modern reader may wish to look at Scottish banking. This study is primarily concerned with institutions but some parts of the subject require analytical treatment. For example certain effects of the Scottish note issues and the consideration of the role of the Scottish banks within credit policy require reference to the modern theory of bank credit. I have tried to keep the references to such theory, as well as other passages of an analytical character, within the bounds appropriate to a book of this nature. I have resisted as far as I could the fascinations of Scottish banking history. But banking, of all economic topics, demands the historical approach, and I have not hesitated to sketch in the historical background where it seemed necessary to a full appreciation of the modern position.

Throughout my research into Scottish banking I have been helped by a large number of people who have answered my questions or commented on my work. I have been more than fortunate in my colleagues in the University of Glasgow, to all of whom I am indebted in some measure. Among present and former colleagues there are four to whom I wish to acknowledge a special debt: Professor A. L. Macfie, Dr A. K. Cairncross, Professor T. Wilson and Professor D. J. Robertson. Both Professors Wilson and Robertson read sections of this book in draft and their comments were of great value to me.

Outside the circle of my colleagues I owe much to bankers, businessmen and journalists, within Scotland and outside it, whom I have consulted at various times on questions of banking and finance. Among them I would especially mention the many Scottish bankers whom I have approached for information: they have been invariably helpful and patient with my inquiries, and I hope that such shortcomings as they find here will not make them think that their assistance was in vain. To Mr F. S. Taylor, Secretary of the Institute of Bankers in Scotland, I am especially indebted for the help he has given me in many personal discussions and for much that I have learned from his own extensive writings on Scottish banking. In one part of this book, a section of Chapter 12, I have been greatly helped by some unpublished writings of Mr Roger Alford on the London Discount Market which he kindly let me read. I am also grateful to Mr John Sherret for access to a useful unpublished thesis by him on Scottish banking. Finally, however, let me add that the views and conclusions expressed in this book, as well as any errors that remain, are entirely my own.

Some sections of this book are based on articles which I have published in the *Scottish Journal of Political Economy* and the *Scottish Bankers' Magazine*. I am grateful to the editors of both journals for their permission to reproduce certain passages from these articles. I am greatly indebted to the Court of the University of Glasgow who have provided the financial guarantee which has made possible the publication of this volume. I wish to acknowledge the work of Miss C. S. MacSwan and her colleagues Mrs I. Finlay and Mrs T. Campbell: their secretarial assistance has made the work of drafting so much easier than it might have been. Above all I owe an immeasurable debt to my wife who has borne with me in the writing of this book and whose encouragement and support have materially helped me to finish it.

University of Glasgow   **M. G.**
August 1964

CONTENTS

CONTENTS

TABLES

CHAPTER 1

INTRODUCTION

The Scottish banks, now five in number, form a distinct regional group of banks within the British banking system. There is a considerable overlapping of ownership between the English and Scottish banks. Two of the Scottish banks, the *British Linen Bank* and the *Clydesdale Bank*, are wholly owned by English banks—by Barclays and the Midland respectively. Another English bank, Lloyds, has a very substantial minority interest in the *National Commercial Bank of Scotland*. On the other hand one Scottish bank, the *Royal Bank of Scotland*, owns the two English banks of Williams Deacons and Glyn Mills and Company. Only the *Bank of Scotland*, the oldest of the Scottish banks, is without connections of ownership with one or other of the London Clearing banks. But with or without these connections all the Scottish banks operate as distinct bodies with full powers of independent action. They are not confined to Scotland, either legally or practically. They all have offices in London which carry on an important volume of business; but elsewhere, if we ignore the English subsidiaries of the Royal Bank, their interests as joint-stock bankers are negligible. Within Scotland they have the field of joint-stock banking to themselves; there they compete with one another to about the same extent as the English banks within their domain. This regional separateness does not amount to any degree of monetary separation. The British monetary system is a completely unified one, controlled by a single authority; the Scottish banks are an integral part of the system and as subject to the forces and policies that control it as any other domestic banks. But the fact that they exist as a distinct group of banks is there and should command the interest of all who study the British money and banking system. If there were nothing more to it than a matter of banking geography it would still be of great importance to examine the operations of a group of banks which serves one-tenth of the country's population and disposes of about the same proportion of domestic

13

banking funds. But the interest goes beyond this. The Scottish banks have a long history of separate development behind them; and although in this century this development has increasingly converged with that of English banking, differences of practice and outlook remain. At some points these differences are important: for example, where they condition the relations of the Scottish banks to the mechanisms of monetary policy. But they also invest the Scottish banks with an individuality which gives them their own place within the wider family of sterling area institutions.

The present position of the Scottish banks is the result of their history.[1] We shall make use of the historical approach throughout this book, wherever it is necessary to illuminate the modern position, and some parts of the history of the Scottish banks will be looked at in more detail later. But a conspectus of the whole development of banking in Scotland, bringing into relief the broad pattern rather than individual features, is an essential introduction.

Banking in Scotland is as old as it is in England; its roots lie back in the days before the Union of the kingdoms when Scotland was a separate country. It developed strongly in the eighteenth and nineteenth centuries when banking everywhere was a regional, if not a local, business; and this long and separate history gave it traditions of its own and a marked individuality. But traditions and 'character' are as little resistant to strong economic forces in banking as in other spheres of economic life; those of the Scottish banks would not have withstood the forces which, during the last seventy years, have been making for the concentration and complete integration of the British banking system had not another important element been present. The Scottish banks have always been subject to separate laws; to a different general system of law and, more specifically, to separate laws applying to the practice of banking itself.

The effect of law on the history of Scottish banking has been profound. In particular, when the Bank of Scotland was established as the first joint-stock bank in Scotland, one year after the foundation of the Bank of England, it was given a monopoly of joint-stock banking for twenty-one years. When this term expired the monopoly was not renewed and the result was that in Scotland, unlike England where

---

[1] There is no adequate modern 'History' of Scottish banking. The standard works in the past were A. W. Kerr's *History of Banking in Scotland*, 4th Edition (London, 1926), and W. Graham's *The One-Pound Note in the History of Banking in Great Britain*, 2nd Edition (Edinburgh, 1911). There is a useful short account in W. F. Crick and J. E. Wadsworth, *A Hundred Years of Joint-Stock Banking* (London, 1936), Ch. XIII.

the Bank of England's monopoly was continued for well over a century, there was no legal barrier to the setting up of other joint-stock companies for carrying on the trade of banking. In addition, under Scots law there was, even at that time, a generally available form of legal incorporation in the 'contract of copartnery'. Thus, although over much of eighteenth-century Scotland banking was a small-scale, local affair, as in England, two other powerful joint-stock banks were established, the Royal Bank of Scotland in 1727 and the British Linen Bank in 1746, and their presence prevented the reproduction of the English pattern of one large bank dominating all the others. Later, in the first half of the nineteenth century, a new group of joint-stock banks arose to join the three ancient institutions, to supplant the remnants of private banking, and to establish branch systems. This led to an early consolidation of the Scottish banking system.

In the early phase of banking note issue was assumed to be a necessary attribute of banks. Later, in the first half of the nineteenth century, the opinion grew up that note issuing and banking were separable activities, and that note issue as such required separate regulation.[1] This trend of opinion led to the Bank Acts of 1844 and 1845 in which Sir Robert Peel erected a system of very stringent control over the issue of bank notes in Britain. Broadly the effect of Peel's Bank Acts was to provide for the eventual extinction in England and Wales of the right of note issue by any bank other than the Bank of England; in Scotland and Ireland, on the other hand, they allowed an indefinite continuance of the banks' own note issues although preventing the formation of any new note-issuing banks. This distinctive treatment was born partly of deference to the national sentiments of these countries, but mainly of recognition of the firmness with which the Scots in particular were attached to the use of small-value notes. In the 1840s powerful political forces could be fielded in Scotland against any attempt to abolish the one-pound notes while almost equally strong prejudices against them existed in England. Peel met this by dividing the currency realm and in doing so incidentally provided a legal reinforcement of the separate identity of Scottish banking. Before 1900, at a time when Scottish banks were among the giants of the British banking world and could easily have spread southwards, the separate note issues effectively kept them within Scotland since they exposed them to

[1] A fuller account of this passage in British banking history may be found in A. E. Feaveryear, *The Pound Sterling*, 2nd Edition (edited by E. V. Morgan; Oxford, 1962), Ch. X.

political attack from the less favourably treated English banks. The possession of the right of note issue remains a distinguishing mark of the Scottish banks; and while from a monetary point of view it has little significance now, it continues to affect the reserve practices and the asset structure of the banks in ways which we shall examine later.

The Scottish banks had very early to adjust themselves to the predominance of London in finance though for a time, in the eighteenth and early nineteenth centuries, Edinburgh had its moments as a local financial centre. A notable milestone in this process of adjustment was the action taken by the Bank of Scotland and the Royal Bank, in the third quarter of the eighteenth century, to stabilize the exchange between Edinburgh and London. To do this they set up what was one of the earliest examples of the now familiar stabilization reserve. Towards the end of that century they took to holding reserves of marketable securities and to regarding London as a money market on which to fall back in time of crisis. In these developments they were evolving mechanisms which the banks and monetary authorities of many countries outside the British Isles were later to adopt. Scotland, in short, was the first member of the sterling area.

These innovations in the techniques and organization of banking were far from being the only ones to emerge from Scotland. Scottish bankers originated the overdraft form of lending and with it an important type of personal security. They were the first British bankers to put emphasis on the wide gathering of deposits. Above all, they pioneered the modern system of branch banking. To the observer of one hundred years ago the most obvious difference between English and Scottish banking was that of structure: Scotland with its fourteen banks and England with four hundred seemed poles apart in banking organization. The structural difference combined with other, connected elements of Scottish banking, especially note issuing and the emphasis on deposit gathering, to form a system of banking which impressed contemporaries as very different from that of England and which, in fact, they designated 'the Scotch system of banking'.

But the intervening years between then and now have transformed this picture. The consolidation of the English banking system into a handful of banks has eliminated the contrast of structure. The extension of the cheque-using habit in Scotland, and of deposit banking in England, have muted other differences. One notable feature that, with note issuing, continues to distinguish Scottish banking is the hundred and thirty year old arrangement whereby the Scottish banks agree on a common set of interest rates and charges. The cry of 'banking monopoly' is an old one in Scotland and it has been repeated under very recent and distinguished auspices,[1] with what justification we shall try to assess in due course. But even in this area of banking practice there has been some convergence of the English and Scottish systems. Today no one would regard the 'Scotch system of banking' as a *highly* individual species of banking practice and organization. But differences remain. If in the following chapters we seem to stress the contrast with England this is not because they are more important than the similarities—the reverse in the case— but because these contrasts are frequently the more interesting where the facts about English banking are already so well known and have been so long discussed.

II. THE STATISTICS OF SCOTTISH BANKING

Banking is a field of economic inquiry which, for a longer period than most, has lent itself to statistical measurement and analysis. This has been partly because of the very nature of the banker's operations which are readily, and indeed naturally, expressed in money terms; and partly because various factors such as the pressing need to maintain the confidence of the public in themselves and, later, the requirements of public policy, combined to cause or compel the banks to publish their balance sheets from an early date. We shall be making much use of the available statistics of Scottish banking in this book and it will be as well therefore if before we close this introductory chapter we take a brief look at the major sources of these figures and notice some of their limitations.

Just over a hundred years ago—in the 1850s—some of the Scottish banks began to publish their annual balance sheets: at the time they led the way in providing the public with information about themselves. Soon all the Scottish banks were publishing annual figures, and for the final decades of the nineteenth century the Scottish

---

[1] *Report of the Committee on the Working of the Monetary System*, Cmnd. 827 (H.M.S.O., 1959), para 159. In future, and for brevity, this Report will be referred to as '*Radcliffe Report*'. Similarly the published '*Minutes of Evidence*' will be denoted as '*Radcliffe Evidence*' and the three volumes of memoranda submitted to the Committee as '*Radcliffe Memoranda*, vol. 1, 2 & 3'. We will do the same with the Report and Evidence of another committee to which we shall be making a good deal of reference. The *Report of the Committee on Finance and Industry*, Cmnd. 3897 (H.M.S.O., 1931) will be referred to as '*Macmillan Report*', and the published *Minutes of Evidence* (in 2 volumes) as '*Macmillan Evidence*'.

figures are unique for their complete coverage. The figures we obtain from these balance sheets are tremendously useful, indeed indispensable, for mapping the course of Scottish banking almost up to the present day; but they have three main defects. The first is that the balance sheets were drawn up by each bank on different dates, and this indeed is still the case. Consequently one cannot compute aggregates of the figures of all the banks which relate to a common date in the year. We can total the figures from the various balance sheets appearing in a given year; for certain periods we have to do this if we want any aggregate figures at all. But the resulting aggregates must be known for what they are: a compound of figures relating to different, arbitrarily chosen, dates.

The second defect of the balance sheet figures is that until very recently there has been no complete uniformity of practice in the definition of various items—cash, loans and advances etc.—on the balance sheets. Individual banks have changed their own definition from time to time and this affects the compilation of historical series of figures. Then thirdly, annual balances appear only once in every year: as far as conveying a picture of a bank's position it is a mere snapshot of what this was on one day out of three hundred and sixty-five. It is well-known that the amount and structure of a banker's assets and liabilities are subject to important seasonal movements which may be in full flood at a time when a given bank draws up its balance sheet. It is equally the case that all sorts of purely fortuitous influences can distort the figures of a bank on any one day—particularly a bank that is on the small side as the Scottish banks now are.

Until recently the annual balance sheets were the main source of statistical information about the Scottish banks. There were other lesser sources. Peel's Act of 1845, regulating the Scottish note issues, required the publication of a Bank Return every four weeks. This Return, which still appears, shows two things: the amount of each bank's notes in circulation (with a division into £1 notes and others) and the amount of Bank of England notes and coin held at all offices and 'on deposit' (i.e. as cover for Scottish notes in circulation) at the Bank of England.[1] In each case the figures are averages of the position on four consecutive Saturdays.

Another source of figures which can, on occasion, be useful is the half-yearly statements which all the Companies Acts from 1862 onwards have required the banks (along with certain other financial

[1] Originally—before 1914—the cash figure required was of the amount of gold and silver coin held at all offices of each bank.

18

bodies, e.g. insurance companies) to make. These are statements of assets and liabilities and they have to be posted every six months in all the offices of a bank. As sources of banking information they have their uses but they are less serviceable than appears at first sight. For one thing, the breakdown of assets which the Acts require is couched in very general terms and a good deal of variation is possible—and exists—between the banks. Then in the case of the Scottish banks there is a major defect of coverage. Until 1948 only those banks registered under Companies Acts were required to publish them and this excluded three of the Scottish banks: the Bank of Scotland, incorporated by an Act of (the Scottish) Parliament, and the Royal Bank and the British Linen Bank which operate under Royal Charters. The 1948 Companies Act applied this provision to all banks except those incorporated by Act of Parliament, so that now only the Bank of Scotland is exempt.

Until 1960 the monthly Bank Return, the bi-annual statement and the annual balance sheet were the only continuing sources of Scottish banking statistics. However, for one period of twelve years there is a series of much more useful figures which must be mentioned. A number of Scottish banks (for most of the period six out of eight) provided the Macmillan Committee with monthly analyses of assets and liabilities for the years 1919–30, and these are to be found in Appendix 1 of the Report. After the appearance of the Macmillan Report the Scottish banks continued to provide the Bank of England with these monthly figures but, unlike those of the London Clearing banks, the Scottish figures were not published.

In 1960 the Evidence and Memoranda submitted to the Radcliffe Committee were published. Volume 2 of the Memoranda contains a statistical appendix in which appear the monthly totals of the assets and liabilities of the Scottish banks for the years 1951–8. Following the publication of these figures the Scottish banks decided to publish a monthly statement of their main assets and liabilities and this series now appears in the *Bank of England Quarterly Bulletin*, and in *Financial Statistics* and other publications of the Central Statistical Office. Until October 1960 each of the Scottish banks made up its monthly statement on a different day of the month; but since then a common day—the third Wednesday—has been adopted. The Scottish banks' statement differs in one very important respect from the corresponding emission of the English banks. It shows only the aggregate figures for all five banks; we are still not given the monthly position of each bank individually. There is one other set of figures which the English banks publish regularly, but which the Scottish banks do not release: the totals of their cheques passing through the clearing house.

The last few years have thus seen an enormous improvement in the amount and type of statistical data which the Scottish banks publish. Of course, as with all banking statistics, there is a deceptive precision about these figures: when one probes into them various omissions and 'impurities' come to light. These defects must always be borne in mind and where they are of particular significance here they will be mentioned. Nevertheless the improved statistics begun in the published Memoranda of the Radcliffe Committee allow us to describe and analyse Scottish banking movements in the 1950s and 1960s much more fully, and on a much surer footing, than has been possible for any previous period of Scottish banking history.

In the following three chapters we shall look at questions of structure and organization in the Scottish banking system: at the evolution of the present group of institutions and their links with the world of English banking; at the branch structure and its problems; and at the emerging prospects of automation. Chapters 5 to 9 will survey the main groups of liabilities and assets—the sources and uses of their funds—and will examine their behaviour in recent years and the features peculiar to Scottish banking. In Chapter 10 we shall take a close look at the Scottish banks as providers of finance to the private sector of the Scottish economy, and in the following Chapter their policy and practice in the matter of interest rates and charges. Chapter 12 will examine the London link in its more technical aspects and this will prepare the way for a consideration, in Chapter 13, of how the various weapons of monetary policy impinge on the Scottish banks. Chapter 14 is a summing up of the present position and the future prospects.

CHAPTER 2

MERGERS AND OWNERSHIP

In its broad structure the contemporary Scottish banking system reproduces, on a smaller regional scale, the pattern of English banking. It is a highly concentrated system composed of a small number of banks operating through countrywide networks of branch offices. The pattern of concentration, now carried to such an extreme in the case of England and Wales, is actually much older in Scotland. The following table gives a view of its evolution in the two systems:

TABLE I

Number of Banks in Scotland and England and Wales, 1844–1960

YEAR	SCOTLAND	ENGLAND AND WALES
1844	19	441
1900	9	106
1960	5	10[1]

[1] This is the number of the London Clearing banks minus the National Bank which operates mainly in Ireland.

As lately as the beginning of the present century the English banking system still presented a picture of localized banking, though the process of concentration was by then moving on very rapidly. At that time some of the Scottish banks ranked among the largest institutions of the British banking world and this had hitherto almost always been the case. Scotland had had its phases of local banking. Many small local banks were set up in the late eighteenth and early nineteenth centuries; but the foundations of the branch system of banking were even then being laid by the Bank of Scotland and the British Linen Bank. Moreover, among the new formations of the first quarter of the nineteenth century were the Commercial Bank of Scotland (1810) and the National Bank of Scotland (1824), which, though established in Edinburgh, were planned from the outset to operate throughout the country. They were joined by others like the Aberdeen Town and County Bank (1825), the Caledonian Bank

21

(Inverness, 1832) and the Clydesdale Bank (Glasgow, 1838), banks which, though distinctly regional in their interests, aimed to operate over wide areas like the North-East or the West of Scotland. During this phase of Scottish banking history most of the smaller, local banks were absorbed by their larger brethren to give, by the third quarter of the century, a relatively concentrated structure of large banks several of which were national, and the rest regional, in scope.

The consolidation of the Scottish banking system was probably helped by the provision of Peel's Bank Acts which restricted the right of note issue to the existing banks. At any rate no new banks successfully established themselves after 1845, and a process of amalgamation, aided by the disastrous failures of the Western Bank in 1857 and the City of Glasgow Bank in 1878, caused the number of separate banks to fall. As the number fell the pace of mergers became slower, and after the absorption of the Caledonian Bank by the Bank of Scotland in 1907 there was a long pause until 1950 when a new phase of concentration opened. In the 1950s three amalgamations, that of the Clydesdale and North of Scotland Banks in 1950, of the Bank of Scotland and the Union Bank in 1954, and of the Commercial and National Banks in 1959, have brought the number of banks down to the present five. These five banks, with some of their leading statistics, are as follows:

TABLE II

The Scottish Banks at the end of 1963[1]

	TOTAL RESOURCES[2] £ mns.	DEPOSITS £ mns.	OFFICES[3]
Bank of Scotland (28/2/64)	247·3	204·9	439
The Royal Bank of Scotland (31/12/63)	184·0	143·2	246
The British Linen Bank (30/9/63)	118·4	98·5	208
National Commercial Bank of Scotland Ltd (26/10/63)	300·4	243·6	462
Clydesdale Bank Ltd (31/12/63)	241·2	208·1	355

[1] The totals of deposits and the numbers of offices relate to the banks themselves exclusive of all subsidiaries and affiliates.

[2] In each case this comprises total assets net of customers' obligations under acceptances and engagements.

[3] All branches, including those outside Scotland.

I. THE RECENT MERGERS

The motives behind the three recent unions between Scottish banks may probably be traced on the one hand to the general advantages of large-scale banking, and on the other to circumstances peculiar to Scottish banking. There is scope for economies of scale in banking particularly at the higher levels of management. General managers and their deputies, secretaries and treasurers and, in the case of the Scottish banks, London managers, do not have to increase in number when the banks increase in size, and the same is true of some kinds of specialist staff. Another factor which in the end may have important consequences for the scale of operation is the automation of accounting work and record-keeping. At present the automative systems with which the banks are experimenting involve the centralization of the accounts and records of groups of branch offices, and, although in two cases this now covers a quarter of their total branches, the overall size of the branch networks is not yet important. But as the machines get larger and faster the time may well come when there will be a premium on being able to feed them with as large a volume of work as possible, and this may provide an incentive to further mergers.

One of the traditional motives for bank amalgamations, the desire for a wider and more diverse spread of lending business, played a part in one of the mergers. The union of the Clydesdale and North Banks (both wholly-owned subsidiaries of the Midland Bank) in January 1950 brought together what were really the last remaining regional banks. The Clydesdale Bank had actually spread out quite widely from its original territory in the West of Scotland, but it still had a marked bias towards that region. The North of Scotland Bank with its headquarters in Aberdeen was very heavily localized in the north and north-east, and brought to the union particularly strong connections with agriculture and the fishing industry. In the case of all three mergers there was a desire for the wider spread among individual customers which a larger total of resources permits. In these days of giant firms a small bank finds itself at an increasing disadvantage in dealing with its larger customers in that their borrowing needs are very large in relation to the bank's total lending. The short-term borrowings of the biggest Scottish firms would consume a very substantial proportion of the total advances of a single Scottish bank, and though in cases like these the element of risk is negligible no bank likes to be so heavily committed in its lending to one customer, or even a small group of customers. The mergers of recent years have gone some way, though not very far, to mitigate this disadvantage of the small scale of the Scottish banks.

Finally, there is one feature of the Scottish banking system, peculiar to it, which furnishes an incentive to the fusion of banks into larger units. This is the over-extension of the branch networks. Due to over-enthusiastic policies of branch opening in the past, there is today some duplication of branch offices. The greater concentration of the banking system through mergers gives scope for the unification of branches, and so leads to reductions in cost. The recent mergers have already produced some seventy closures of branches, but we shall look into this in detail in the next chapter.

The question that now hangs over the Scottish banking scene is whether or not the process of amalgamation will go any further. At present one bank, the British Linen Bank, is markedly smaller in resources than the other four; these, if we disregard the English subsidiaries of the Royal Bank of Scotland, are of roughly the same order of size. It used to be thought that the English ownership of some of the Scottish banks would ultimately interfere with the process of concentration; if this were true the candidature of the British Linen for the next amalgamation would be ruled out, owned as it is by Barclays. However the union, in 1958, of the 'independent' (i.e. unaffiliated) Commercial Bank of Scotland with the National Bank of Scotland, which was owned by Lloyds, has demonstrated that English ownership need not necessarily obstruct further amalgamations. On the pattern of the National Commercial it might appear that the easiest merger would be between the British Linen and the one remaining Scottish bank which has no affiliations with, or interests in, English banking, the Bank of Scotland. But there are precedents for the joint participation of the large English banks in the ownership of other, non-English banks, so that a union between the British Linen and, say, the Clydesdale is not necessarily ruled out.

II. OWNERSHIP AND THE SCOTTISH BANKS

Today two of the five Scottish banks are wholly-owned affiliates of English banks, while a sizeable fraction of the share capital of a third is also in English banking hands. On the other hand one Scottish bank owns two English banks. How did this pattern of interlocking ownership come about and why did it take this particular form?

During the nineteenth century the Scottish and English banking systems remained structurally separate from one another. English bankers of the second half of the century regarded the right of note issue, preserved to the Scottish banks by the Act of Sir Robert Peel, as a barrier to any attempt on their part to extend their activities into Scotland. But this was hardly the effective reason why there was no attempt by English banks to extend northwards. The fact is that until the closing years of the century the Scottish system was composed of banks which were big, some of them very big, by English standards. The consolidation of the English system, which began so much later than in Scotland, proceeded by numerous amalgamations and until the process had gone a long way there were very few English banks which were big enough either to absorb a Scottish bank, or to be able to attempt a competitive incursion into Scotland. Furthermore, right up to the First World War the possibilities of amalgamations within England and Wales were sufficient to absorb the full energies of the expanding banks.

In fact, the more pertinent question is why a unified banking structure did not emerge through the movement of Scottish banks into England. The Scots did make some moves in this direction. For example, the majority of them opened London offices in the 1860s and 1870s. But the main reason for these was the close and necessary contact which they afforded with the financial markets of London. One Scottish bank, the Clydesdale, did open a small number of branches in Cumberland in 1874. This aroused a storm of opposition from the English country bankers to which the London banks lent their support. The campaign which they mounted was able to obtain some political leverage from the note-issuing character of the Scottish banks and the apparent anomalies and inequities with which this surrounded their presence in England, where the law in these matters was different from the corresponding Scottish law. This opposition did not succeed in dislodging the Scottish banks from their English footholds but at the time it effectively frightened them off further expansion in England either by opening branches or by absorbing English banks.[1]

By 1917 the English banking system had largely completed its process of concentration. The number of banks was still higher than it was to become, but the future pattern was unmistakable and the 'Big Five' had clearly emerged. Now that they were within sight of the complete consolidation of banking within England and Wales the expansive energies and the competitive pressures generated by the 'amalgamation race' caused the big English banks to look outwards. Two avenues of expansion seemed to offer themselves. One was through extension into those parts of the British Isles which had so far retained their own banking systems, namely Scotland and Ireland. The other avenue, which at the time appeared equally if not more

[1] For a fuller account of these events see my article 'Anglo-Scottish Banking Conflicts, 1874–81', *Economic History Review*, May 1960, pp. 445–55.

promising, was through expansion overseas. The English banks had turned relatively late to providing the financial facilities required in overseas trade; in fact, in 1914, they were only beginners in this field having hitherto left it to the merchant banks, the British overseas banks and the London offices of foreign banks. During the First War and in the immediate post-war years the joint-stock banks came to entertain large expectations of this line of business and these led them into a variety of arrangements with banks abroad, as well as into a number of outright acquisitions.[1]

It is against this background of widening ambitions and an expansionary impetus which had more or less reached its own domestic bounds that one must view the 'take-overs' of four Scottish banks by English banks. The first to be carried through was the acquisition of the National Bank of Scotland by Lloyds, in 1918. This was followed by Barclay's capture of the British Linen Bank in 1919. Then the Midland Bank acquired the capital first of the Clydesdale Bank, in 1920, and later, in 1924, of the North of Scotland Bank. In all these cases the shareholders of the Scottish banks were offered shares in the acquiring banks, and the offers were made with the agreement and blessings of their directors. All but a negligible fraction of the shareholders accepted.

Why did half the Scottish banks of that time succumb to the forces of expansion in English banking? As far as the shareholders were concerned the decisive fact was obviously the terms which they were offered. In every case these placed a valuation on the Scottish shares well above their current market value, while in some cases they carried the prospect of a larger gross income as well. The liberality of the terms, reflecting the anticipated advantages of the Scottish links to the acquiring banks, were also the major consideration with the directors who were called upon to commend them to their members. Indeed the Clydesdale's board rejected an early offer from the Midland, in 1917, because it was inadequate.[2] But other conditions were present—and are perhaps needed—to explain why institutions with such long, independent histories, were disposed to acquiesce so readily in these amalgamations. During the war years two prospective developments loomed largely in the minds of bankers. One, which we have already remarked, was the expected extension of foreign business and the necessity to meet it by forging as many

[1] See R. S. Sayers, *History of Lloyds Bank* (Oxford, 1957), p. 266; also A. S. J. Baster, *The International Banks* (London, 1935), Ch. VII; and J. Sykes, *The Present Position in Joint-Stock Banking* (London, 1926), pp. 23–9.
[2] See J. M. Reid, *The History of the Clydesdale Bank* (Glasgow, 1938), p. 237.

26

overseas links as possible. The other was the feeling that the trend towards concentration in business was quickening, that this was going to throw up ever bigger units, and that to provide large firms with adequate financial facilities would require large units in banking itself. For the Scottish banks the emergence of giant banking institutions in the South threw a peculiarly ominous light over these prospects. The danger that they would be outmatched in any competition in facilities with the English banks was there, and seemed to become very real indeed when, in 1916, the Midland (the London City and Midland Bank as it then was) acquired a site in Glasgow for a post-war branch offering foreign business facilities.[1] With these anticipations it is very understandable that some at least of the Scottish banks were persuaded that their best policy was to link themselves with the large-scale and widely extending interests of English banking.

One final fact about the Anglo-Scottish unions—the form they took—is very relevant to an understanding of the ease with which they came about. The Scottish move of the English banks followed a new pattern in bank expansion which had been set by the Midland and the Westminster in 1917, when they each bought a bank in Northern Ireland. In all these cases, Scottish and Irish, the banks acquired were 'affiliated' to the parent banks. 'Affiliation' meant that they continued as separate legal entities and actually retained a very considerable measure of independence. At the board level there were exchanges of directors with the parent banks; but, apart from the ultimate control, they remained in every respect Scottish and Irish banks. The reasons for this were of course the particular historical and regional circumstances in which Scottish and Irish banking were embedded.

To the English banks looking northwards at that time, three courses of action offered themselves. They could open their own branches in Scotland; they could acquire one or other of the existing banks and incorporate it completely in their own structure; or they could acquire a bank and keep it as a separate affiliate. As we have seen the first of these courses was, for a time, resolved upon by the Midland Bank. But this was clearly a difficult and dubious way of extending operations into a country already heavily banked. Much

---

[1] At the same time sites were also acquired in Dublin and Belfast: see W. F. Crick and J. Wadsworth, op. cit., p. 406; also J. M. Reid, op. cit., pp. 239–41. According to the Annual Report of the Clydesdale's Chairman, February 1920, the Midland's intention for the proposed Glasgow branch had been 'to give special attention to exchange and foreign business. . . .'

the more attractive course was to acquire one or more of the existing banks; but this still left the choice of whether or not to merge the acquired banks into the structure of the acquiring bank. That this was not done must be put down mainly to the 'goodwill' which, through their long history, the Scottish banks had won with the Scottish public:[1] for an English bank to have absorbed a Scottish bank by a merger so complete as to extinguish its identity would obviously have been to court a very severe set-back. The Scottish note issues were undoubtedly a contributory factor here. The complete absorption of a Scottish bank would have entailed the loss of its right of issue and this would have meant sacrificing the profits of issue, as well as its advertisement value to which some importance is attached by the banks themselves. But the note issues were only one among a whole set of historical elements which made it necessary for the English banks to preserve their Scottish acquisitions as independently operating institutions.

The extension of its banking interests into England by the Royal Bank of Scotland is the only example of this movement in reverse. The Royal Bank actually acquired three English banks in all. The first was Drummond's Bank, the small private bank at Charing Cross, which was taken over in 1924. This was a complete absorption and provided the Royal with its first West End branch. Then in 1930 came the much more important acquisition of Williams Deacons Bank, one of the four remaining provincial banks in England, with its headquarters in Manchester and a heavy concentration of branches in the English North-West. Following the pattern of the English acquisitions in Scotland, Williams Deacons became an independently operating affiliate of the Royal Bank. With this move the Royal Bank became the first Scottish bank to acquire a substantial operating interest outside Scotland and the only one to gain an entrée, albeit vicariously, to the circle of the English Clearing banks. Finally, in 1939, the Royal Bank acquired Glyn Mills and Company, again a private bank, operating mainly in London, but much larger than Drummonds and with some very important customers among the railway companies and the larger industrial firms. It also had some large Forces accounts, and through this the Royal's connection with the Public Departments—it was traditionally the Government's agent in Scotland—was strengthened. Like Williams Deacons Bank, Glyn Mills brought a seat in the London Clearing House, and it has continued as an independent banking entity. The whole group,

---

[1] Cf. T. Balogh, *Studies in Financial Organization* (Cambridge, 1950), p. 11.

known as the 'Three Banks Group', is today the sixth largest in Britain being just ahead of Martins in scale of resources.

All these acquisitions, English and Scottish, took place after the Treasury Committee on Bank Amalgamation, of 1918, had reported in favour of legislation to control further amalgamations in British banking.[1] This Committee had been set up in response to the growing alarm at the degree of concentration in banking that was emerging in England. Its call for legislation was not heeded, but the substance of its recommendation was conceded by the setting up of an informal mechanism whereby all proposals for bank mergers were—and still are—voluntarily submitted for the approval of the Treasury. The English acquisitions of Scottish banks were all approved presumably on the grounds that they involved no further concentration of banking within England, and also that they furthered the knitting together of banking facilities over the country as a whole. The acquisitions of the Royal Bank are in many ways more interesting in that they involved the take-over of banks within the area of English banking where concern about concentration was most intense; and it is natural to speculate on how far Treasury influence determined their outcome. The Royal Bank itself was at that time in a strongly expansionary phase of its history. Its resources were growing more rapidly than those of any other Scottish bank; furthermore it was anxious to expand southwards and had even considered the opening of branches in the larger English towns.[2] The initiative in absorbing these banks was clearly taken by the Royal Bank; but had there been no official intervention, actual or potential, one wonders if it would have stood a chance against the resources and expansionism of the big English banks.[3] In one of its acquisitions of the interwar period the bank was quite definitely the chosen recipient of favour. In 1930 the Bank of England, wishing to divest itself of its West End branch in Burlington Gardens, was able to avoid an invidious choice among the English banks by offering to sell it to the Royal Bank of Scotland. The Royal, here benefiting from its two-hundred-year-old connection with the Bank of England, was only too glad to extend its stake in London.

[1] The *Report* is Cd. 9052 (H.M.S.O., 1918).
[2] See Governor's Address, *Scottish Bankers' Magazine*, October 1930, p. 205.
[3] The Royal was said to have been 'not the sole potential purchaser' of Williams Deacons, so that the Treasury was presumably compelled to exercise a choice: see *The Economist*, August 5, 1939, p. 270.

III. THE MOVEMENT INTO HIRE PURCHASE

Since 1958 we have had a new kind of financial expansion by the banks of this country with the direct acquisition of interests in hire purchase finance companies. The Scottish banks have taken a full part in this development. Indeed the Commercial Bank of Scotland pioneered this movement by its purchase, in 1954, of the Scottish Midland Guarantee Trust Ltd., a hire purchase finance company based in Edinburgh. The Commercial followed this by taking a major part in the founding of finance companies in Southern Rhodesia and South Africa. Then, when the general rush of the banks into hire purchase finance started in 1958, it joined with the National Bank of Scotland—they had not yet merged—and the National's parent bank, Lloyds, in acquiring Old's Discount Company. After the union of the National and Commercial Banks the various holdings in British finance companies of the new bank and Lloyds were reorganized under a holding company, Lloyds and Scottish Finance Ltd. In the main movement of 1958-9, the Clydesdale and the British Linen both joined with their parent banks in taking interests in finance companies, the former in Forward Trust and the latter in United Dominion Trust; the Bank of Scotland acquired the whole capital of North Western Securities Ltd., a finance company based on Chester; and the Royal Bank joined with its two English subsidiaries in taking a 40 per cent interest in the British Wagon Co. Ltd.

This extension of the Scottish banks into the hire purchase field has several interesting facets which we shall discuss later, But one that we should notice here is its effect of broadening the geographical range of the banks' interests.[1] All the Scottish banks now have wide interests in the provision of finance, albeit of the specialized, hire purchase kind, outside the borders of Scotland. It may be doubted if this kind of extension adds as much to the stability of business and the reduction of risk as a similar widening of ordinary banking business is normally supposed to do. In fact, in the short life of the new phase the experience of the Scottish banks in this field has been as unfavourable as that of the rest of the British banking system.[2] But if their home base continues to be a region of difficulty in the economy, and if the real promise of consumer finance is fulfilled and the snags overcome, considerable advantages will flow to the Scottish banks from these wider connections.

[1] Cf. F. S. Taylor, 'Bankers off the Leash', *The Banker*, April 1959, p. 255.
[2] See below, pp. 160-1.

IV. THE HIGHER ADMINISTRATION OF THE BANKS

One by-product of the consolidation of the Scottish banking system has been an increasing concentration of the ultimate management in Edinburgh. In the middle of the last century there was a sizeable and distinct group of banks based in Glasgow, and a small one in Aberdeen. But the ranks of the Glasgow banks were decimated by the failures of the Western and the City of Glasgow Banks; and the merging of the Union, also a Glasgow bank, with the Bank of Scotland has left only the Clydesdale with its head office in that city. (The two former Aberdeen banks first united, and then, as the North of Scotland Bank, were merged with the Clydesdale.) One result of these events has been to enhance Edinburgh's position as a financial city. Besides the banks, several insurance companies and a number of investment trusts are based there, and between these three groups of institutions there are numerous links at the board level.

All the Edinburgh banks have their second main office in Glasgow. Glasgow is the most important single centre of banking business in Scotland. This is due partly to the very size of the place, but also to its position as the hub of the whole industrial West of Scotland : much of the business of the big firms in this area is conducted through the main Glasgow offices of the banks. All the banks have their principal foreign departments in Glasgow; some keep specialists in investment and trustee work there; all have designated their Glasgow chief offices as 'authorized' offices for the purposes of holding the legal tender cover for their note issues. However, in spite of the dominating importance of Glasgow as a business centre the higher administration of the Edinburgh banks is largely conducted from that city. In some cases the boards of directors meet periodically in Glasgow, and Western business interests are represented on them. In one bank a committee of directors meets weekly in Glasgow, and in this case the administration is more or less divided between the Edinburgh and Glasgow offices. But of the other three it would probably be true to say that, apart from specialist departments, their Glasgow chief offices are simply the largest and most important of their branches. Two of the banks, the Bank of Scotland and the Clydesdale, have local boards in Aberdeen, while the former also has one in London. The function of these is the usual one of advising on local conditions, sanctioning loans up to a certain level, and perhaps bringing in some business through the connections of their members.

The main boards of directors vary in size from the British Linen Bank's ten to the Royal Bank's twenty-one plus eight extraordinary directors. The men who compose them are drawn fairly widely from industry and finance: such Scottish industries as shipbuilding, shipping, heavy engineering and jute are all represented. But, if anything, the strongest links, at the board level, are with those other notable fields of Scottish financial enterprise, the insurance companies and the investment trusts. In the case of the affiliated banks there is, as we have mentioned, an interlocking of directors with the parent banks, and in the case of the Royal Bank with its English subsidiaries. At the very top of their hierarchies the three oldest banks—the Bank of Scotland, the Royal Bank and the British Linen Bank—have 'governors'; the other two have 'chairmen'. In all but the National Commercial Bank these positions belong (to borrow Bagehot's distinction) to the 'dignified' rather than the 'efficient' organs of Scottish banking; they are filled mostly by members of the Scottish aristocracy, ancient and modern, and they carry no administrative responsibilities. When the National Commercial Bank was formed from its two forebears it was decided to break with this tradition. The post of Governor which had existed in both the uniting banks was discontinued, as also were the 'extraordinary' directorships. The new bank adopted the usual English structure of a board of 'ordinary' directors with full administrative responsibilities, headed by a chairman who is a full-time administrator of the bank. The first to occupy the chair, Mr Ian W. Macdonald, was formerly the General Manager of the Commercial Bank; and the board over which he presides has been slimmed, from twenty-two at the time of the merger, to sixteen.

CHAPTER 3

BRANCHES AND OVERBANKING

The obverse of concentration in a banking system is branch banking. This, as we mentioned earlier, was a development in which Scottish bankers led the way; indeed, for long, they were so far ahead that branch banking was regarded as one of the prime distinguishing marks of the 'Scotch system of banking'. It had appeared even before the end of the eighteenth century, but it was in the nineteenth century that it went forward most rapidly. In the present century the number of bank offices continued to rise up to the outbreak of the Second World War. There was a particularly rapid growth in the interwar period with the establishment of branches in the new suburban areas. The Second World War not only brought this to an end but partially reversed it by an agreed policy of closures to economize manpower. Since 1945 there has been a further, slight decline in the total number of bank offices although, as we shall see, the stagnation of the global figure masks a considerable amount of change within the structure.

TABLE III

Number of Bank Offices in Scotland, 1844–1961

1844	375
1872	912
1895	1,015
1914	1,253
1921	1,343
1938	1,831
1951	1,699
1961	1,683

I. SOME FACTORS PROMOTING BRANCH BANKING IN SCOTLAND

The result of her early and vigorous development of branch banking is that Scotland is by all standards a 'highly banked' country. To take one measure that is commonly quoted, in 1951 she had one bank office for every 3,000 people compared with one for every 4,500 people in England and Wales. Many believe that Scotland is 'overbanked', but before we examine this contention let us ask why there has been this proliferation of bank branches. Historically three main reasons seem to have been responsible. One was the stress placed from an early period in Scottish banking on the collection of deposits. During much of Scottish banking history the deposit-gathering function predominated to a greater extent than, for example, in England where the business of transmitting money and effecting monetary payments was an important part of the country banker's operations. The Scottish banker regarded many of his branch offices, especially in the smaller towns and villages, as collecting centres for deposits to be used in the commercial and industrial centres, and the importance which he attached to this was reflected in the exuberant expansion of branch networks. The two other factors encouraged this by reducing the cost of running the branches. First, the one mainly stressed by the bankers themselves, was the right of note issue. It has always been claimed that this significantly reduces the cost of branch operation since the till-money needs of the offices can be largely met by holding supplies of the banks' own unissued notes. The currency which a bank must hold in the tills of its branches to meet withdrawals by depositors must normally be supplied out of its total assets, and the cost to the individual bank of supplying it is the return which it could have obtained by holding another asset, such as a loan to a customer, instead. The Scottish banks, however, have always been able to hold their own unissued notes in their tills; and as these are not held at the expense of any other asset the only 'cost' to the banks is that of printing them. The use of unissued notes in branch tills is actually a complicated matter that requires careful analysis; it will be examined, along with the other aspects of note issuing, in Chapter 7. But we may very briefly anticipate our conclusion on this question by saying that the effect of note issue has been, not to reduce the total amount of legal tender (or its equivalent) held, but to transform the cost of till money from one which could be directly attributed to individual branch offices into a fixed cost at the centre. The effect has therefore been to encourage the opening of branches.

The other factor which historically reduced the cost of branch operation and made the extension of branch networks more practicable was the agency system. During much of the nineteenth century the salaried bank manager, though by no means unknown, was not the typical head of a bank branch in Scotland. Instead bank branches were usually agencies conducted by men who combined banking with

34

some other profession, usually the law, or with business. This practice was not unknown in England, but it was not so general as in Scotland. It is an appropriate system wherever the sparsity of population, the low development of the banking habit, or simply the scarcity of managerial talent, make it uneconomic or difficult to maintain fully-staffed bank branches. To a bank in process of extending its interests it also has the added advantage that a well-selected agent can bring a ready-made set of business connections in his district. But the counter attractions of the managerial system are very powerful: it offers the advantages of specialization and professionalism as well as permitting more satisfactory control from the centre. When conditions are suitable, and particularly as banking moves away from the relatively simple stage of deposit gathering and bill discounting into a more complex phase, it inevitably prevails. The agency system began to decline in Scotland in the later decades of the last century, although agencies of the traditional kind were still being appointed as late as the interwar period.[1] Shortly after the Second World War the banks agreed to a request by the Scottish Banks Staffs Association that they appoint no more of the old-style agents. Bank employees objected to the 'hereditary' character of the agencies and to the fact that their existence reduced the opportunities for promotion of the full-time servant of the banks; and it was accepted by the banks that the existing agencies would lapse with the retirement of the present incumbents. Today only half a dozen agencies of the old kind remain.

The Radcliffe Committee, in its Report (para. 159), considered that one factor that helped to make Scotland 'one of the relatively "overbanked" countries of the world' was the Scottish banks' practice of agreeing on a common set of interest rates and charges. In the view of the Committee these agreements, by precluding competition by price, have 'meant the encouragement of competition by service'. When we come to look at the Scottish banks' agreements on interest and charges, in Chapter 11, we shall find that the difference that they make to Scottish banking, compared at any rate with the English position, is relatively slight. The absence of price competition in Scottish banking *may* have had some effect on branch expansion, but in a somewhat different way from that envisaged by the Radcliffe Committee. Banking is largely a service industry, in a way which we shall specify in the next chapter; and as in most service industries the marketing of its services depends on a widespread location of 'outlets'.

[1] The loss of trained staff during the First War has been given as a reason for these later appointments: see F. S. Taylor, 'Scottish Banking in the Twentieth Century', *The Bankers' Magazine*, July 1951.

The normal tendency in such an industry is towards multiplication of outlets. The effect of restrictions on price competition is to afford relief from the pressure of an excessive provision of outlets on costs— in a way which is paralleled for example in parts of the distributive trades. The Scottish rate agreements can in principle be used in this way and that they are so used is evidenced by the fact that Scottish bankers usually point to the extensiveness of their branch systems as one cause of the higher level of interest charges in Scotland compared with England.[1] But the significance of the agreements as such can be exaggerated—after all, competition by price is hardly a notable feature of English banking. Now that the question of 'overbanking' has been raised let us examine it more closely.

II. IS SCOTLAND OVERBANKED?

If cost factors encouraged the extension of branches in Scotland in the past the result is a branch structure which all admit to be relatively costly in the present day. Does this then mean that Scotland is 'overbanked'? Two ratios are frequently quoted as evidence that this is the case: the ratio of population to branch offices and the ratio of deposits to branch offices. In both cases the Scottish ratios are below those of England and Wales and, as Table IV shows, this condition goes back a long way.

A hundred years ago the disparity in these two ratios between Scotland and England was very great indeed. Since then the more rapid growth of branch banking in England and Wales has considerably reduced the difference; but it is still there. Looking at the matter in these broad terms it certainly appears that Scotland is generously provided with banking facilities; but whether this amounts to an excessive provision, it is not easy to judge. The usual implication of the term 'overbanking' is that, due to competitive branch opening in the past, there is now in many places in Scotland an excessive number of bank offices. If true this could certainly be the cause of the low ratios, per bank branch, of the Scottish population and Scottish bank deposits. But it need not be the only cause. Another, obviously important, element in the situation is the fact that much of Scotland is only sparsely inhabited. Banking is in large measure a service industry, and the distribution of its facilities is moulded by the distribution

---

[1] See David Alexander, 'Scottish Banking Policy', *Accountants' Magazine*, October 1956, p. 542. Mr Alexander, formerly General Manager of the Commercial Bank of Scotland, is now General Manager of the National Commercial Bank of Scotland.

TABLE IV

Ratios of Population and Deposits to Bank Offices, 1881–1951

YEARS	INHABITANTS PER OFFICE		DEPOSITS PER OFFICE £000's	
	SCOTLAND	ENGLAND AND WALES	SCOTLAND	ENGLAND AND WALES
1881	4,300	14,000[1]	89[4]	173[6]
1911	3,800	6,800[2]	86[4]	150[6]
1951	3,000	4,500[3]	429[5]	641[3]

[1] The number of offices is taken as the number of offices of joint-stock banks (see *The Economist*, Banking Supplement, October 21, 1881) plus a pure guess for the private banks of two offices per bank.

[2] The number of offices of the joint-stock banks only is used here and is taken from *The Economist*, Banking Supplement, October 21, 1911. (There were only nine private banks in 1911.)

[3] The number of offices is taken from C. G. D. Tennant, 'The Structure of Scottish Banking', *Scottish Bankers' Magazine*, January 1952.

[4] Deposits are aggregated from the annual balance sheets of these years.

[5] Deposits are the average of ten monthly totals.

[6] These figures refer to the joint-stock banks only; they exclude a small number of joint-stock banks not then publishing balance sheets as well as all the private banks. Deposits are the balance sheet totals given in *The Economist*, Banking Supplements.

of population. If the people are thin on the ground the provision of anything like a reasonable level of service will impose a comparatively large number of bank offices in relation to population, and there will be a concomitantly low level of deposits per branch. A rough indication of this kind of extensiveness in the Scottish branch system is provided by the fact that there are some 300 places in Scotland where there is only one bank office; and these branches account for between one-fifth and one-sixth of the total. It may be argued, of course, that this is still a kind of overbanking in that the inhabitants of these sparsely peopled areas are being provided with a level of banking service for which, since banking charges are the same everywhere, they are probably not paying a price that covers the full cost of provision. But for the moment let us leave aside the supplying of banking services to the thinly populated regions of Scotland and try to determine how far there is 'overbanking' in the more usual sense of an unnecessary *duplication* of bank offices.

In 1952, C. G. D. Tennant analysed[1] the position by calculating banking densities for towns and places of different sizes, making use of the 1951 Census figures. We have now had another decennial

[1] 'The Structure of Scottish Banking', *Scottish Bankers' Magazine*, January 1952.

census and the Preliminary Report,[1] giving us some of the collected data, has been published; in Table V I have used this to make a similar analysis to that of Tennant's showing the position in the two years 1951 and 1961. In this table the burghs are classified by their population sizes in 1961, and their banking densities refer to the same year. But at the time of preparing this table we had not yet been given the 1961 figures for the places which do not have burgh status,

TABLE V

Distribution of Bank Branches in Scotland, by Town Size Groups,[1] in 1951 and 1961

	TOTAL BANK OFFICES IN EACH GROUP		AVERAGE NUMBER OF BANK OFFICES PER PLACE, IN 1961	POPULATION PER BRANCH IN 1961
	1951	1961		
Cities and burghs				
4 Cities	501	480	–	3,900
20 Burghs, 20,000 and over	185	181	9	4,800
23 Burghs, 10,000 and under 20,000	121	119	5	2,800
44 Burghs, 5,000 and under 10,000	186	178	4	1,800
51 Burghs, 2,000 and under 5,000	157	152	3	1,100
56 Burghs, under 2,000	107	102	2	670
Other towns and villages				
5 Towns, 10,000 and over	14	14	3	6,000[2]
16 Towns, 5,000 and under 10,000	32	33	2	3,400[2]
94 Places, 1,000 and under 5,000	130	134	1	1,700[2]
258 Other, mainly small, places	266	290	1	
	1,699	1,683		
Non-Scottish offices				
Berwick and N. England	11	11		
London	23	22		

[1] Cities and burghs are classified by their populations in 1961. 'Other towns and villages' are classified by their 1951 populations.

[2] These ratios are calculated from the 1951 Census figures.

[1] *Preliminary Report on the Sixteenth Census of Scotland*, 1961 (H.M.S.O., 1961).

and for them the 1951 figures have had to serve. This affects the comparability of the results between the burghs and the non-burghs, but the effect of using different population dates will be so small that we can safely ignore it. Also included in the table is a column showing, in rounded figures, and for all but the four cities, the average number of offices per town or place in each group, in 1961.

Tennant made the assumption that a 'reasonable' banking density was one bank to every 4,000 people; this was an arbitrary figure apparently based on the density for the larger towns and cities. From this he argued that the greatest 'surplus' of branches was in the places falling within the 5,000–20,000 population range. In these groups the ratio of bank offices to population was, and still is, in the region of 1 : 2,000. Towns of under 5,000 population had then, as now, markedly higher banking densities than this (the figure for the burghs of under 5,000 people is about 1 : 900) but Tennant argued that at this level the 'reasonable' standard should not be applied on the general social grounds of the importance of the banks to the communities concerned.

Now quite apart from the obvious difficulties surrounding the conception of a 'reasonable' standard, the use of banking densities of this kind in order to make comparisons and derive conclusions about efficient levels of operation is (as Tennant himself was aware) subject to important qualifications. Banking habits and population structure differ very widely and these differences affect the interpretation of the results. This is obviously so when international comparisons are in question, but even within a single country important differences of these kinds exist. A much more reliable index of banking density, if we could calculate it, would be the ratio of bank offices to what we can call the 'banking population' rather than the total population, meaning by the 'banking population' that portion of the total population who are users of banking facilities or, roughly speaking, depositors and borrowers. The relationship between the banking population and the total population is neither direct nor constant; this explains some of the differences in banking densities between the various groups of Scottish towns and places. Take for example the twenty burghs of 20,000 and over, with a banking density of 1 : 4,800, and compare them with the sixty-seven burghs in the 5,000–20,000 range, with a density of 1 : 2,200. The former group is made up predominantly of industrial towns with large, working-class populations among whom the banking habit is so far undeveloped. In the latter group on the other hand there are many of the smaller, older burghs which have comparatively high numbers of the commercial and professional classes, and which in many cases are market towns with extensive rural connections. The same factor, incidentally, accounts for the marked general contrast in banking densities between the burghs as a whole, and the group of 'other towns and villages' or 'non-burghs'. For historical reasons, the non-burghs contain a high proportion of towns and villages that grew up during the industrial revolution; these places have few connections with agriculture, and their banking populations are small. Thus the ratios for the non-burgh categories understate their banking densities just as, at the other end of the scale, the figure for the small burghs (1 : 900) overstates theirs.

Clearly then, banking densities in themselves give us no firm pointers to the existence of overbanking. At best they can indicate roughly where one might expect to find it. It seems very likely, for example, that the 107 burghs with populations of under 5,000, which in 1961 had 254 bank offices and an average banking density of 1 : 900, were overbanked in the sense with which we are concerned here. Tennant placed these towns in the group which, on grounds of social policy, he exempted from the application of his 'reasonable' standard of 1 : 4,000. But in this particular case the social argument hardly applies. Of these 107 burghs, in 1961, only twenty-six were served by a single bank office. The rest had at least two offices; consequently a reduction of the number of offices in these places would not necessarily mean the withdrawal of banking facilities. In spite of their agricultural hinterlands burghs such as Huntly with seven bank offices, Duns with five, and many others besides, could get along with smaller numbers.

As we ascend the scale of town size groups we begin to meet more industrial towns; due to differences of banking populations this introduces rather more variability in banking densities within the size groups and makes it even more difficult to generalize. Still, within the 5,000–10,000 range one can point with some confidence to the market towns—places like Cupar, Brechin and Lanark—as over-equipped with bank branches. While above the 10,000 mark it is the country towns, both small ones like Forfar and Elgin and large ones like Ayr and Perth, which seem very lavishly endowed with banks and well capable of sustaining some concentration of facilities. In the larger towns of course one must take account increasingly of the factor of situation. The larger a town is the less easy is it to say how much unnecessary multiplication of bank offices there is without actually looking at their situation on the ground. However, as far as the cities and some at least of the larger towns are concerned, this is not so important as, at first sight, it appears. Contrary to what one might think the effective dispersion of bank offices is no wider in large cities than in small towns. Our cities, or at least older parts of them, show distinct nodes of commercial activity scattered over their area. Historically they have usually grown by engulfing villages and small towns on their fringes (Glasgow is a prime example of this), and the old commercial centres of these places live on, preserving something like a village pattern beneath the urban tide. The offices of the banks naturally tend to cluster round these nodal points, with the result that one's impression of an excessive multiplication of bank offices is apt to be as strong in the big cities as in the smaller towns. Certainly, the situation factor seems no less favourable to the concentration of bank offices and when, in a moment, we look at the evidence of branch closures following the recent mergers we shall see that this is strikingly borne out in one case.

There remains the question of overbanking in areas of very sparse population. To say that these are overbanked is in most cases to imply not that there is a duplication of offices but that the demand for banking services is insufficient to sustain even a single office. It may well be that the provision of banking services in these places is being subsidized by the banking public elsewhere. If this is the case then it does, of course, merely add banking to the already extensive list of subsidized elements in the life of the remoter parts of Scotland. But the position is not so clear-cut as this. In these areas many of the bank offices are 'sub-offices', that is to say they are run by the staff of other, larger branches, or as part of a circuit of similar offices, and they are usually only open for a short period—in some cases as little as one hour—during the week. The costs of running these offices reckoned, say, per £100 of deposits collected (or services dispensed) are no doubt higher than they would be in a large and active town office. It is not possible indefinitely to scale down everything necessary to the running of a bank office, in proportion to the level of demand. But the disparity of unit costs between branches in large and small places is not so great as, for example, the relative population ratios might suggest.[1] In this connection it is noteworthy that one bank, the Bank of Scotland, has opened or re-opened as many as sixteen small offices in the crofting counties in recent years. Another device by which two of the Scottish banks provide banking services in some remote and scattered communities is the use of mobile offices. The Clydesdale and the National Commercial have both introduced these in Highland districts and the latter even has a

[1] This is actually another criticism of banking ratios as indications of 'overbanking'; in taking no account of differences in the size of bank offices they tend to exaggerate it.

waterborne branch sailing round the Orkney settlements. However, despite the usefulness of sub-offices and mobile branches in these areas, banking costs would seem bound to be higher there than in the more populous places.

III. BANK MERGERS AND BRANCH UNIFICATION

Granted that Scotland is an overbanked country, how is it to be remedied? To the extent that the problem arises from sparsity of population the remedy is, of course, a retraction of banking facilities from those places where the level of demand is not high enough to permit economical branch operation. This brings in social issues: it may be the national policy to preserve the communities concerned, and banking facilities are certainly among the ingredients of this preservation. The banks themselves are not insensitive to this point, but it may be remarked that the burden falls unequally in that some banks have a larger proportion of their offices in these areas.

Where overbanking is the result of duplication of bank offices there are two possible cures. One would be an agreed policy between the banks of closing branches. Under the pressure of emergency conditions this happened during the Second World War; but in peacetime it is an unlikely event, at any rate on a large and general scale. Alternatively, redundant branches may be eliminated through mergers between the banks, and indeed the unification of branch offices is regarded as one of the advantages which will flow from the greater concentration of the Scottish banking system. Let us take a look at what has happened so far in the way of branch unification as a result of the three recent mergers.

The earliest of the post-war amalgamations, that of the Clydesdale and North Banks in 1950, was the least promising from the point of view of producing a more streamlined branch network. The two banks had a differing regional bias in the distribution of their offices: the North Bank was very heavily localized in the north-east and north, while the Clydesdale had its main strength in the west and south-west. Outside the four cities there were only twenty-one places where both banks had offices. Between the date of their union and 1961 twelve branches in these places had been closed, and another three had been closed in Edinburgh and Aberdeen. Much more could be expected from the merging of the Bank of Scotland with the Union Bank, in 1954. At that time there were forty places, outside the four cities, where both banks had branches, and as most of these were small there was clearly scope for reduction in the number of branches.

In fact, by 1961, fourteen of these offices had been closed but, in the light of our discussion of duplication of offices in the larger towns and cities, it is significant that a further nineteen had been eliminated in Edinburgh and Glasgow. The last of the three mergers, that of the National and Commercial Banks in 1959, would seem to promise most in the way of branch concentration: at the time of the union there were seventy-four places, outside the cities, where both had branches. Two years later, in 1961, twenty-two offices in these places had been eliminated leaving another fifty or so which, on the face of it, were in line for closure. In the four cities, however, the pace of closures had been much slower: there had only been five during these three years, though there seemed to be scope for more.[1]

The rate at which branches which appear to duplicate one another can be amalgamated is, of course, subject to some strong and well-known retarding influences. There is the problem of redundancy among staffs, particularly at the managerial level; as this is probably one of the major sources of cost reduction the need to carry redundant managers may mean that for a time the full economies of unification are not obtained. Another difficulty springs from the smallness of many bank premises in Scotland. Frequently in the cities bank offices are little more than converted shops; the possibility of concentrating staff and equipment in one of two very closely situated offices may be limited by sheer lack of physical space. Last, but not least, there are all the uncertainties about how the banks' customers will react. Just how far people object to having their accounts transferred to a new office, possibly some distance from the old one and staffed by strangers, is open to question. But it is safe to assume that bank customers do not positively welcome a change of this kind, and the banks certainly are disposed to tread cautiously in the matter. Here again the conditions for rapid unification of branches will probably be quite favourable in the large towns and cities. Commercial dealings, like other human relations, are more impersonal in the cities and this mitigates the more intangible grounds for objection by customers.

IV. THE GEOGRAPHICAL DISTRIBUTION OF BRANCHES

We have seen, in the case of the Clydesdale and North, how regional bias can limit the effects of a merger on branch consolidation. This was an extreme case and there no longer remain banks with such degrees of regional concentration; nevertheless some differences between the banks in the spread of their branches do persist. One or

[1] Three of the London offices were also closed during this period.

two of these divergences, particularly as they affect representation in the cities, are brought out in Table VI.

TABLE VI

Distribution of Branch Offices between Certain Places in 1961

	BANK OF SCOTLAND	BRITISH LINEN	CLYDESDALE AND NORTH	NATIONAL COMMERCIAL	ROYAL BANK
Total branches in Scotland	438	204	345	460	236
Percentage of sub-offices	14·4	8·3	8·1	12·2	14·8
Percentage of offices in 4 cities	27·6	34·3	28·4	25·0	27·5
Percentage of offices in Glasgow	14·4	20·1	15·7	12·2	12·3
Percentage of offices in Edinburgh	9·8	11·3	5·5	10·2	14·4
Percentage of offices in crofting counties	14·6	5·9	8·4	13·2	7·6

The remaining geographical differences in branch networks are to be explained in part by the history of amalgamations between the banks. The Clydesdale Bank is the outstanding example of this: it has a very heavy weighting of branches in Aberdeen and the north-east, inherited from the old North of Scotland Bank; at the same time it has the largest number of Glasgow offices, most of them the legacy of the original Clydesdale Bank. But on a lesser scale some of the other banks carry the marks of their past history. The Royal Bank of Scotland is very strongly represented in Dundee as a result of its absorption of the Dundee Banking Company in 1864; while the Bank of Scotland's strength in the Highlands and Islands has its roots in the absorption of the Caledonian Bank, a Highland bank, in 1907. There appear to be no reasons of this kind to explain the strength of the National Commercial Bank in the crofting counties: this was contributed equally by the banks' two forebears and must stem from their branch policies.

Table VI reveals some interesting contrasts in the degree of concentration of the various banks on the cities. Particularly striking is the high proportion—one-third—of the British Linen's branches which are in the four cities. This goes with a low representation in the remoter parts of the country, which in turn is reflected in a low proportion of sub-offices; this branch structure no doubt does something to offset the disadvantages of the small overall size of the bank. There are some interesting differences in the relative strengths of the banks in Glasgow and Edinburgh. The British Linen Bank again stands out with a fifth of its offices in Glasgow. We have remarked already on the bias of the Clydesdale in this direction; more surprising is the similar, though lesser, bias of the Bank of Scotland—a bias which, contrary to what one might think, antedated the amalgamation with the Union Bank.

V. THE FUTURE PATTERN OF BRANCH BANKING

So far, then, the three mergers have led directly to the closing of some seventy branches, or about 4 per cent of the total. These represent the main bloc of branch closures during the 1950s, although there have been others. But, as Table III shows, between 1951 and 1961 the overall total fell by only seventeen, pointing to the fact that the opening of new branches went on during this decade. In fact, with the exception of Berwick and northern England, there were openings of new branches in all the groups of Table V.[1] All the banks opened some new offices during this period, and one must keep this in view when considering the process of change in branch structures: it highlights the point that changes in the distribution of branches are really as important as an alteration in their total number.

The direction in which branch networks should develop must be one of the most perplexing questions facing the banks today. Many factors, both external and internal, impinge on it. One is the form which an inevitable and potentially vast urban re-development will take: how far, for example, will it involve the establishment of new towns or the expansion of suburban areas? And another major influence will be the effect of the motor car on shopping habits and the location of shops and other services. These are just two of the many external forces shaping this problem, but there are important internal factors also—'internal', that is, to the operation and evolution of banking itself. The spreading use of cheque facilities and credit transfers will inevitably increase the counter work of branches and enhance the service element in the banker's function. This development in itself will tend to create a need for a wider dispersion of bank offices, but the degree of dispersion will be subject to the external factors already mentioned. What forms the branches will take, what range of duties they will need to fulfil, will be largely determined by other internal developments, above all by the progress of automation (which we shall review in the next chapter). If, as at present seems likely, this leads to the concentration of accounting work and records

[1] In London too there were both openings and closures of branches. Consideration of the London offices is deferred until Chapter 12, pp. 182–4.

in large central offices where the expensive products of the electronics industry can be economically employed, the effect will be to reduce the size of branch offices. The future need may thus be for a large number of comparatively small and widely scattered offices. This is to look at the question in terms of the developing use of the current account and other banking services and this, of course, is not the whole of the matter. The needs of the borrowing customer are important, in some cases predominantly so. But future developments in this field may actually reinforce the need for dispersion of offices. If, for example, the banks move more firmly into the direct provision of consumer finance this, too, will point in the direction of a dispersed pattern of branch offices in which counter and consultative work together play the major part.

Could this mean that in the end the wide extension of the Scottish branch structure will 'pay off' and prove to be right? The answer, I think, is no. As we have seen, a good deal of the high banking density in Scotland is due to the large area with a scattered population. It is doubtful if any future developments will turn many of the branches in these areas into more desirable assets than they are now. On the other hand, we have seen that in those areas where the growth possibilities may be greatest because of the poor development in the past of the banking habit, namely the industrial towns, banking densities are actually rather low. If now we add the inevitability of great changes in the location of population within and around the existing urban areas, I think that we have reasons enough to conclude that the present pattern of Scottish branch banking will confer only limited advantages in the future. Whatever direction events take, it is clear that continual adaptation of branch networks will be necessary. In this connection there will be an undoubted advantage to the Scottish banks flowing simply from the smallness and unspecialized character of many of their branches, making it relatively easy and cheap to close branches which the march of events have made uneconomic. The further effects of the last three mergers will continue to work themselves out: the Treasurer of the Bank of Scotland, speaking on this point in evidence to the Radcliffe Committee said,[1] 'In the case of my own bank we have not yet got anywhere near the final possibilities', and this must be even more true of, for example, the National Commercial Bank. However, unless the number of banks falls to three or two, any reduction in branch numbers due to the unification of branches or the closure of other unwanted offices will probably continue to be offset by further openings of new branches.

[1] *Radcliffe Evidence*, Q. 4771.

CHAPTER 4

AUTOMATION AND STAFFING

Banking is a service industry in the sense that it does things for people without producing a tangible product. It is generally held that in a progressive economy the service industries are condemned to an upward pressure on their costs. The basic cause of this is that in such an economy incomes, measured in real terms, rise due to increases in the quantity, and improvements in the quality, of mechanized operations. Industries whose processes cannot be mechanized easily are forced sooner or later, by competition, to pay higher incomes to their employees; but because they cannot offset this by resort to ever more labour-saving methods and equipment the unit costs of their outputs are bound to rise.

As far as the so-called service industries are concerned this prognosis is probably only completely applicable to those which produce personal services, that is, services involving actual personal contact. Some bank services are of this kind, or involve it. But the most important service of all that the banker renders—that of the current account—contains only a small element of such direct personal contact. Practically all the work that goes into the servicing of current accounts is process work, performed within the banking system, and much of which is now capable of being committed to machines. Mechanical accounting machines have made great strides in recent years and they are widely used in the branch offices of all banks, including the Scottish banks. But the technical limits of strictly mechanical aids of this kind appear more or less to have been reached;[1] in any case, they can only be used to speed up a part of the total work involved. Increasingly, therefore, further advance is seen to lie in the adaption of electronic data processing equipment for banking operations. Such equipment can be made to record, store and operate on vast amounts of information at high speeds. In principle this seems to contain the answer to the problem of pro-

[1] See 'Thoughts on Electronic Banking', *Three Banks Review*, December 1961, p. 19.

cessing the immense and growing numbers of cheques and other items which current accounts entail; and of processing them not only more quickly, but also more fully, than the mechanical equipment now in use. Hence the interest of the banks in 'automation'.

Three Scottish banks are currently developing advanced electronic systems of accounting and other banking operations and a fourth is about to do so. The Bank of Scotland is perhaps the most advanced at the moment and indeed lays claim to being a pioneer in the matter of centralized posting of customers' ledgers. By the end of 1963 more than a quarter of customers' current accounts was handled by a computer in a central office, in Edinburgh. Information is supplied to this machine from a widely scattered number of branches, partly by telex, but increasingly by a newer and more rapid system of transmission. The National Commercial Bank is moving along the same path and it too handles about a quarter of its current accounts with advanced data processing equipment in Edinburgh. The Clydesdale, after an initial experiment with electronic machines of intermediate capacity, has now ordered a more complex machine of the computer type. Both the Clydesdale and the National Commercial have installed electronic cheque-sorting machines. Finally, in May 1964, the Royal Bank announced an ambitious programme to set up a computer centre in Edinburgh.

The pattern which all of these developments seem to be following is that of a large, central machine handling work for branch offices. With the machines at present in use, this is the inevitable line of development; they are complex, expensive and of a high capacity. To be economically employed they must be supplied with a large volume of work, much greater than that of any single branch. Whether this will be the ultimate pattern depends on the development of the electronic computer. If, for example, it ever becomes possible to make small computer-type machines which can be economically employed in branch offices, then the present trend to concentration of work may be reversed. It seems unlikely that every branch office will ever be able to sport its own computer; but it is possible that the machines may become cheap enough for each bank to operate several of them installed in regional centres. However, the present prospect is of computers for banking operations becoming larger and more elaborate, and hence of even greater centralization of work to keep them economically occupied. Indeed the question for the Scottish banks is whether in the end they will be individually big enough to make efficient use of the products of the electronic engineers. This may strengthen the forces making for further concentration of the

Scottish banking system. On the other hand there are many ways in which the part use of equipment may be enjoyed by organizations not large enough to make full use of it. We may yet see the establishment of a common computer centre serving all the Scottish banks, and perhaps hiring out spare capacity to other users.

Enough has been said to show the uncertainties which surround the future development of electronic banking aids. If we add to the many unknowns in the technological field, others concerning the possible effect on the level of service which can be offered to the customer and his reactions to this (centralized posting, for example, may involve a lower level of service), we have ample reasons to explain the caution with which the banks are proceeding. It may also explain why one of the Scottish banks has so far given no indication that it is experimenting on these lines. The automation of banking is one of those developments in which much of the problem lies in the timing of progress. It is safe and easy to predict that in thirty years' time electronic processes will be extensively used in banking; what is much more difficult is to predict at what stage a bank should be in the adoption of these techniques three or five years from now. The operation calls for an attempt to cost the penalties of both over-slow and over-rapid development.

Automation is closely connected with problems of staffing. Automatic equipment replaces human effort of the repetitive kind. This may lead to a smaller demand for bank staff although the immediate prospect is that it will merely mitigate or offset a rising demand due to the expansion of banking services. More important perhaps, it will in the end alter the character of staff needs. There will obviously be a need for technically trained staff to programme and operate the new machines, but this may not run into large numbers. A more significant effect will be a relative reduction in the numbers of people needed to perform the lower grades of clerical and accounting work. At the same time, relatively (though probably absolutely as well), the number of posts in the more responsible types of administrative, consultative and specialist work will increase. This, as bankers these days never tire of proclaiming, will make banking a more promising and more interesting career for a much higher proportion of male recruits.

Actually, this improvement in the prospects for male staff has already happened. In the battle with rising costs the Scottish banker has resorted to female labour on a scale that is apparent in every branch office. These women are mostly young and—with increasing exceptions—engaged in the lowlier clerical tasks; eventually

D 49

the progress of electronic banking may supplant more of them than of men. The male staff of the banks will in future need to be, on average, more educated than in the past and the problems that this poses are being pondered by the banks.[1] The re-thinking which it has produced has had a practical result in a reshaping of the structure of the examinations of the Institute of Bankers in Scotland, which is the professional, educational and examining body of the Scottish bankers.[2] But of course educational effort, however well conceived, may see its achievements limited by the human material on which it works. A major uncertainty facing the Scottish banks is whether or not they can continue to get recruits of the quality that they have had in the past. Indeed they really need a higher average quality in their new entrants since whereas at one time one in every six could expect to rise to the managerial level, today the proportion is one in two.[3]

The recent experience of other professions and businesses, including banks elsewhere, which recruit at the same level as the Scottish banks—straight from school—has allegedly been that of declining quality. The usual explanation is that the extension of university and other higher education is taking off a rising proportion of the brightest school children leaving ever fewer for the traditional recruiters of school-leavers. One response by some employers has been an increased intake of graduates. The English banks have been doing this for some years now, but so far as is known only two Scottish banks have recruited graduates for general duties, and that in very small numbers. In their public pronouncements Scottish bankers disavow any suggestions of lowered quality in the young men joining them, and indeed it is said that in recent years the quality has been rising.[4] There are reasons why the Scottish banks may not have met the staffing problems experienced elsewhere. For example the increase in university entrance has not been, relatively, so marked in Scotland (where it has always been high) as in England. Also there has been a drop in bank recruitment compared with some earlier periods. In the ten years after 1918, 3,400

[1] See the Presidential Address of Mr R. D. Fairbairn, June 1963, reprinted in *Scottish Bankers' Magazine*, August 1963, pp. 70–6.

[2] See 'The Examinations of the Institute', ibid., May 1960, pp. 6–13.

[3] See the Presidential Address of David Alexander, June 1960, ibid., August 1960, p. 69.

[4] According to a recent statement out of all first-year students registered with the Institute about one-fifth had qualifications 'on or very close to' University entrance standards (three 'Higher' passes) and about one half had some 'Higher' passes in the Scottish Certificates of Education: Presidential Address of R. D. Fairbairn, ibid., August 1963, pp. 73–4.

candidates completed the first of the Institutes examinations; in the ten years after 1945 the corresponding number was 1,600.[1] The earlier period was one of particularly heavy recruitment while the later one was a period of low intake. At the present time the number completing the examination in each year is in the region of 200–250, which is probably equivalent to a somewhat lower annual intake than before the war. Thirdly, there has been some decline in the loss of staff to overseas banks, compared with earlier periods. Scotland has for long exported bankers as she has exported practically every other sort of professionally trained men. Many Scottish bankers, when they complete their training, are attracted to the British overseas and dominions banks; and the intake of recruits by the Scottish banks must take this into account. In the 1920s this outflow was very high, but in the 'thirties it came to an abrupt halt, causing a troublesome distortion in the age structure of Scottish bank staffs.[2] It was resumed after the Second War and is now far from negligible, although not so high as in the 1920s. The future prospect here is probably one of a slowly declining demand on the part of many of the overseas banks that previously recruited in Britain, due to the greater employment of indigenous staff. This, by reducing the wastage of trained staff from the Scottish banks may help to relieve some of the pressures that may develop in the future.

The idea that the quality of school-leavers must be declining because of the higher intake of the universities and other institutions of higher education derives from the 'reservoir' theory of the quantity of talent in the community. This theory is far from proven; at any rate there is evidence that the supply of school-leavers of reasonable accomplishments, and the ability of good teaching to increase that supply, have been underestimated. But what is true in the present may not always be true in the future: the hypothesis may simply have been applied too early. If the proportion of young people taking some form of higher education is substantially increased—and this is the avowed policy of all political parties in Britain today—the process may go far enough to have an appreciable effect on the quality of those who leave school to take up a job immediately. In this case institutions like the Scottish banks are bound to feel the pinch if they still confine their recruitment to school-leavers.

[1] Presidential Address of Sir John J. Campbell, June 1955, reprinted in *Scottish Bankers' Magazine*, August 1955, p. 74.

[2] F. S. Taylor, 'Scottish Banks in the Twentieth Century', *The Bankers' Magazine*, July 1951.

There is another aspect of the problem of recruitment which opens up an even less promising prospect. In recruiting the staff who will eventually rise to the managerial grade, the banks are faced with more than the problem of simply keeping up a good general level of talent in their new entrants. They must also ensure that they recruit a certain number of men who are capable of rising to the very highest posts. This is really a separate problem from that of keeping up the standards of the ordinary managers, and it may well prove the more difficult if they persist in their policy of recruiting staff at the age of seventeen. In recent years two of the Scottish banks have recruited their chief executives from outside the banking world, and while one should not make too much of this at the moment, it may be a foretaste of the future.

CHAPTER 5

PROBLEMS OF CAPITAL AND DEPOSITS

The ultimate sources from which a banker draws his funds can be divided into two: the proprietors, or shareholders, and the public. Roughly speaking—but only roughly—the proprietors' interest is represented on the bank's balance sheet by the capital, reserves and profits, while the public's share is measured by the total of deposits plus, in the case of the Scottish banks, the volume of the bank's own notes in circulation. It is a distinguishing mark of banks, shared with certain other financial intermediaries, that their liabilities to the public are far and away the most important source of their funds. The Scottish banks today obtain somewhere in the region of 90–94 per cent of their total resources from the public, through deposits and note issue. The note issues are a peculiar feature of Scottish banking: to say something about their history and to analyse their present position and effects will require a couple of chapters in themselves. The present chapter will concentrate on the other liabilities of the Scottish banks, mainly capital (considered along with reserves), profits and deposits.

TABLE VII

Scottish Banks' Liabilities in 1963–4[1]
£ millions

	CAPITAL	RESERVES AND CARRY FORWARD	DEPOSITS	NOTES
Bank of Scotland (28/2/64)	6·3	6·8	204·9	29·0
Royal Bank of Scotland[2] (31/12/63)	11·4	12·0	143·2	16·8
British Linen Bank (30/9/63)	1·3	3·5	98·5	15·1
National Commercial Bank (26/10/63)	9·3	11·9	243·6	41·6
Clydesdale and North of Scotland Bank (31/12/63)	3·4	4·3	208·1	25·3

[1] The figures are taken from annual balance sheets and refer to the dates given for each bank.

[2] The total of deposits relates to the Royal Bank of Scotland itself, and excludes its English subsidiaries.

I. 'THE SHAREHOLDERS' MONEY'

The distinction between the proprietors' provision of funds and the public's is important, but certain well-known features of the published balance sheets of the banks prevent any precise allocation between these two sources. The valuation of capital and the assessment of profits present accounting difficulties in any enterprise; but quite apart from these, the law, as embodied in successive Companies Acts, allows banking companies (along with some others, e.g. insurance companies) certain privileges of concealment of their true financial position. Banks are permitted to maintain hidden reserves and to make undisclosed appropriations of profits to them. In order to support this concealment it is obviously necessary for total real profits to be concealed, and the profits figures that are made public bear no ascertainable relation to the amount of the true figures.

The effects of these privileges on the banks' balance sheets are not confined to reserves and profits; items on the assets side are necessarily affected. For example, there is invariably a substantial undervaluation of buildings and property owned by the banks, and generally some undervaluation of portfolio investments; these match the understatement of reserves on the other side. But as well as, and perhaps more important than, straight omissions like this, a good deal is concealed in one of the figures actually published. 'Deposits', as they appear for example on the annual balance sheets of the Scottish banks, include contingency reserves and various other internal accounts of the banks. This meant that before the appearance of the improved statistical series which began with the published evidence of the Radcliffe Committee, it was not possible to put a precise figure on the public's ownership of bank deposits. It is still not possible to be absolutely precise about it but current banking statistics do give a breakdown of total deposits into 'current accounts', 'deposit accounts' and 'other accounts'; the 'other accounts' include contingency and other reserves (which belong to the banks themselves), though along with a certain element of the public's funds in the shape of credit transfers[1] in course of transmission. This improvement, welcome though it is, is a mere flicker of light in the darkness which surrounds the capital and reserve position of the banks: anything one says about this must be either general, or conjectural, or must at any rate lack reliable quantitative evidence.

[1] The growth of credit transfers in recent years has actually led to doubt as to whether it is an improvement to separate 'other accounts' from current and deposit accounts: see below, pp. 66–7.

Proprietors' capital and reserves form a section of the banker's resources which outside commentators have usually disregarded. This is partly because, in modern times, it has been completely overshadowed by the deposits of the public; and partly also because interest in banking has largely centred on their monetary function and this too has put the spotlight on deposits. Furthermore, the stability of British banking over a long period, and the strong controlling position of the Bank of England, have contributed to the general feeling that capital and reserves are not very important elements in the banking picture. Bankers themselves do not share this disregard. For them the proprietors' interest, both hidden and disclosed, forms a disposable margin of assets of great importance, necessary to meet sudden depletions due to bad debts and to fluctuations in the market values of investments. In spite of the tremendous scale of banking resources today losses from these causes can be very large in relation to current income, and reserves of some kind must be available to meet them.[1] The importance that the banks attach to the proprietors' stake in total resources is made evident by their constantly voiced concern about the depletions of reserves caused by inflation, and by their overt efforts, through capital issues, to repair these. As Lord Franks, then Sir Oliver Franks and Chairman of Lloyds Bank, put it, in 1960, '. . . the whole history of the last fifteen years has been an effort to get the shareholders' money in the business into a proper trading relationship to the deposits.'[2]

Just what constitutes 'a proper trading relationship' between capital and reserves and the banks' liabilities to the public, in the present day, is not very clear. Historically bankers have expressed varying views which have altered as the circumstances and stability of banking have developed.[3] *The Economist* recently declared that 'there is a general principle that capital funds should cover at least fixed assets'.[4] But there are so many ambiguities surrounding concepts like 'capital funds' and 'fixed assets' in the sphere of banking, that this is

---

[1] Falls in the market values of securities may only cause 'accounting' losses, in the sense that the securities may well be held to maturity, and no actual losses realized. But unless the balance sheet values are shown in excess of the market values there must be some reserve element on the liabilities side which can be correspondingly written down. During the 1950s four of the Scottish banks adopted the practice of valuing investments at 'under cost and below redemption value' with a note giving the market value: see below, p. 140.

[2] *Company Law Committee* (Jenkins Committee), *Minutes of Evidence*, Q. 3108.

[3] See H. Brough, 'Fresh Capital for the Banks', *Scottish Bankers' Magazine*, August 1959, p. 81.

[4] July 15, 1961, p. 271. Also see Brough, ibid., p. 82.

hardly an illuminating statement. In any case, it smacks of one of those rules of thumb that are followed gregariously without any deep rationale. But if it has indeed been the guiding star of the English banks then the Scottish banks have not followed it since the *published* figures of their capital and reserves have traditionally stood in a much higher ratio to their deposits than those of the English banks, and it has usually been assumed that this does reflect the real position. In 1938 the published capital and reserves of the Scottish banks were equal to $11 \cdot 9$ per cent of deposits compared with $6 \cdot 2$ per cent for the Clearing banks. At the end of 1960 the corresponding ratios were $7 \cdot 3$ per cent and $3 \cdot 7$ per cent, but by 1963 the English ratio had risen to $5 \cdot 2$ per cent whereas the Scottish figure had only gone up to $7 \cdot 8$ per cent. But within the Scottish system there is a marked difference between the two affiliated banks and the three independents; taking the latter banks alone, in 1963 their average ratio of capital funds to deposits was $9 \cdot 8$ per cent.

Another indication of reserves—still an imperfect one—may be found in the 'other accounts' component of total deposits; this item, we have seen, embraces some of the internal reserve accounts of the banks. In 1938 'other accounts' averaged 11 per cent of total Scottish deposits, and 6 per cent of English deposits. In 1963 the figures were 14 per cent and 10 per cent, but these recent figures must be treated with even greater caution because credit transfers are now on the increase and will be affecting the size of 'other accounts'.

Why have the Scottish banks maintained such comparatively large capital and reserves? The practice probably has historical origins which we can now no longer trace, but two conditions may have been important during the last hundred years. One is the note issue itself: the continuance of the right of issue after 1845, together with the fact that for most of the period a majority of the banks were subject to unlimited liability for their notes in circulation (two are still in this position), probably induced an early conservatism in the holding of capital reserves. The other influence has been the high investment portfolios which have been a feature of Scottish banks' assets during most of this period and which have involved them in a comparatively heavy provision against the risks of fluctuation in market values.

As they are largely embodied in monetary assets the capital funds of the banking system have been subject to the shrinking effect, in real value terms, of the inflationary process through which we have been living; and high though the Scottish banks' reserve funds were at the beginning of this phase, they are now felt to be inadequate. As one banker put it to the Radcliffe Committee: '... my predecessor of fifty years ago had more real money behind him than I have today ... [his reserve funds] formed a bigger buffer against unforeseen circumstances than our contingencies account does today, looking to the heavy inflation of the intervening periods.'[1] And so the rebuilding of reserves, hidden and disclosed, goes on, assisted in some degree by resort to the capital market. Since the relaxation of controls on borrowing in 1958 all three of the 'independent' Scottish banks have raised new money, in each case by the inevitable 'rights' issue. Neither of the two affiliated banks have brought in any new money from outside, but they have been noticeably conservative in declaring profits and in paying dividends to their parents. In 1963 both increased the amount of their 'issued capital' by transfers from reserves—in the case of the Clydesdale from 'hidden' reserves.

One other change in the capital structures of the Scottish banks in recent years has been the virtual elimination of uncalled or 'reserve' liability on the shares of certain of the banks. The Scottish banks, with the exception of the three ancient foundations which were limited companies from the beginning, achieved limitation of shareholders' liability under the Companies Act of 1879.[2] Prior to 1882, when, in concert, they registered under this Act, they were mostly 'co-partneries' possessing the privileges of incorporation, but with unlimited liability. One provision of the 1879 Act allowed banks registering under it to create a 'reserve liability' which would be callable only in the event of liquidation. They could do this either by increasing the nominal value of their shares or by setting aside part of any existing uncalled liability. At the time great importance was attached to this measure; it was regarded by the banks as a means of reassuring the public, offsetting to some extent the reduction in the security of the banks' creditors which the adoption of limited liability appeared to bring. As all these steps, including the Act itself, followed the appalling experience of the failure of the City of Glasgow Bank,[3] in 1878, it is not difficult to see why the questions of security and liability were so closely linked and treated with such

---

[1] The General Manager of the British Linen Bank, *Radcliffe Evidence*, Q. 4854.

[2] Of the three 'old' banks, the Bank of Scotland was founded by an Act of the Scottish Parliament, and the Royal Bank and the British Linen by royal charters. In all three cases limitation of liability was assumed and was presumed to extend to note issue, although Professor R. H. Campbell informs me that the legal position was never entirely clarified. The banks registering under the 1879 Act (42 and 43 Vict. c. 76) retained unlimited liability for their notes in circulation with the public.

[3] It failed for more than £6 million.

caution. Indeed, so much importance was attached to the matter that, in 1881, the three old banks tried unsuccessfully to promote private legislation to enable them to assume reserve liability.[1] In the present day the need for such assurances to the banks' creditors has evaporated, and uncalled liability on bank shares has come to be viewed as something of a nuisance, impairing, however slightly, their marketability. The reserve liability of the Union Bank of Scotland was extinguished when it was merged with the Bank of Scotland, and at the amalgamation of the National and Commercial Banks there was a similar extinction of the uncalled liabilities on the capital of both banks. Only the Clydesdale Bank retains an uncalled liability on its shares, and these, of course, are all owned by the parent bank.

Scottish Banks' Profits

Profits, to which we turn next, are not a continuing liability of the banks in quite the same way as capital or deposits. They accrue progressively during the course of a year's operations, and they are run down when they are paid out as dividends or appropriated to reserves or other uses. In the banking sphere there is little one can say about them other than to report the movement of the *published* totals. These bear no relation in point of scale to true profits. We do not even know if the Scottish banks follow the convention of the English banks of allowing the movement of their published profits to reflect the *trend* of real profits,[2] though it is probably safe to assume that this is so. At the beginning of the 1950s the aggregate published net profits of the Scottish banks, at £2½ million, were about the same as they were in the early 'twenties, though if we make allowance for tax changes between these two periods this figure represented an increase in published gross profits. Dividends also showed a similar stability, which meant that in real terms they had declined considerably.

During the 1950s the movements of published profits were variable, falling in 1952, rising in 1953 and 1954, falling again between 1955 and 1957, and rising in 1958, although with individual exceptions in some years. In 1959 and 1960 there were substantial rises which, with the conspicuous exception of the National Commercial with its very heavy stake in hire purchase, continued, though more slowly, in 1961. In 1962 they levelled out once more. Dividends have shown less variability in that, with odd exceptions, they have remained stable when declared profits have fallen; but the trend has been upwards, sharply so in 1959 and 1960. After 1957 there was a notable diver-

[1] See Gaskin, op. cit., pp. 451–2.
[2] See *Company Law Committee, Minutes of Evidence*, Q. 3087.

gence between the three 'independents' and the two banks affiliated to English banks. The two affiliates showed markedly smaller increases in published profits and very much smaller increases in dividends. This, presumably, has been their way of increasing the proprietors' interest in their capital structure: an overt introduction of new capital was, no doubt, felt to be unnecessary in view of the size and standing of their parents.[1] The dividends declared by the independents actually rose faster than published profits between 1957 and 1962.

One particular movement in profits deserves notice as it was connected with a peculiarity of Scottish bank deposits which we shall examine later. There was an almost general decline in Scottish banks' profits in 1956 which was in marked contrast with the trend of English bank profits. This was attributed to the effect of higher levels of interest rates (compared with earlier years) operating on a peculiar conjunction of deposits and assets. Scottish bank deposits contain a relatively high proportion of interest bearing deposits; as a consequence, the interest cost to the banks is comparatively sensitive to a general rise in rates. Assets, on the other hand, were at that time heavily weighted with gilt-edged securities, the yield on which changes only slowly. This situation, which in any case only presented a problem of *short-run* variability of profits,[2] has been relieved by the big change in the banks asset structures after 1959 (which we shall examine in Chapter 9).

The broad trend of Scottish banks' profits over the last decade has been upwards reflecting the attainment of much greater profitability in banking by the early 'sixties. Higher levels of interest rates and a more favourable distribution of assets were the chief causes of this, with the newly acquired hire purchase subsidiaries bringing profits and losses. But it cannot be too often repeated that the movements we have been tracing here, while possessing interest in themselves, are no more than indications of the trend of true profits. Do we know anything about true banking profits? How do they compare with the declared figures? Recently some interesting attempts at estimating the profits of British banks have appeared in the pages of *The Bankers' Magazine*.[3] The results of these exercises in financial

[1] The Royal Bank of Scotland on the other hand used part of the money it raised in 1960 to increase the capital of its two English subsidiaries.

[2] See Gaskin, 'The Scottish Banks' Interest Rates', *The Scottish Journal of Political Economy*, February 1958, pp. 72–4.

[3] These articles, under the pen-name 'Phaedra', have appeared in the August 1961, May 1962, and June 1963 numbers. The third article is confined to the Scottish banks, though these are treated along with the Clearing banks in the previous two articles.

detection are obviously subject to wide margins of error, but they furnish interesting and useful indications of the order of magnitude of real profits and their relationship to declared profits. They show, as one might expect, a substantial difference from the declared profits. For the Scottish banks the estimated real net profits in 1959–62 are broadly twice the published profits in the case of the three independents, rather more than this for the British Linen Bank, owned by Barclays, and in the case of the Midland's subsidiary, the Clydesdale, they are three times the published total. These last two results are interesting as being very similar to the relationships between the declared and estimated real profits of their parent banks. In the other three cases the relationships are broadly similar to those of the smaller Clearing banks.[1]

II. DEPOSITS

In the nineteenth century the intensive gathering of deposits was regarded as one of the great distinguishing marks of Scottish banking. Before the consolidations of the big joint-stock banks of deposit in England, the Scottish banks were the outstanding examples of institutions that set themselves to attract the unused liquid balances of the public on a wide scale. The prime instrument of this was the 'deposit receipt', a form of interest-bearing deposit which is still important although now yielding ground to the 'deposit account'. In the nineteenth century there was a minimum of £10 on the amount that could be placed on deposit-receipt, but above that the smallest sums were accepted. In the early part of the century, before the inception of the modern savings bank movement, the many small savings

---

[1] Apart from the reserve with which, as the writer of these articles himself insists, these calculations must be treated, the present writer has some special reservations about the Scottish estimates. To begin with, the figure used for staff and other costs seem to me to be on the low side when compared with the Clearing banks, and in the light of the smaller scale of operations of the Scottish banks and their more expensive branch systems. In the article of June 1963 two alternative methods of estimation of true profits are used. The starting point of the second method consists essentially in taking an aggregate block of assets, based on the monthly figures, and dividing it up between the banks according to the relative size of their note circulation. To this it must be objected that the relative sizes of individual note issues diverge to some extent from the relative quantities of assets of each bank. Also, within the assets of individual banks, there are divergences which are ignored by the author of this article. He does consider one such divergence, that in regard to cash holdings, but this is not the most important (and some of his statements about the relationship between cash and note issue are wrong).

banks which sprang up after 1810, on the models of the Ruthwell and Edinburgh pioneers,[1] acted as feeders to the joint-stock banks. When a depositor's balance in one of these small savings banks reached £10 it was transferred to a joint-stock bank and he became a deposit-receipt holder.[2] The funds of the savings banks themselves were deposited with the joint-stock banks.[3] In this way the Scottish banks were in some measure an extension of the savings banks.

Even the note issues themselves came to be regarded as deriving their chief importance from the fact that they sub-served the collection of deposits. Where an earlier generation of bankers had looked on them primarily as a source of funds, after the middle of the nineteenth century their prime function in the eyes of the Scottish bankers was to make possible a wide spread of branches which in turn produced a more effective 'draining' of the country of deposits than would otherwise have been possible.[4] Thus note issuing, branch banking and high deposits were viewed as three interlocking elements which gave Scottish banking its distinctive character. The early success of the Scottish banks as gatherers of the public's deposits produced the situation in the middle of the nineteenth century where the level of commercial bank deposits per head of population was almost certainly higher in Scotland than in England. In the latter half of the century, with the growth in England of institutions more strongly orientated towards deposits banking, this disparity was progressively narrowed. The Scottish figure may have remained the higher of the two until the Second World War: the figures we have for that period certainly show this but, apart from other objections, they are totals of gross deposits and for reasons which we shall shortly examine they probably overstate the Scottish position. For what they are worth they are given in Table VIII, along with some more reliable indicators for recent years.

Comparisons of deposit holdings are affected by the nature of the deposits concerned and compared with the English system the Scottish banks have always shown a distinctively high proportion of time deposits. But before we examine this we must say something about the actual types of deposits in Scottish banking. There are three of these today: current accounts, deposit receipts and deposit

[1] See H. O. Horne, *A History of Savings Banks* (London, 1947), Ch. III, pp. 39–57.

[2] See *Committee of Lords on the Circulation of Promissory Notes, 1826, Evidence*, pp. 114–15.

[3] See Horne, op. cit., pp. 40, 45.

[4] The restrictions on note issue imposed by Peel's Bank Acts encouraged this view: see below, p. 95.

TABLE VIII

Bank Deposits per Head of Population, 1901–61

YEAR	SCOTLAND £	ENGLAND AND WALES £
1901[1]	24	21
1938[2]	65	55
1951[3]	146 (119)	141 (126)
1961[3]	156 (119)	161 (137)

[1] Gross deposits as shown on annual balance sheets. The deposit total for England and Wales covers joint stock and private banks as given in W. T. Layton and G. Crowther, *The Study of Prices*, 3rd edition (London 1938), Appendix C Tables II and IV.

[2] Scottish deposits are totalled from annual balance sheets; for England and Wales the annual average of monthly figures is used.

[3] Deposits are annual averages of monthly totals of gross deposits, with net deposit totals in brackets. The net deposits total for England and Wales, shown against 1951, actually relates to 1952.

accounts. Current accounts need little explanation: as elsewhere, they may be operated on by cheque, without notice; they earn no interest; and they are subject to a system of charges the evolution of which, in Scotland, will be described in Chapter 11. The deposit receipt, on the other hand, is a peculiarly Scottish institution with a history going back to the earliest years of the last century. It takes the form of a document held by the depositor which he must present for encashment if he wants to withdraw the money, or annually if he wishes to realize the interest which only accrues at simple interest. There is now no minimum amount on a deposit receipt, and they may be encashed without notice[1] at any bank office in Scotland, whether of the issuing bank or not. (They are also issued at the London offices where the London deposit rate is applied and where, incidentally, 'deposit accounts' of the English type are also held.) The rate of interest paid on deposit receipts varies with Bank Rate and is at present normally $2\frac{1}{2}$ per cent below that Rate; it is payable on a balance only after it has been on deposit for thirty days.

What the Scottish banks term 'deposit accounts' are a comparatively recent innovation. They were introduced under that title in 1928; later, they were re-named 'savings accounts' and it was only in March 1964 that the banks decided to revert to the original title.

[1] The fact that both deposit receipts and the Scottish 'deposit accounts' may be encashed without notice means that to call them 'time' deposits is something of a misnomer. We shall use the term however as a convenient label for balances other than current accounts.

For anyone reared in English banking terminology the discarded designation, 'savings accounts', gives a near enough indication of what was the original purpose of these accounts; as to their present role, it is now probably a less accurate description than formerly and this may be one reason for the recent change of name. The Scottish banks introduced their deposit accounts (on an English model) specifically to appeal to small savers. Sums as low as a shilling may be deposited or withdrawn; and balances are recorded not on a deposit receipt, which the small saver finds inconvenient, but in a passbook. They are a highly liquid asset since, under present arrangements, the depositor may uplift his whole balance without notice at the branch office at which he holds his account; while he may withdraw up to £10 without notice from any office of his bank. The rate of interest on deposit accounts, calculated on the minimum monthly balance and credited automatically each year, is $\frac{1}{2}$ per cent higher than the deposit receipt rate when this is 4 per cent or below; above that level the two rates are the same. Originally there was a limit of £500 on deposit accounts, but this is no longer applied except as a limit to the amount of interest payable at the deposit account rate whenever this is higher than the deposit receipt rate.

Why did the Scottish banks introduce the savings-type 'deposit account' when they did? In the published history of the Commercial Bank of Scotland there is a revealing passage on its inception.[1] The author ascribed the initiative in adopting it to Alexander Robb, then General Manager of the Commercial Bank and, obviously quoting him, says: 'He was fully alive to the changing ownership of money, and he foresaw that the Scottish banker of tomorrow would have to depend upon the small depositor. The drift southward was steadily leading to business of magnitude being arranged in London, and it was in view of this that he urged the need of widening the scope of the clientele and introducing supplementary methods to attract depositors.' Today, a generation later, we see the same situation producing basically similar remedies; but more of this shortly. The question that imposes itself at this point is: why should it have been necessary to introduce the deposit account in Scotland at all? Had the deposit receipt ceased to fulfil its original role as a popular savings asset, widely held by the Scottish public and in particular by those small savers at whom the deposit account was explicitly aimed?

The answer to the second of these questions is clearly, yes: it is implied in the passage just quoted, and it is also a matter of observa-

[1] See *Our Bank: The Story of the Commercial Bank of Scotland Ltd. 1810–1941* (Edinburgh, 1941), pp. 58–9.

tion that the Scottish banks, although probably drawing on a wider clientele (socially speaking) than those of England, have to this day very few customers among the manual workers. But at one time, in the first half of the last century, they apparently had them. A witness before the 1826 Committee on the note circulation was asked: 'What classes of persons form the large and steady depositors in the Scottish banks?' He replied: 'The middling and lower orders of society; industrious poor people who are saving their money; and small capitalists, who have realized a moderate sum of money, upon the interest of which they live.'[1] The interesting question, of great point today when new policies are in the air, is when and why did the Scottish banks lose the custom of the 'industrious poor'? The answer is that they lost them in the second half of the nineteenth century and for three reasons. One reason—the most speculative one—may simply have been that the descendants of those early working-class accumulators of deposit receipts graduated to the middle classes, leaving behind them a working class which then, as now, was largely untouched by the commercial banks. But a more certain cause was the development and success of the trustee savings banks. In 1835, George Rose's Savings Bank Act (of 1817) was extended to Scotland;[2] this ushered in a new phase of the movement in which the re-formed savings banks no longer passed on their depositors and their savings to the joint-stock banks, but kept them, and placed the funds with the National Debt Commissioners. Since that time the trustee savings banks of Scotland have grown so strongly that today two Scots in every five hold accounts with them—a much higher proportion than for Britain as a whole—and the average balance per head of the Scottish population is twice the national average.[3] There is also evidence that the Scottish savings banks have been much more successful than those elsewhere in attracting the custom of the manual worker.[4]

The third reason for the loss of the working-class depositor by the joint-stock banks was that the banks themselves lost interest in him.

[1] *Committee of Lords on the Circulation of Promissory Notes (1826), Evidence,* p. 104.

[2] See Horne, op. cit., p. 55.

[3] In 1961 balances in the special investments departments of the Scottish savings banks were 22 per cent of the national total. This must be set against the Scottish population ratio which is 11 per cent.

[4] A study of the clientele of the Glasgow Savings Bank before 1914 has been made by Dr P. L. Payne of Glasgow University, and will shortly appear in a volume entitled *Studies in Scottish Business History,* edited by Dr Payne.

This did not happen immediately: in the 1840s and 1850s some of them, at any rate, put up strong competition with the savings banks.[1] But the leaders in this were the Western and City of Glasgow Banks. These two banks established many branches and, by opening in the evening and pushing up their deposit rates, they aimed to attract the small deposits of the manual worker.[2] The other banks, partly no doubt in revulsion from these two, whose methods and general philosophy they disliked, were less keen; and this was confirmed by the failure of the Western, and the temporary closure of the City of Glasgow, in 1857.[3] This crisis was marked by a panic among small depositors, including those of the savings bank. Henceforth small deposit business was regarded not only as imprudent in itself[4] but also as likely to arouse suspicions of unsoundness. As the general manager of the Clydesdale Bank put it: 'For our credit we must not have it said that we are collecting business in shillings and sixpences.'[5]

Nevertheless, in spite of this loss of an earlier clientele among the manual workers, it remains true that the Scottish banks were comparatively successful in attracting the deposits of a thrift-conscious people, and that the deposit receipt was, and to some extent still is, an important savings asset for people of moderate means. But the deposit account, having been designed originally to recapture the small saver, is now replacing the deposit receipt over a wider field than this, and is probably beginning to approach the English deposit account in character. This may be partly due to the more favourable rate of interest (on the first £500) when Bank Rate is low. But equally, if not more, important is the greater flexibility and convenience of the deposit account: the depositor holds a pass-book instead of receipts, and interest is credited automatically. The deposit receipt still possesses advantages for some users.[6] Solicitors, for example, make considerable use of them for trust monies and for the holding of temporary balances in real property transactions. But the trend is towards deposit accounts: numerically they now exceed deposit receipts, although the volume of funds held in

[1] Horne, op. cit., p. 139.
[2] *Select Committee on the Bank Acts*, 1858, *Minutes of Evidence*, Q. 4381-4. The minutes of the Clydesdale Bank refer to the breaking of the rate agreements at this time.
[3] Ibid., QQ. 4590-1.
[4] Ibid., QQ. 4381, 4390-3.
[5] J. M. Reid, op. cit., p. 147.
[6] It possesses a tax advantage in that income tax is not chargeable on the interest until the receipt is actually encashed.

them is probably still not equal to the amount held in the older form.

Deposits, 'Gross' and 'Net'

Before we examine the movement of the Scottish deposit totals through time there is a statistical problem that must be faced. Totals of bank deposits are, like many other items of banking statistics, very slippery things when one tries to handle them firmly. The most commonly used measure is that of 'total' or 'gross' deposits; for example, it is customary to calculate such widely quoted ratios as the cash ratio and the liquidity ratio on the basis of this figure. But the 'gross deposits' figure is not, of course, a true measure of the banks' deposit liabilities to the public. We have already seen that one component of it, 'other deposits', represents various reserve accounts within the banks as well as credit transfers 'in transit'. The 'gross deposits' figure also contains a measure of double-counting stemming from three other sources. One is cheques and other items 'in course of collection' on other banks. At any given moment every bank is either holding, or has just transmitted to the clearing or collecting agents, cheques which have already been credited to accounts of their own customers but which have not yet been debited to the accounts of the payees because these are held in other banks. The second source of double-counting lies in what are usually termed 'transit items'. These, again, are mainly cheques in course of transmission, but in this case they have passed between customers of the same bank and are in course of collection by one branch of the bank from another. Thirdly, inter-bank balances—funds held by one bank with another—introduce a further bit of distortion.

To get somewhere near a figure which measures the 'true' bank balances of the public at a given point of time, it used to be the practice to deduct all four of these items from gross deposits to leave a total which was termed 'net deposits'. Recently however a change has been made in official statistics. It has always been recognized that the deduction of 'other accounts' actually led to some under-estimation of net deposits in that credit transfers in course of transmission, which are submerged in this item, represent funds belonging to the public which have been deducted from the payer's balances but not yet lodged in payee's accounts. But before 1963 the amount involved was regarded as small. In 1963 this view changed: it was decided that a larger distortion—particularly in regard to changes from one period to another—was introduced by omitting 'other accounts' (and so ignoring credit transfers 'in suspense'), than by including them (and so admitting some internal bank funds into the total). The Bank of England has therefore recalculated its series of net deposit figures of the English and Scottish banks.[1]

A further example of unavoidable distortion is peculiar to the Scottish banks. In a largely enclosed banking system any balances held by one bank with another should be deducted since they are an addition to gross deposits and are not held by the public. But in the Scottish case 'balances with other banks' are held wholly with banks outside the system, and consequently there is no corresponding addition to the total of Scottish deposits. Hence they should not be deducted from gross deposits in the calculations of Scottish net deposits. But here we run into a problem. These balances are lumped together (in the monthly statements) with 'cheques in course of collection'. We cannot deduct the one without the other. There is no question that the 'cheques' item should be deducted in the Scottish case as in other cases. It is true that these cheques in course of collection are very largely drawn on banks outside the Scottish system and are indeed regarded by Scottish bankers as potential additions to their 'external' balances.[2] But it is equally true that at any given moment these outward cheques are more or less counterbalanced by a flow of inward cheques which, in the course of a day or two, will be debited to Scottish accounts and will reduce Scottish deposits. Hence there are no grounds for treating this item any differently in the Scottish case than in the English: cheques should be deducted from gross deposits. But to do so means in practice that we also deduct 'balances with other banks', and whether or not we should in fact make the deduction depends on the view we take of the relative importance of 'balances' and 'cheques'. In 1962 the whole item was $5 \cdot 2$ per cent of gross deposits. In my view 'cheques' accounted for about three-quarters of this, and 'balances' for the remaining quarter.[3] If this is correct it means that if we deduct this item we underestimate net deposits by about 1 per cent whereas if we fail to deduct it we overestimate them by about 4 per cent. Hence in this chapter 'cheques in course of collection' are deducted from

---

[1] See the *Bank of England Quarterly Bulletin*, December 1963, pp. 285–94. This article gives a good account of the statistical difficulties surrounding the concept of 'net deposits'.

[2] The significance of this item for the liquidity of the banks is discussed below, pp. 126–7.

[3] This is based on conclusions about the size of 'balances with other banks' in Chapter 8, pp. 115–16.

gross deposits to arrive at Scottish banks' net deposits. But this practice is not followed by everybody.[1]

This statistical snag is, of course, well understood, but it has a special bearing on the interpretation of Scottish banking statistics which is perhaps not so well known. In the Scottish banks' figures the combined total of 'other accounts', 'cheques etc.' and 'transit items' is a much larger proportion of gross deposits than in the case of the English figures. The obverse of this is that Scottish 'net deposits' are a significantly smaller proportion of gross deposits than in the English case: in 1962 the respective ratios were 75 and 84 per cent.

TABLE IX

Components of Gross Deposits, 1938–62
Per Cent of Total

YEAR	SCOTTISH BANKS			CLEARING BANKS		
	OTHER ACCOUNTS	CHEQUES ETC.[1]	TRANSIT ITEMS[2]	OTHER ACCOUNTS	CHEQUES ETC.[1]	TRANSIT ITEMS[2]
1938	10·7[3]	4·9[3]		5·8	2·6	0·8
1952	8·6	9·7		3·9	3·6	1·3
1962	12·9	5·2	7·3	8·9	6·9	

Sources: 1938 and 1952: *Radcliffe Memoranda*, Vol. 2, Statistical Appendix Tables 2 and 3.

1962: *Financial Statistics* (H.M.S.O.), October 1963, Tables 27 and 28.

[1] 'Cheques etc.' includes balances with other banks.

[2] 'Transit items' signifies items in transit between offices of the same bank.

[3] These figures cover six only of the eight banks then in existence.

As Table IX shows, the smaller relative size of the adjusted total of Scottish deposits, compared with the English banks, is due partly to the bigger proportion of 'other accounts' (probably reflecting hidden reserves), but partly also to the larger float of collection items which, at any given moment, are in the pipeline. Within the latter total the

[1] In the officially published banking statistics different procedures are adopted in different places. In *Financial Statistics*, October 1963, Table 28 (the Scottish banks table), in the calculation of net deposits 'items in transit between offices of the same banks' are deducted, but 'balances with, and cheques in course of collection on other banks' are not; and this is also the case in the *Bank of England Quarterly Bulletin*, December 1963, Table 10. This is apparently because the official statisticians take a different view from mine on the relative importance of 'balances' and 'cheques'. On the other hand in *Financial Statistics*, Table 17, the table showing consolidated figures for the English and Scottish banks, this item is deducted from the Scottish banks' deposits, on the correct grounds that within the combined system *both* balances and cheques introduce an element of distortion.

big difference is obviously in 'transit items'. The Scottish and English ratios of 'cheques etc.' are fairly close (that is, if we put the Scottish figure for 1962 alongside the English figure for 1952); and if we take into account the fact that the 'balances with other banks' included in this item are almost certainly proportionately larger for the Scottish than for the English banks, the difference becomes smaller still. The main peculiarity of the Scottish figures (apart from 'other accounts') is the high ratio of 'items in transit between offices of the same bank'; this must be due to differences either in accounting procedures or in the speed of handling these items compared with the Clearing banks.

The import of this digression into banks' statistics is that if we use the Scottish banks' gross deposits figure for comparative purposes we shall be exaggerating the comparative scale of Scottish bank deposits, as owned by the public[1] (it will also have some effects on the asset ratios which we customarily use). Furthermore, the effect is not confined to static comparisons: as Table IX shows, the items we deduct to arrive at 'net deposits' have been growing relatively during the last decade, and although their rates of growth have been roughly similar in the English and Scottish banks, there has been a slight difference. This leads to some overstatement (by just under 3 per cent) of the rate of change in Scottish deposits if we use the 'gross' figures. For tracing the movement of deposits over time the figure of net deposits, while not ideal, is obviously the more satisfactory of the two, but it is only available, for the whole group of Scottish banks, from 1952 onwards. However, before we look at the actual trend of Scottish deposits and the interesting questions that arise from it, there are some points to notice about the composition of these deposits.

Deposits, 'Time' and 'Current'

Within Scottish bank deposits, in contrast to English deposits, 'time' deposits exceed 'current' deposits, and this has for long been the normal position. In his evidence to the 1826 Committee the cashier of the Glasgow branch of the Royal Bank of Scotland said that in his office balances on deposit receipt and balances in 'operating accounts', which were the forerunners of the present-day current accounts, were about equal.[2] But, as a commercial centre, Glasgow was not typical. In the country offices of the banks deposit receipts

[1] We must also bear in mind that if by 'the public' we want in some sense to mean 'the Scottish public', some Scottish bank deposits are owned by members of the English public and presumably vice versa.

[2] *Committee of Lords on the Circulation of Promissory Notes, 1826, Evidence,* p. 114.

probably predominated to an extent sufficient to swing the overall position in this direction.[1] The balance may have swung even further in favour of deposit receipts after 1892 when the banks ceased to pay interest on current account balances. The first year for which we have published figures of any kind is 1919 when the Macmillan statistics begin, and the changes in composition since then are shown in Table X.

TABLE X

Composition of Scottish Bank Deposits, 1919–63

	PER CENT OF TOTAL OF TIME AND CURRENT DEPOSITS	
YEAR	TIME[1]	CURRENT
1919[2]	68·5	31·5
1928[3]	62·6	37·4
1938[4]	56·8	43·2
1951[5]	46·9	53·1
1955	46·9	53·1
1960	51·9	48·1
1963	52·8	47·2

[1] 'Time' deposits comprise deposit receipts and, after 1928, savings accounts.
[2] Three banks only: *Macmillan Report*, Appendix 1, Table 2.
[3] Six banks only: ibid.
[4] Six banks only: *Radcliffe Memoranda*, Vol. 2, Statistical Appendix, Table 3.
[5] Average of ten monthly figures only: ibid.

For comparison, the time deposits of the English banks were 40 per cent of the total both in the early 1920s and 1962, although they varied somewhat in between. The high proportion of time deposits in Scottish banking has been a reflection partly of the greater use which the Scots have traditionally made of their banks as savings institutions, and partly of the slower development of the use of cheques within Scotland. The first cheque clearing house was established in Scotland only in 1856. In earlier periods bank customers had withdrawn cash from their 'operating' or 'drawing' accounts—one cheque per day was normally allowed—for their local payments and used bills or drafts for long-distance payments. The lag of Scotland in the use of cheques probably persisted for a long time; as

[1] Records in the Bank of Scotland, which the Bank has kindly allowed me to see, show that in the early 1840s deposit receipts normally exceeded 'current deposit accounts' by a small margin in Edinburgh. In the branches however, judging by the amounts of interest paid, deposit receipts appeared to account for about 60 per cent of the joint total.

we have no figures of cheque clearings for Scotland it is not possible to draw any conclusions about the present day.

The ratio of time deposits is now distinctly lower than it was forty years ago. This decline is presumably related to the increased use of the current account, but a reduced appeal of bank deposits as savings assets may also be part of the answer. However, while this may be the long-run trend, in the short- or medium-term the ratio shows fluctuations which are closely linked with interest rate movements. The proportion of time deposits was markedly lower in 1951, when the post-war figures begin, than in 1938; it probably fell during the Second World War with the high liquidity and low interest rates that accompanied war finance. It remained low until the mid-'fifties when, with higher interest rates, it began to show a rise which has gone on to the present, and which has also affected English bank deposits.[1] One consequence of the high proportion of interest-bearing deposits within total Scottish deposits is, as we have said, to make the cost of them to the banks rather more sensitive to interest rate movements than is the case with the English banks. It is interesting to notice however that, over Scottish banks' liabilities as a whole, this is partially corrected by the presence of the note issues, the costs of which are completely insensitive to interest rate changes.[2]

The Lag of Scottish Bank Deposits

The available indexes of the trend of bank deposits show that the growth of Scottish deposits is lagging behind that of English deposits and this appears to have been the case since the 1920s. The most satisfactory—or least unsatisfactory—figure with which to trace this trend is that of net deposits but this is only available for the Scottish banks from 1952 onwards; for earlier periods we have to use the distinctly unsatisfactory total of gross deposits derived from annual balance sheets. Both series of figures are used in Table XI to compare the trends of Scottish and English deposits since 1938.

The indexes of gross deposits, for what they are worth, suggest that Scottish banks' deposits did not grow as rapidly as English deposits during the Second World War. Since the early 1950s the improved figures give much more reliable evidence of a lag in Scottish deposits. During this period, compared with the growth of the liabilities of other financial intermediaries, the growth of bank

[1] A similar fluctuation in this ratio, related to interest rate movements, can be observed in the years 1919–21: see the figures in *Macmillan Report*, Appendix 1, Table 2.

[2] See below, p. 103.

71

TABLE XI

Trends in Bank Deposits, 1938–63
1952=100

| YEAR | NET DEPOSITS[1] | | GROSS DEPOSITS[2] | |
	SCOTTISH BANKS	CLEARING BANKS	SCOTTISH BANKS	CLEARING BANKS
1938	..	..	43	37
1948	..	..	99	97
1952	100	100	100 (100)	100
1955	104	105	102 (107)	106
1960	106	117	108 (107)	119
1963	112	128	118 (115)	131

[1] For both groups of banks 'net deposits' are taken as total deposits minus 'balances with and cheques in course of collection on other UK banks' and 'items in transit between offices of the same bank'. In each case annual averages of monthly totals are used.

[2] For the Scottish banks 'gross deposits' are the aggregate of the deposit totals shown on annual balance sheets appearing near or just after the end of the year indicated; the figures in brackets are indexes of the annual average of monthly totals. In the case of the Clearing banks, gross deposits are the annual averages of the monthly figure of 'total deposits'.

deposits has been slow throughout the British system; but the rate of growth of Scottish deposits has been well below that of the Clearing banks.

Today, all bankers are worried about the failure of their deposits to expand as rapidly as those of other financial intermediaries, such as building societies and hire purchase finance companies. During the 1950s the overall level of bank deposits, although rising only slowly, did not in any way limit the expansion of bank lending. The extension of bank loans and advances was subject to more or less continuous restriction by official policy, but even apart from this the banks, partly as a result of war and post-war finance, held far more investments than they normally like to carry. To the extent that government policy allowed they were always willing and able to find the resources for increased loans and advances by liquidating securities. But today the position is different: following a remarkable upsurge of advances, largely at the expense of securities, between 1959 and 1961, all the British commercial banks have reached a point where their advances ratios are nearing what they have traditionally regarded as the safe limit. This means that they are approaching the point, if they are not already there, where further expansion of their lending totals can only come through a higher overall level of deposits. This has turned their attention sharply to the reasons for the slower

72

growth of their resources, compared with other institutions, and to possible remedies.

The main influence on the trend of bank deposits in recent years has clearly been Government policy. The position of the banks is such that the monetary authorities can control the volume of bank deposits through their control over the volume of liquid assets in the financial system.[1] The financial conditions of the country over the last decade have been such as to allow them to exercise this control effectively. There is however a persistent feeling among bankers that the poor performance of their deposits has been due in significant measure to the competition of other financial institutions for deposits. As far as the flow of funds into national savings and the trustee savings banks is concerned this is unquestionably true. How far the deposit-attracting activities of non-state financial institutions do in fact nibble into the deposit totals of the commercial banks is a much more complicated and obscure issue. It is arguable that it can happen[2] and that the banks by adopting a more competitive policy in their interest rates can meet the trend and reverse it. The Radcliffe Committee clearly believed this[3] and, in a recent exhortation to the banks to be more competitive, the present Governor of the Bank of England has also endorsed it.[4]

Whatever the truth regarding the behaviour of the deposit totals of the banking system as a whole—and the present writer does not accept all of the current argument on the matter—there is no question that the Scottish banks are peculiarly vulnerable to loss of deposits due to their special position as a regional system. Many of the financial institutions which compete for deposits, but particularly the building societies, have their headquarters in England and keep their accounts with English banks. Whenever such bodies successfully attract deposits from the Scottish public they necessarily reduce the level of Scottish deposits. To the extent that such institutions lend to borrowers in Scotland, deposits flow back; but the probability is that the net movement is outwards.

Judging by the remarks of Scottish bankers they seem to consider the trustee savings banks as their most dangerous competitors. They are very vocal in their criticism of the favoured tax treatment of

[1] This is discussed more fully below, in Ch. 13, pp. 192–5.

[2] See A. N. McLeod, 'Credit Expansion in an Open Economy', *Economic Journal*, September 1962, pp. 611–40.

[3] *Radcliffe Report*, para 132.

[4] Earl of Cromer, in a speech at the quatercentenary dinner of Martins Bank, April 25, 1963.

interest on small deposits in the savings banks, and it is undoubtedly the case that these banks are particularly strong in Scotland. Two elements expose the Scottish banks to losses of deposits to state and private institutions alike. One is their own past success in attracting savings balances and the resulting high proportion of time deposits within their deposit totals. This is bound to leave them more exposed than the English banks to loss of deposits when interest differentials are markedly in favour of other repositories of such balances. The second element reinforces this: the deposit receipt rate of the Scottish banks has in recent years usually been ½ per cent below the deposit rate of the Clearing banks, thus increasing any differential between their rate and those of competing institutions.

The regional position of the Scottish banks exposes them to loss of deposits in other ways than by competition. There has been in this century a southward drift of the control of business. In some cases firms which originally grew up in Scotland have moved their headquarters to London, to be at the centre of business and financial life. More commonly the effective control of undertakings has moved south through the absorption of Scottish enterprises by firms based in England. There is evidence that the concentration of British business, apparently halted during the war years and the immediate post-war period,[1] has now been resumed, and this seems bound to lead to an even greater concentration of control in the South. Whenever the control of a Scottish business moves to England the tendency is for the main accounts to be transferred to an English bank with a consequent loss of deposits and business to the Scottish banks. This trend may be accentuated, though this is less certain, by the comparatively small size of the Scottish banks and the handicap that this imposes on them in dealing with the very largest national concerns.

For all these reasons the deposit problem is felt even more acutely in Scotland than in England. As Table XI shows, since the mid-1950s Scottish bank deposits have been growing at less than half the rate of English deposits. There is not much that the Scottish banks can do about the loss of deposits due to the integration of industry, though the activities of their London offices probably have some counteracting influence here. But their regional position while increasing their vulnerability to deposit loss from all causes, also puts them in a special position in relation to one possible response: the offer of higher interest rates for longer-term deposits. When the point has

[1] See P. E. Hart and S. J. Prais, 'The Analysis of Business Concentration', *Journal of the Royal Statistical Society*, Part II, 1956, p. 175.

been put to them that they might do this the general reaction of bankers has been that, as a group, they would gain no increase in deposits: higher interest rates on certain types of deposits would merely cause balances to be transferred from existing time or demand deposits.[1] There are signs that this attitude may be changing and that bankers, influenced by those recent currents of thought that we have mentioned, are seriously considering a change of policy. What is clear is that the regional situation of the Scottish banks places them in a different position from the banking system as a whole: they could offer higher interest rates and expect to attract funds, or at least to diminish any outflow. There would undoubtedly be some transference of balances from deposit receipts and deposit accounts, but assuming that they took this step on their own they should be able to draw some money from the South.

A strong objection of bankers to any move of this kind is that even assuming that they would secure more deposits, they would have to lend them at interest rates higher than their customary rates in order to make a profit on them. One answer to this—the Governor of the Bank gave it in the speech referred to—is to say that bank lending in this country is too cheap anyway, and that the whole structure of the banks' interest rates should be reconsidered and reformed. Among Scottish bankers Ian W. Macdonald, Chairman of the National Commercial Bank of Scotland, is a notable proponent of reform. In his annual address, dated November 26, 1963, he quoted experience abroad as supporting the view that deposits 'with graduated rates and, above all, with negotiability' are effective in attracting new funds. After considering the implications of such changes for the lending side of the business he concluded, 'There is much to be said in favour of a longer and more flexible price list both for money-in and money-out.' Short of a dramatic reform of interest rate practices the Scottish banks, if they were acting alone, might find a solution by expanding the newer types of lending such as personal loans and term loans which yield higher rates of return than the customary overdraft. (At present, four banks offer personal loans, and one offers term loans.) But the practical difficulties, and even risks, connected with expanding and administering these innovations in lending should not be underrated. We shall return to this question later when we examine the lending policy and interest rates of the Scottish banks.[2]

[1] See *Radcliffe Evidence*, QQ. 3906–16, 4784–97. From the figures, the recent rise in time deposits in the Scottish banks seems to have resulted from the transfer of balances from current accounts.   [2] See below, pp. 159–61, 173–4.

Of course, if the Clearing banks decide to compete for deposits by raising their interest rates the Scottish banks will be compelled, from sheer self-defence, to follow them. But if the Clearers decide against this course the way will still be open for the Scottish banks to experiment on their own, and an experimental attitude is what is needed at this stage. For example, it would seem to be only a short step from the present Scottish deposit receipt to the issue of some kind of negotiable deposit certificates with a definite maturity and a higher rate of interest than the present receipt. But there is another way in which deposit totals may be increased without involving the question of interest rates. If the banking habit can be extended to those sections of the population, chiefly the manual workers, which are so far untouched by it, the demand for banking services will increase and with it the level of the balances held by the public with the commercial banks. Recent developments in advertising by the banks, including the National Commercial Bank's foray into television advertising, are clear indications that the Scottish banks see this as one remedy for the stagnation of their deposits. It is no easy remedy, but it is an important possibility and we raise it again in later chapters.

Yet another influence accounting for the poor showing of Scottish bank deposits in recent years has been the comparatively poor performance of the Scottish economy itself. The slower economic growth of Scotland, compared with the country as a whole, must necessarily retard the development of banking business and even tend to produce some outward drain of deposits. That deposits did not rise more rapidly than they did after 1960 may reflect the greater intensity of the recession in Scotland in 1961–2. Any success which current and impending government policies have in stimulating the growth of the lagging regions will, as far as Scotland is concerned, have an expansive effect on the business and deposits of the Scottish banks. It will certainly do something to mitigate the current disparity of developments between the Scottish and English banking systems. But it will not do more than this and the deep-seated forces which threaten to retard the impetus of banking development, generally, in the second half of this century, have still to be reckoned with.

Individual Deposit Trends
The recent improvements in Scottish statistics have not gone far enough to permit firm conclusions on the position and progress of the individual banks since, unlike the English figures, the published monthly totals of the Scottish banks are undivided aggregates for the whole group. The only individual figures we have—apart from the

statistics on the monthly returns of the note issue—are those obtained from the annual balance sheets of the banks, and from the semi-annual statutory returns which four of the five banks are obliged to publish. In Table XII the balance sheet totals of deposits are used to show movements of individual banks' deposits since 1938, and to provide an estimated distribution of total deposits between the banks. To show the growth of the banks' deposits, the balance sheet totals are averaged over groups of three years. To estimate the distribution of deposits, the balance sheet totals of the individual banks have been averaged over a period of eight years and then adjusted to take account of the average seasonal variation of the particular months in which the balance sheets individually appear.

TABLE XII

Movement and Distribution of Scottish Bank Deposits by Banks, 1920–2 to 1960–2

BANK	MOVEMENT OF GROSS DEPOSITS[1] 1936–8 = 100			AVERAGE DISTRIBUTION OF GROSS DEPOSITS, 1955–62[2]
	1920–2	1950–2	1960–2	PER CENT OF TOTAL
Bank of Scotland	97	247 ⎫	262	23·1
Union Bank	100	225 ⎭		
Royal Bank	58	196	201	15·7
British Linen Bank	82	207	249	10·7
Commercial Bank	94	273 ⎫	281	28·7
National Bank	99	259 ⎭		
Clydesdale Bank	102 ⎫	239	295	21·7
North Bank	78 ⎭			
				———
				99·9

[1] In each case an average of three consecutive balance sheets is taken. Balance sheets are dated not by calendar years but by the cycle beginning in September of the year indicated and extending to February or March of the following year.

[2] In each case an average of eight seasonally adjusted balance sheet totals are used; percentages are of the aggregate of these average totals. Seasonal adjustment is based on the average seasonal movements of Scottish banks' monthly totals during the eight calendar years, except for the Royal and Clydesdale Banks. The balance sheets of these two banks show the position on December 31st whereas the December figures of the Scottish monthly statement relate to a date in the middle of the month. Because of the special movements affecting the end-December totals the adjustment for these two banks has been based on the seasonal variation of Clearing bank figures which show the end-December position.

From our earlier excursion around the pitfalls of deposit statistics it is obviously dangerous to base any ambitious conclusions on the figures in Table XII. The averaging of sets of three annual balance sheets probably irons out most of the fortuitous movements of individual years, but the figures are still gross totals, and differences of practice in the inclusion and treatment of the multifarious elements contained in 'other accounts' may well explain some of the apparent divergences of trend. The comparatively slow expansion of the Royal Bank's deposits since the war seems sufficiently marked to suggest that there had indeed been a lag here: it contrasts sharply with the truly remarkable advance of this bank in the interwar period. From the balance sheet figures the fastest grower in the 1950s appears to have been the Clydesdale Bank, and here again there is a contrast with the interwar years in that the old Clydesdale, then separate from the North, was among the slowest growers. The second fastest grower in the 'fifties may well have been the British Linen Bank, which suggests that it has not been hampered by its small size.

CHAPTER 6

THE NOTE ISSUES–I FACTS

One fact that clearly marks off the Scottish banks from the English banks is that they issue their own bank notes. Traditionally the individual note issues were regarded as an important feature of Scottish banking, responsible for some of its most characteristic elements. This partly reflected the fact that before 1914 bank notes were a much more important medium of exchange in Scotland than in England, the £1 note taking the place occupied by the gold sovereign in the south. Today, while no one would regard the note issues as a major element in Scottish banking, they are nevertheless something more than a picturesque survival of a bygone banking age. For one thing they account for 13 per cent of the total of the Scottish banks' note and deposit liabilities—a much higher proportion, incidentally, than at any time since Peel's Bank Acts. But more than this they have effects on the asset structure and reserve practices of the banks from which flow a variety of secondary effects: on the money supply; on the branch system; on the profitability of Scottish banking. None of these effects is of immense importance; but neither, within the Scottish context, are they negligible. To examine them adequately, as well as to convey the factual background to the business of note issuing in Scotland, will occupy two chapters. The present chapter will stick, broadly, to facts: the regulations governing the issues, their practical operation by the banks, and a number of interesting statistical trends will all be examined. In the following chapter we shall analyse the effects of the note issues on those aspects of Scottish banking on which they impinge.

I. THE STATUTORY POSITION

The present note-issuing powers of the Scottish banks derive from two statutes, the Bank Notes (Scotland) Act of 1845 and the Currency and Bank Notes Act of 1928, although the latter merely gave permanence to an arrangement that had originated in emergency legislation passed at the outbreak of the First World War. The 1845 Act is the basic statute: along with a companion Act for Ireland it was part of the edifice of legislation erected by Sir Robert Peel to regulate the British monetary system according to the monetary doctrine known as the 'Currency Principle'. The central measure of Peel's banking laws was the Bank of England Charter Act of 1844, and the whole system was founded on two basic propositions: that the money supply consisted of the total of coin and bank notes (i.e. currency) and that this total should 'fluctuate precisely as if the currency were entirely metallic' if periodic disorders of the monetary system were to be avoided. Peel took three main steps to give effect to his policy in England. First, he prohibited the founding of any new banks of issue; and this provision of the Act applied throughout the British Isles. Secondly, he placed a ceiling on the note issues of existing banks of issue, with the proviso that their rights of issue would lapse if they united with any other banks. Thirdly, he gave the Bank of England the right to issue notes up to a fixed limit against holdings of government securities—this was the original 'fiduciary issue'[1]—and beyond this against holdings of gold on a one-for-one basis, the whole business of issue to be segregated from its other banking business and conducted in a separate department, the Issue Department.

The basic difference between Scottish and English opinion on the question of small-value bank notes made it necessary to treat Scotland differently. The necessity to maintain the £1 note in Scotland—and in Ireland as well—while excluding it rigorously from England precluded any attempt to extend the dominance of the Bank of England's issue over the three kingdoms. The solution, embodied in the Scottish and Irish Bank Acts of 1845, was a neat one. The 1844 Act had frozen the right of issue on the existing banks of issue in all three countries: the 1845 Acts now applied to each separate bank of issue in Scotland and Ireland a form of regulation which in essence mirrored that imposed on the Bank of England. Each bank was given a fiduciary issue of fixed size which was actually termed its 'authorized circulation'; but it could circulate notes beyond this limit provided it held an amount of gold, equal in value to the 'excess' issue, in two authorized offices of the bank. But the differences from the English legislation were important. There was, for example, no attempt to impose a separation between note issuing and the other banking business of the Scottish and Irish banks as in the case of the Bank of England. This meant that there was no prescription of the

---

[1] The fiduciary issue of the Bank was originally set at £14 million but it was subject to increase by two-thirds of the value of any lapsed issues.

assets to be held against the fiduciary issues nor was there any special earmarking of the gold held as 'cover' for the excess issues to that function. It also implied an absence of any attempt to reserve the profits of the Scottish note issues to the state, as with the Bank of England's issue, although they were of course subject to stamp duty.[1] Finally, there was a significant omission of any provision for the lapsing of Scottish and Irish note issues when banks amalgamated; and, indeed, the only occasions when rights of note issue have lapsed have been on the failures of the Western and City of Glasgow Banks.

This system of regulation has been modified by two developments, one statutory, one practical. Under an emergency arrangement of 1914, made permanent in 1928, gold was replaced as the 'cover' for excess note issues, first by Currency notes, and then (in 1928) by Bank of England notes. Further, by the same Acts, the Scottish banks were allowed to hold such notes 'on deposit' at the Bank of England, as well as in the traditional authorized offices. This was a welcome measure of convenience which should have come much sooner: before 1914 the gold required to cover the seasonal increases in the Scottish note issues had to be hauled into Scotland from the New-castle branch of the Bank of England only to be taken back when the circulation had subsided. From the figures of the Bank of England notes of denominations over £1,000, which are used only within the Bank to represent the cover deposited by the Scottish and Northern Irish banks,[2] it appears probable that these banks now hold the bulk of their note cover in this way; the significance of these notes placed 'on deposit' therefore needs a little more explanation. The important point is that these notes *remain* notes in principle, whatever their form: that is to say, they form part of the Bank of England's own note circulation and are liabilities of the Issue Department. They are quite distinct from the balances which the Scottish banks, like the English banks, maintain with the Bank: these are liabilities of the Banking Department and cannot be treated as cover for note issues. But the facts that the notes are held within the Bank and are not in principle earmarked to the cover function inevitably raise the question of their significance for the reserve position of the Scottish banks; to this we shall return later.

[1] From 1853 this was compounded by a payment at the rate of 8s 4d per £100 of annual average circulation.

[2] See the Bank of England's *Report for the Year Ended February 28, 1963*, p. 11, note (b). This states that £1,000 notes are 'used only within the Bank of England for internal purposes, e.g. for transfers made by banks of issue in Scotland and Northern Ireland as cover for their excess note issues'. I am assuming here that there are in fact no other significant internal uses of these notes.

The other development has followed from the fact that the fiduciary issues of the Scottish banks have never been altered in size since 1845, when they were equal to the whole circulation of each bank; in the aggregate they have actually fallen, as a consequence of two failures. During this period the volume of the currency circulation has expanded many times and the Scottish note issues have more or less kept in step. The result has been that the fiduciary portion of the issues—they amount in all to £2·7 million—have sunk to an insignificant 2 per cent of the total, and this makes it almost true to say that the Scottish banks must hold an equal amount of Bank of England notes against their own notes in circulation. This has had effects on the cash holdings of the banks to which we shall return shortly.

II. THE OPERATION OF THE NOTE ISSUES

There are two important points to notice about the way in which the Scottish banks conduct their note issues. The first is that they do not attempt to control the circulation of their own notes. When customers withdraw cash—other than coin or 10s notes—the Scottish banks have the choice of issuing their own notes or Bank of England notes. They could, if they wished, limit the circulation of their own notes by issuing English notes,[1] but there are no signs that they do this in any consistent way. If they are asked for Bank of England notes they will issue them and some customers do express a definite preference in this matter: for example, the Armed Services prefer to use Bank of England notes for pay purposes, and there are of course always people travelling to England who ask for them. But failing requests of this kind the banks tend to issue their own notes, if only because the branches are much more plentifully supplied with Scottish than with English notes. A Scottish bank does not have to provide statutory cover for its notes until they actually move across its counter into circulation. They can hold as many of their own unissued notes as they like and, as the cost of doing so is merely that of manufacturing the notes, this is much the cheapest way of providing money 'in the till'. As the Bank of England notes have to be acquired at full value, the holding of them involves the locking up of resources which have to be paid for; there is therefore a premium on keeping the stock of them in the branches at a minimum. We can get a fairly accurate indication of how much English money is held in Scottish bank branches.

---

[1] They are said to have done this during the Second World War when supplies of their own notes were short.

The monthly Bank Returns give the figure of total holdings of Bank of England notes and coin in *all* offices of the banks: if we deduct from this an amount equal to the excess note issues (since this amount must be held either at the Bank of England or in the authorized offices) we get a figure which represents the maximum amount that could be held in all offices other than the authorized offices. In 1963 this figure averaged £10·3 million over all the banks, or slightly more than 1 per cent of total deposits. This is a Saturday figure and may therefore be on the low side by one or two million;[1] but if we consider that it contains coin and 10s notes as well as the cash in their English offices, which must be wholly English money, and then compare it with English banks' till money ratio of nearly 5 per cent, it is clear that the Scottish banks hold very low stocks of Bank of England notes in their branches.

The second practical point about the conduct of the note issues is that no Scottish bank re-issues the notes of other Scottish banks which it acquires. Such notes are presented to the originating banks through regular 'note exchanges'. In other words notes are cleared like cheques, and indeed historically the note exchanges preceded the organized clearing of cheques in Scotland by a century.[2] At one time Scottish bankers attached great importance to the note exchanges as a means of preventing the over-issue of notes. This they certainly did as far as over-issue by individual banks was concerned, since any disproportionate increase in the note issue of one bank would be quickly returned to it through the exchanges. How far the exchanges inhibited over-issue by the whole group of Scottish banks is disputable: in principle the check would be removed if all acted together; but it is not impossible that the restraint on the banks as individuals added up to an overall moderating influence. With the relegation of currency to a subordinate role in the monetary system, over-issue of any kind has ceased to be a danger: the main function of the note exchanges today is to keep to a minimum the amount of one another's

[1] Apart from the week-end drain of cash into circulation, the figure may be depressed by another practice. At least one bank calls in to its authorized offices the Bank of England notes held in the larger offices within range, on a Saturday morning. The object of this, of course, is to swell the total of available cover.

[2] The earliest recorded agreement on exchanging notes is one of 1752, between the Bank of Scotland and the Royal Bank. Later other banks were admitted to the exchange. The first Clearing House in Scotland, in Glasgow, was instituted in 1856: see J. O. Leslie, *The Note Exchange and Clearing House Systems*, Institute of Bankers in Scotland, 2nd ed., pp. 30–4, 45–50. Today, the note exchanges are held on most days of the week wherever two or more of the banks are represented; the net balances are passed into the next cheque clearing and from this point onwards the two settlements are merged.

notes that each bank holds, and so to keep down the amount of statutory cover that each must hold. Indeed an exchange is held on a Friday afternoon in order to minimize the Saturday circulation on which the cover requirement and stamp duty are reckoned.

III. TRENDS IN THE SCOTTISH NOTE ISSUES

As has so often happened, the statutory regulation of the Scottish note issues had a useful by-product of statistics. The 1845 Act required the Scottish banks to make a weekly return of three figures: their notes in circulation, their *total* holdings of legal tender and their holdings of legal tender in the authorized offices, all at the close of business on Saturday. For the purpose of determining that the requirements of the law were met, these figures were to be averaged over periods of four weeks, and the first two of them, the note circulation and the total legal tender held, were to be published in a four-weekly Bank Return. These provisions are still in force; indeed, as we have seen, until the Scottish banks began to publish regular monthly figures of their assets and liabilities, in 1960 (and with the exception of the statistics published by the Macmillan and Radcliffe Committees), the Bank Return was our only source of monthly data on Scottish banking.

Since 1960, we have had two monthly figures of the volume of Scottish bank notes in circulation: the Bank Return figure which is an average of the position on four Saturdays, and the monthly statements which give the position on the third Wednesday of each month.[1] The annual averages of these two figures, for 1963, were respectively £125·8 million and £122·6 million. The Saturday figure is the larger since, mainly because of the payment of wages on the previous day, this is a weekly peak of note circulation. As the Wednesday circulation is probably very near the low-point of the week, the mean value of the two figures is a reasonable indication of the average circulation through time. But, here, we shall actually have occasion to use all three figures in varying contexts.

The Scottish note issues have been subject to the same expansionary forces as the currency circulation of the country as a whole during the last quarter century, and the present level is higher than at any time in the past. Since 1945 the Scottish note issues have actually risen faster than the total currency circulation, causing a slight increase in their relative importance.

[1] Before October 1960 the individual monthly totals of the banks, including the Radcliffe series (1951–8), referred to varying dates in the month.

TABLE XIII

Scottish Note Issues and the UK Currency Circulation, 1938–63

YEAR	SCOTTISH NOTES IN CIRCULATION[1]		AVERAGE CURRENCY CIRCULATION WITH THE UK PUBLIC[2]		SCOTTISH NOTE ISSUES AS A PER CENT OF UK CIRCULATION
	£ m.	INDEX 1938=100	£ m.	INDEX 1938=100	%
1938	23·5	100	446	100	5
1945	64·9	272	1,263	283	5
1950	70·1	298	1,255	281	6
1963	125·8	531	2,220	498	6

[1] Annual averages of Scottish Bank Return totals.
[2] Average estimated circulation with the public as given in the *Annual Abstract of Statistics*.

The Significance of the Note Issues in Scotland

In 1963 the Scottish note issues formed roughly 6 per cent of the total currency in circulation with the British public. If we adjust the British total to exclude coin and an estimate of the circulation of 10s notes (a denomination which Scottish banks cannot issue) the proportion rises to nearer 7 per cent. But, of course, a more interesting figure would be the percentage of Scottish bank notes within the total currency circulation of Scotland. We have no means of calculating this precisely but we can attempt to place it within certain limits. If we assume that currency needs are exactly proportional to population then, as Scotland has 11 per cent of the British population, she will also account for the same percentage of the total currency circulation. The Scottish banks would thus appear to supply about six-elevenths of the currency needs of Scotland. But the assumption of proportional currency needs may well be wrong: Scotland as a region is poorer than the British Isles as a whole and this will reduce her total demand for currency; on the other hand a smaller use of cheques—itself connected with the lower level of incomes—will go some way to offset this. An alternative estimate may be obtained by comparing ratios of currency circulation to current bank deposits. For the country as a whole the currency in circulation with the public, in 1961, was equal to 44 per cent of current deposits; for Scotland the ratio of Scottish bank notes to current deposits was 36 per cent. The crude ratio of these two percentages would indicate that the Scottish notes serve about nine-elevenths of the currency needs of the Scottish public. But this again assumes uniformity between Scotland and the rest of the country, this time in the holding and use of current deposits, and the result is almost certainly too high. The true proportion must be between these two values, and my guess is that it is somewhat nearer to the lower than the higher figure.

The Composition of the Note Issues

A striking fact about the Scottish note issues is the very marked rise in importance of the high-valued notes (i.e. £5 and above) during the last twenty-five years. The obverse of this has been a decline in the £1 note—traditionally the staple note of Scotland—from 62 per cent of the total circulation in 1938, to 32 per cent in 1960.

TABLE XIV

Composition of the Scottish Note Issues, 1850–1960

YEAR	PERCENTAGE OF £1 NOTES[1]
1850	77
1910	69
1920	62
1938	62
1945	48
1955	36
1960	32

[1] Averages of the figures in the first three Bank Returns in each year.

In February 1963, the £5 denomination of the Bank of England's note issue accounted for 51 per cent of its total circulation.[1] During the previous six years the whole growth of the English note issues was in this component, the £1 note declining absolutely as well as relatively. This suggests that the trend in Scotland has anticipated a country-wide movement in currency-using habits, a movement caused by the great rise in the level of prices and money incomes during the last quarter century. The Scottish lead in this matter has surely had something to do with the fact that the £5 notes of the Scottish banks were of a size and texture which made them much more acceptable to the public than the old, flimsy £5 notes of the Bank of England; at any rate, the rising trend in the Bank of England's £5 notes began after the introduction of the new note. But the present low proportion of £1 notes in the Scottish issues cannot be attributed wholly to this trend. In part it must reflect the use of English notes in Scotland. Bank of England notes make up an appreciable fraction of the Scottish circulation, due to the fact that some bank customers

[1] Bank of England, *Report for the Year Ended February 28, 1963*, p. 11. In calculating this percentage I have excluded notes of the over £1,000 denomination from the total, as these are held only within the Bank.

—the Services for example, and some industrial concerns—express a definite preference for them when withdrawing cash. It is possible that hitherto these demands for English notes have been biased towards the £1 denomination, thus restricting the circulation of the corresponding Scottish notes. Now that the English £5 note is in every way more sensible its use in Scotland may increase (one has the impression that it is increasing); and in the end this may halt, and even reverse, the upward movement in the proportion of high-valued notes within the Scottish issues.

Seasonal Variations

As with the national currency circulation the Scottish note issues are subject to a clear seasonal variation, and the pattern is much the same, showing peaks in July and December. There is a slight difference in that with the Scottish issues the July peak is the higher of the two, but the degree of variation—in recent years about 8 or 9 per cent from low to high—is close to that of the British currency as a whole. In the nineteenth century the Scottish issues varied much more widely than this during the course of the year—by something like 20 per cent from low to high—while the movement of the English issues was narrower than it is today. In those days, in Scotland, the payment of rents, mortgages and the wages of farm servants was made bi-annually at the terms of Whitsuntide and Martinmas; the withdrawal of notes to make them produced a peak in June, and made the November circulation almost as high as that of December. This wide seasonal variation was regarded by some, on rather slender evidence,[1] as tending to destabilize interest rates in the London money market, since funds had to be withdrawn to provide the gold cover.

Today, with modern monetary management, even were the Scottish note issues much larger and more significant than they are, there would be no question of their seasonal peaks producing unwanted stringencies in the money market. As it is they merely present the Scottish banks with a comparatively small problem of providing cover at the appropriate times. As far as the mid-year peak is concerned they appear to do this by withdrawing funds from the London

[1] R. H. I. Palgrave was the leading exponent of this view and he assembled a vast quantity of statistics to support it in his *Bank Acts and the Bank Rate, 1845–1891* (London, 1892). Palgrave actually underestimated the seasonal variation of the Scottish note issues during this period by an erroneous use of averages, but in any case his evidence of its effects on Bank Rate was pretty slender. Palgrave attributed the wide variability of the Scottish note issues to the £1 note: in two years which I have examined, 1880 and 1881, the variation of the high denomination notes was nearly twice that of the £1 notes.

money market: at least, more often than not, July brings a dip in the total of money lent 'at call'. Towards the end of the year the seasonal rise in deposits seems to provide for the extra cover need of the higher note circulation without any net withdrawal of funds from the market. It is possible that if there were no seasonal swings in the note issues the banks could maintain slightly lower average levels of liquid assets and correspondingly higher amounts of advances and investments, but the amount involved is not more than a few millions over all the banks. Indeed, it must be stressed that the seasonal variation of the note issues, and their effects on liquid assets, are small compared with the similar movements caused by the seasonal swing in deposits.

The Note Issues within Liabilities
Today the Scottish note issues are 13 per cent of the total of Scottish banks' notes and deposits, a level which, perhaps unexpectedly, is higher than at any period since 1845—as Table XV shows.

TABLE XV

Notes as a Percentage of Scottish Banks'
Notes and Deposits,[1] 1845–1962

1845	9·0
1908–10	6·3
1918–20	9·8
1936–8	6·8
1950–2	9·3
1962	13·0

[1] For 1845 the deposits total is that given in *Select Committee on Banks of Issue 1875, Minutes of Evidence* Q. 768, and the note total is the average circulation from Bank Returns. For all other periods except 1962, both totals are taken from annual balance sheets and averaged over groups of three years. The figures for 1962 are annual averages of the published monthly figures. All deposit totals are of *gross* deposits.

The ratio has fluctuated but for much of the period since 1845 it has been below the 9 per cent at which it stood then. It rose sharply in the last war, subsided a little in the immediate post-war years, but has been rising steadily since 1950. This apparent buoyancy of notes within the Scottish banks' liabilities may come as a surprise to those who have in mind a picture of the declining relative importance of currency within the money supply, during the last hundred years. The fact is of course that the ratio of currency to bank deposits is a misleading guide to the comparative monetary significance of the two media. As we saw in the last chapter, bank deposits are not a homogeneous quantity. They are the major medium of exchange in the economy, but they are also a savings asset. The total of bank deposits contains a significant but indeterminable savings element, and this has always been very much the case with Scottish bank deposits. Furthermore, since the beginning of this century this element has not been constant: in the Scottish case it has probably been declining and this means that a rising ratio of notes to deposits is consistent with a declining importance of currency as a means of payment. However, even the ratio of notes to *current account* deposits, which might be thought to be a more accurate indicator, yields no evidence of a declining relative importance of bank notes. In 1961 the Scottish figure was 36 per cent; in 1921, using an estimate of Scottish current account deposits based on the Macmillan Committee's statistics, it was in the region of 32–33 per cent.[1] But even this measure is unreliable in that the total of current account deposits is almost certainly not very closely related to the volume of payments settled by cheque. Whatever the reason for, and the monetary significance of, the continued buoyancy of bank-notes within the total liabilities of the Scottish banks, the fact of it has some clear consequences for their asset structures to which we shall shortly turn.

Distribution of the Issues

The distribution of the total circulation of Scottish bank notes among the individual banks calls for the final comments in this survey of the statistical aspects of the Scottish note issues. The trend of this distribution over the last half century is shown in Table XVI.

The most remarkable feature of the pattern of note issues over these years is its steadiness. The shares of the National and Commercial Banks, first individually and now jointly, have increased. Before its amalgamation with the Bank of Scotland the Union Bank's share was declining, and this may account for the fall in the combined figure for these banks between 1947 and 1962. But one should not read too much into movements of this kind. The relative size of a Scottish bank's note circulation is undoubtedly influenced by its share of the country's banking business and changes in this are responsible for part of the long-term trends in the distribution of note

---

[1] The Macmillan totals, which give a breakdown of deposits into current and deposit accounts, only cover six banks; at the same time they omit the corresponding total of notes in circulation. I have therefore taken the proportion of current accounts as shown in Table II of Appendix 1 of the *Report*, applied it to the balance sheet total of deposits for 1921, and calculated the ratio of the balance sheet note totals to this figure.

TABLE XVI

Distribution of the Scottish Note Issues by Banks, 1910–62

PER CENT OF TOTAL AVERAGE ANNUAL CIRCULATION

	1910	1938	1947	1962
Bank of Scotland	16·9	14·7	15·5⎫	
Union Bank of Scotland	12·9	11·2	9·5⎭	22·3
Royal Bank of Scotland	13·8	13·1	13·5	13·9
British Linen Bank	11·2	11·7	11·4	11·7
Commercial Bank of Scotland	13·2	15·5	16·6⎫	
National Bank of Scotland	10·9	12·1	12·6⎭	32·9
Clydesdale Bank	10·6	12·2	11·0⎫	
North of Scotland Bank	10·5	9·6	9·9⎭	19·3
	100·0	100·1	100·0	100·1

Source: Scottish Bank Returns.

issues. But this is not the only factor: another, probably of equal importance, is the differences between the banks in the make-up of their clienteles. This should be considered along with another aspect of the distribution of the issues.

If we compare the banks' individual shares in the total note circulation, in 1962, with the distribution of deposits between them as shown in Table XII (p. 77), some divergences appear. For example, the National Commercial has a high note circulation relative to its deposits, the two percentages being 33 and 29. The Royal Bank on the other hand has about 16 per cent of the total deposits of the Scottish banks compared with about 14 per cent of the total note circulation. These divergences, again, are probably related to the clienteles of the banks concerned. The note issue of the Royal Bank has for long been low in relation to its deposits, and this may be due to its connections with state departments. The Royal was traditionally the Government's banking agent in Scotland and it may still hold more public accounts than the other banks;[1] this would tend to keep down the circulation of its own notes since some of the public departments are more inclined than other customers to make use of Bank of England notes in their cash transactions. The relatively high note issue of the National Commercial may arise from especially strong connections with large industrial customers who make heavy and regular withdrawals of cash for wage payments.

[1] For example, it has the Post Office account. One important public account, that of the Inland Revenue, circulates annually between the banks.

CHAPTER 7

THE NOTE ISSUES–II EFFECTS

The immediate and most general effect of their power to issue bank notes is that it enables the Scottish banks to hold a greater quantity of assets than they would hold were they restricted to deposit banking alone. This extra quantity of assets cannot be smaller in amount than the volume of the note circulation at that time. When a note is passed into circulation it is given either in exchange for an asset (e.g. as part of an advance to a customer), or for an equal reduction of the bank's deposit liabilities (i.e. when a customer encashes a credit balance). In the second case assets do not increase, but the composition of liabilities changes and there is, as it were, a transference of an asset from 'matching' a deposit balance to 'matching' a note. Thus, in their note-issuing activities, the banks will always acquire an amount of assets at least equal to their circulations. The proviso 'at least' is entered here because, as we shall see later in this chapter, the Scottish note issues—or at any rate the reserve practices associated with them —have a small expansive influence on the level of the deposit liabilities, and hence on the assets, of the whole banking system. But here we may disregard this deposit effect and treat the assets held on account of the note issues as equal in amount to the volume of notes in circulation. The question that now immediately poses itself is: which particular bank assets are affected by the existence of Scottish bank notes in circulation?

I. THE NOTE ISSUES AND THE CASH POSITION

The primary effect of the note-issuing activities of the Scottish banks is on their cash position. This effect is determined both by the statutes which govern these activities and by the way in which the banks conduct them. We have seen that all but a now negligible fiduciary quantity of Scottish notes in circulation must be 'covered' by holdings of Bank of England notes of equal amount. We have also seen that in practice the Scottish banks do not exercise any positive

91

control over the extent of their note circulations: these are determined by the public's requirements for currency as modified by its demand for coin and English banknotes. As the cash held for note cover purposes represents the major part of the aggregate cash of the Scottish banks—in 1963 it was about 84 per cent of it—and as the remainder contains little if any margin over their other needs for cash, the consequence is that the level and movements of total cash are largely determined by movements in the note circulation. Furthermore, not only is the absolute amount of cash almost wholly determined by the note issues, but its ratio to deposits, the 'cash ratio', is also largely the consequence of the ratio which Scottish notes in circulation bear to deposits. This is shown very clearly, by the movement of the various ratios, in Table XVII.

TABLE XVII

Scottish Banks: Note Issues and Cash Ratios, 1938–63

1	2	3	4	5
YEAR	RATIO OF TOTAL CASH TO TOTAL DEPOSITS[1]	RATIO OF TOTAL NOTES IN CIRCULATION TO TOTAL DEPOSITS[2]	RATIO OF TOTAL EXCESS ISSUES TO TOTAL DEPOSITS[2]	RATIO OF UK CURRENCY CIRCULATIONS TO TOTAL UK BANK DEPOSITS[3]
	%	%	%	%
1938	8·3	7·3	6·5	17·1
1945	13·5	11·0	10·5	23·9
1951	11·5	10·0	9·6	18·7
1955	14·8	12·9	12·4	22·9
1960	17·9	15·5	15·1	25·7
1963	17·3	14·5	14·2	25·6

[1] Ratios for 1938, 1951, and 1955 are calculated from averages of monthly figures as given in *Radcliffe Memoranda*, vol. 2, p. 206; that for 1960 from similar averages now published in *Financial Statistics*. The 1938 figures cover six of the then eight banks; and the 1951 figures relate to ten monthly figures. 'Cash' comprises coin, notes, including the banks' holdings of each other's notes, and balances with the Bank of England. The 1945 figure is calculated from annual balance sheets of six banks, appearing between September 1945 and April 1946, and the 'cash' figure includes some holdings of Scottish notes and some balances with banks other than the Bank of England.

[2] Sources of figures are the same as in (1) above with the exception that for 1945 the figure covers eight banks, and the note total used is the annual average of the Bank Return totals for the calendar year. In calculating the total excess issues of the six banks covered by the Radcliffe figures for 1938, I have simply taken three-quarters of the total authorized circulations and deducted this from the Radcliffe figure of the average note circulation in that year.

[3] Ratios of estimated annual average currency circulation with the UK public to the total of Scottish and English bank deposits. English deposit totals used are the annual averages of monthly figures. Scottish totals are annual averages as in (1) above, except for 1945; for this year deposits are totalled from the annual balance sheets of the eight banks, appearing between September 1945 and April 1946.

The marked surges, of recent years, in the ratio between the currency circulation and the level of bank deposits have had clear reflection in the cash ratios of the Scottish banks. This shows itself in the close correspondence between the movements in the percentages of columns 2 and 4 of Table XVII. The correspondence is least close between 1945 and 1951 but the larger drop in the cash ratio between these dates is explained by differing definitions of 'cash': for 1945 we have had to use the 'impure' balance sheet totals.

There has been one long-term force at work tending to increase the influence of the note issues on the Scottish banks' cash position. This is the rise in the proportion of the excess issues within the total note issues, itself the inevitable result of the fixity of the fiduciary elements and the general currency expansion of the last fifty years. Before the First War the excess issues were around 60 per cent of the total; to-day they are 98 per cent. This trend has exerted a long-term upward pressure on the Scottish banks' cash ratios and caused them to reflect more closely the circulation of Scottish bank notes. Working against it however has been a tendency, since the early 1950s, for the non-cover elements of cash to rise slightly.

Let us now revert to the bloc of extra assets which, on account of their note issues, the Scottish banks are enabled to hold, and consider more closely what is its actual composition. At first sight, and in the light of what we have just said about their effect on the cash position, the note issues—apart from the small fiduciary issues—seem simply to entail the banks in holding an extra quantum of cash. But how far is this cash, the amount of which is admittedly and practically determined by the note issues, to be regarded as a purely adventitious element, there simply because of the fact of note issue? Are there any grounds for regarding it as, in some degree, forming a necessary part of the asset structure quite apart from its formal connection with the note issues? The position of the cover fund within the Scottish banks' assets is admittedly a peculiar one. It is passively determined by the public's demand for Scottish bank notes; it is held in the form of currency—or at any rate quasi-currency—and as we shall see in the next chapter when we examine the liquidity of the banks it seems to be treated for the most part as an unusable fund. It could almost be regarded as vicariously forming part of the general currency circulation: if the Scottish note issues were abolished, and ignoring the small fiduciary elements, we could conceive of the Scottish banks as simply withdrawing their own notes from circulation and replacing them with the English notes which at present they hold as cover. But if they did no more than this they would be left with cash reserves of between 2 and 3 per cent of deposits (the difference between columns 2 and 4 in Table XVII), and on operating grounds alone this would not be enough. There is one bit of their cash reserves which is large enough for their present working needs and that would be unaffected by such an operation—their free balances in London. But what would most certainly be inadequate in the absence of the note issues is the present stock of English money in the tills of Scottish bank branches; at about 1 per cent of deposits this would clearly need to be augmented to replace some, if not all, of the stocks of unissued Scottish notes which at present supply the main need for money in the till.

How much till money the Scottish banks would need to hold is difficult to say. In 1961 the English banks held cash in hand equivalent to 4·8 per cent of deposits. Scottish needs would not be less than this and in view of the smaller average size of Scottish branch offices in terms of deposits lodged they would probably be higher, though the higher proportion of time deposits might offset this to some extent. If we allow for the English money which they already hold in branch offices we can say that in the absence of note issue their till money needs would require them to hold additional cash equal to at least 4 per cent of deposits over and above their present non-cover cash. This would make an overall cash ratio, reckoned purely on working needs, of at least $6\frac{1}{2}$ per cent. But, of course, cash ratios are not determined solely by working needs. In the past they have frequently contained a conventional element felt to be necessary to manifest the soundness of the banks. Today this conventional element is still there but, as far as the English banks are concerned, it rests on an explicit agreement with the Bank of England. The nature of this agreement—to avoid window-dressing and maintain a stable ratio of around 8 per cent—is aimed essentially at stabilizing the cash ratios rather than maintaining them above any particular level. Nevertheless it is a plausible assumption that, in modern conditions, the Scottish banks would probably not wish to show cash ratios lower than those of the English banks, especially as this would only mean a small increase above the level dictated by working needs.[1]

If we accept that in the event of their ceasing to issue notes the Scottish banks would have to hold an amount of cash greater than their

[1] But this is pure speculation: there have been long periods in the past, for example throughout the interwar years, when the Scottish banks have shown lower cash ratios than the English banks. It is arguable that there is more pressure towards uniformity today, and that the authorities might require it—if only to obtain the slight extra amount of interest-free finance that it would bring to the State.

present non-cover cash, then clearly some part of the cash now held as cover would have to be retained. The important corollary to this is that the bloc of assets which they would relinquish would contain earning assets, including some loans and advances, as well as cash. Further conclusions follow from this. One is that some part of the resources which the Scottish banks acquire through the circulation of their own notes is to be regarded as being made available to the Scottish economy and not simply passed on to the State through the holding of Bank of England notes. Another is that the presence of earning assets among the total of assets held on account of the note issues means that the gross income of the Scottish banks is increased by the possession of this right. Whether or not their *net* income is higher depends also on the cost of operating the issues. Later in this chapter we attempt a rough estimate of the net profits of note issue: the conclusion reached there is that at the present time these are probably positive but not large.

II. NOTE ISSUE, TILL MONEY AND THE BRANCHES

It is time to look more closely at the connection between note issue and the till-money needs of Scottish bank branches. As we have seen, these needs are largely supplied by holding stocks of unissued Scottish bank notes, the stocks of English money being correspondingly low. This 'cheap' till money has long been regarded by Scottish bankers as a prime advantage of the right of note issue, in that it reduces the cost of branch operation; indeed, the nineteenth-century banker took the view that it was more or less the *only* advantage of note issue since he argued that the excess issues merely involved the holding of cash and therefore yielded no profit. Along with the argument for a general till-money advantage there is an extension of it which holds that without this source of cheap till money the Scottish banks would be unable to maintain many of their smaller branch offices;[1] but this is a separate argument and needs to be kept apart from the more general proposition which we shall examine first.

Clearly a general advantage from cheap till money, applying to *all* bank offices in Scotland, is possible. If it exists it must take the form of reducing the level of the Scottish banks' cash holdings so that if at any time they ceased to issue notes they would have to hold proportionately more cash. The advantage would then be measured by the

[1] For a modern statement of this view see F. S. Taylor, 'Differences in English and Scottish Banking—I, The Note Issue', *The Banker*, December 1950, pp. 371–2.

yield on a quantity of earning assets equal to the extra cash that the banks would have had to hold, due to till-money needs. Stated in this way the till-money argument is seen to be inconsistent with the view, once prevalent and just mentioned, that the excess issues are unprofitable because they involve the banks in holding cash for which they would otherwise have no need. From the one side, through the till-money advantage, the note issues were regarded as permitting a lower cash holding than would have been possible without them; from the other, they were regarded as causing cash to be greater than it otherwise would be. Both contentions could not be true at the same time; but the problem is admittedly a tricky one and there were reasons why the older bankers should have held the views they did.[1]

We have seen that in analysing the effects of the note issues on the asset structures of the Scottish banks we can only proceed by comparing the actual position with a hypothetical one which, we postulate, would exist in the absence of note issue. This applies with equal force to the dissection of the till-money argument. Indeed, assumptions about till-money needs played a part in the analysis of the previous section: to arrive at a feasible assumption about the cash ratio which would be maintained in the absence of note issue we had to make an estimate, based on the special conditions of the Scottish branch systems, of till-money needs. We concluded there that on the basis of working needs, including the need to hold legal tender in branch tills, the minimum total cash reserve that the Scottish banks would need to hold in the absence of note issue might be as low as $6\frac{1}{2}$ per cent of deposits, and would in any case not exceed the 8 per cent which they would hold if they followed the English convention. Thus, having arrived at an estimate of cash reserve needs which takes account of till-money needs we may say that so long as it is exceeded by the cash ratio actually maintained under present arrangements no till-money advantage can be said to accrue from these arrangements. Now whatever one thinks about the suggested figure of 8 per cent, it is beyond question that the present cash ratio of 17–18 per cent exceeds any feasible alternative value that one might choose. Hence we may conclude that the fact that they can stock their branch tills with their own unissued notes is of no *general* advantage to the Scottish banks at the present time.

[1] The principal one is that when they spoke about the advantages and disadvantages of the Scottish note issue under the Peel system, they were really comparing it with the pre-1844 system when all banks had a natural right to issue notes without statutory cover requirements. That is to say, they were not setting it alongside the English system as it has now developed, with explicit and uniform practices in the holding of cash.

But admittedly this is not all that can be said on the matter. There is, in fact, a till-money *effect*, and the isolation of it throws light on the contention that without the ability to use unissued notes in branch tills many of the smaller Scottish branches would be unprofitable. The precise effect of the Scottish right of note issue, and the use of un-issued notes as till money that goes with it, is that it converts what is normally an avoidable cost of branch operation into an unavoidable or fixed cost. However much cash the note issue and its cover require-ment cause the banks to hold, the amount is unaffected by the size of branch offices, and hence from that point of view—regarded, so to speak, as vicarious till money—it becomes a *fixed* cost. If the Scottish banks surrendered their note issues they would be able to supply their till-money needs from a cash ratio of about half the present level. But in this situation the incidence of till-money costs would be felt in the individual branch offices, such costs would become avoidable, and it might then be found, as is frequently argued, that the net revenue of the banks could be increased by closing certain branches.[1] The pre-sumption is that it would be the smaller offices where, already, other costs are comparatively high which would be affected. Much however would depend on the actual business of individual branches: some of the very small branches with a low and predictable cash turnover might still prove workable.

III. MONETARY EFFECTS OF THE NOTE ISSUES

What are the monetary effects, if any, of the Scottish note issues? If we conceive of such effects as proceeding simply from an addition to the supply of currency, then clearly, except for the small fiduciary element, they do not exist. This is because, in the first place, Scottish notes in circulation merely immobilize an almost equal amount of Bank of England notes; and secondly, and more fundamentally, because currency is a subsidiary means of payment the quantity of which is determined by the volume of bank deposits which are the dominant form of money. If, however, we look at the effects of the Scottish banks' operations on the quantity of bank deposit money, and take account of the way in which these operations are moulded

---

[1] This does not mean that because of note issue the Scottish banks are main-taining branches which, on a real-cost calculus, ought to be closed. The cost of cash is unlike other costs in that it does not represent a use of the real resources of the community. One might argue that where, as in England, the holding of cash is a cost item attributable to individual bank offices, the branch network of the banking system is unduly restricted.

G   97

by their note-issuing activities, we get a different answer. This is a matter of some complexity which we shall deal with more fully when we consider the position of the Scottish banks in relation to the various techniques of monetary policy. Here we shall state the argument very briefly in terms which will have to be qualified later.[1]

We have seen that the cover fund is a passive quantity within the assets of the Scottish banks: it is determined by the actions of the public and not by any purposive action by the banks themselves. From this it follows that it plays no part in determining the lending and investing activities of the Scottish bankers, and hence does not in any way determine the effects of these activities on the volume of bank deposits. In the traditional theory of the creation of the stock of bank deposits (and here we leave for later discussion the modern developments of this theory) the size of this stock depends on three things: on the cash ratios maintained by the banks, on the cash demands of the public, and on the quantity of cash supplied to the system by the central issuing authority.[2] In such a system the banks, by virtue of operating on the basis of a fractional cash reserve, will generate a volume of bank deposits which will normally be some multiple of the cash base. The size of this multiple will depend partly on the banks' cash ratio and partly on the public's cash-deposit ratio. Given the public's cash ratio, it will be the larger the smaller is the banks' cash ratio.

Now the cash ratio that matters here is that which actually controls the lending and investing activities of the banks—what is sometimes referred to as the *operative* cash ratio. For the Scottish banks this is not the ratio of total cash to deposits, since this contains the large and passive item of note-cover; it is, in fact, the much smaller ratio of non-cover cash. This ratio has for long been in the region of 2 per cent of deposits compared with an English ratio which before the war was somewhere around 10 per cent, and since 1945 has been 8

---

[1] See below, Ch. 13, pp. 192–200. The main complication which we postpone is the replacement of the 'cash doctrine' by the 'liquidity doctrine' in the analysis of credit creation by the banks. The modern theory of credit creation is very much more complex than that presented here, but not all the complexities are relevant to the present analysis.

[2] Or, for that matter, by the gold-mining industry. In other words, the theory assumes that 'cash' emanates from a source outside the commercial banks themselves; in the British system it is to be regarded as the total of currency and bankers' balances at the Bank of England. For an early statement of this analysis see W. F. Crick, 'The Genesis of Bank Deposits', *Economica*, June 1927, pp. 191–202, reprinted in *Reading in Monetary Theory* (A. E. A. Series, London, 1952), pp. 41–53; also *Macmillan Report*, pp. 33–40.

per cent. The implication of this is that the credit-creating effects of the operations of the Scottish banks are greater than those of the English banks. But what is the connection between this effect and the existence of the note issue? It is simply that the lowness of the *operative* cash ratio of the Scottish banks is a consequence of their possession of the right of note issue. On the one hand the till-money arrangement has reduced the practical need to hold legal tender; and on the other, the very existence of the note cover fund and its integration in the asset structure for balance sheet purposes, has created an appearance of similarity with English practice which has obviated any pressure on the Scottish banks, whether internal or external, to make their reserve practices uniform in substance with those of the English banks.

Thus the Scottish note issues do have a monetary effect which operates circuitously through the reserve practices of the bank; and we shall see (in Chapter 13) that this conclusion is unaffected when we substitute the modern liquidity ratio doctrine for the traditional cash ratio view of the creation of bank deposits. The upshot of this is that the Scottish banking system tends to create a higher volume of bank deposits than the English system. But, obviously, in an economy as closely integrated as the British, any extra expansion of bank deposits of this kind cannot remain within one region: it must spill over into the system at large. Hence the monetary effect of the Scottish note issues is to be found in a slightly higher level of deposits in the British banking system as a whole than would otherwise be the case.

IV. THE PROFITS OF NOTE ISSUE

An obvious and interesting question to ask about the Scottish note issues is: how profitable are they to the banks? We have seen earlier in this chapter that the note-issuing activities of the banks may be presumed to add to their earning assets and the question at issue is whether or not the income which they derive from these assets is outweighed by the costs which the banks incur in operating the issues. We can only get anywhere near to an answer to this question by attempting an actual estimate of the profits of note issue and this we will now do for the year 1962. It must be said at the outset that we do not have enough information to make anything like a precise estimate of these profits. Nevertheless it is useful to carry the calculation as far as it will go: it does at least give an idea of the orders of magnitude involved and it enables us to place some limits on the size of the various unknowns. We shall confine ourselves here to the broader outlines of the argument. Some issues connected with the estimation of income and costs require rather detailed discussion which would unduly prolong this section and these more technical points are consigned to an appendix at the end of the chapter.

In the light of what we said earlier in this chapter[1] let us assume that in the absence of note issue the Scottish banks would maintain an overall cash ratio of 8 per cent. For this purpose we define 'cash' as coin, Bank of England notes, balances at the Bank of England, and balances with London Clearing banks. The last item is appropriately to be regarded as an integral part of the true cash reserves of the Scottish banking system.[2] If in 1962 the Scottish banks had maintained a cash ratio of 8 per cent, the ratios of all other assets would have been higher than they were, since the actual cash ratio in that year was in the region of 18 per cent; we will assume that in our hypothetical situation the main earning assets would have been increased in equal proportions. With a cash ratio of 8 per cent the Scottish banks would have held £65·6 million of cash. If we now subtract this figure from the amount of cash they actually held during 1962 we are left with that quantity of cash which is to be regarded as held wholly on account of the note issues and therefore to be 'set against' them.

Unfortunately, for reasons which will emerge in the discussion of the cash item in the next chapter, we do not have a figure which corresponds exactly to cash as we define it here. All we can do is to build up a total from different sources and hope that it is not too wide of the mark. We shall take the average total holdings of legal tender, as shown on the monthly Bank Returns, and to it add the total balances at the Bank of England, shown separately in the monthly statement, and an estimate of the balances held with the London Clearing banks. The information about these balances is fragmentary[3] but such as it is it points to their being about 1 per cent of deposits overall (though varying between banks). We shall assume that they did in fact amount to 1 per cent of gross deposits in 1962.

The total of these three elements of cash, in 1962, was £143·8 million. If we deduct from this our hypothetical 8 per cent of deposits —the cash ratio in the absence of note issue—we are left with £78·2 million as the amount of cash to be placed wholly to the account of the note issues. The difference between this figure and the total amount of assets acquired through note issue represented the earning assets held on account of the note issues. Ignoring the effects of note

---

[1] Above, p. 94. [2] See below, pp. 114–15.
[3] See below, pp. 115–16.

issue on the level of deposits, since these are small and in any case not confined to Scotland, the total assets held on account of note issue were equal in amount to the volume of the note circulation during 1962. We shall take the note circulation as equal to the average of the Wednesday and Saturday figures for that year: a total of £124·1 million. Deducting from this the £78·2 million of 'surplus' cash, wholly accountable to note issue, we arrive at a total of £45·9 million of earning assets acquired through note issue. We now assume that the composition of these earning assets was the same as that of all earning assets held by the Scottish banks in 1962, and to each type of asset we apply an average rate of return, the derivation of which is described in the appendix to this chapter. The aggregated returns on these assets gives us a figure of the gross income earned by the Scottish banks as a group on their note issues in 1962. The whole calculation can be set out in balance sheet form as follows:

An Aggregated Balance Sheet of the Scottish Note Issues in 1962

Liabilities £m.		Assets	£m.	Rate of Return per cent	Yield £m.
Notes	124·1	Cash	78·2	—	—
		Money at call	4·9	4·13	0·20
		Bills and Special Deposits	2·5	4·17	0·10
		Investments	14·1	4·96	0·70
		Advances	24·4	6·70	1·63
	124·1		124·1		2·63

The uncertainty surrounding this estimate needs no emphasis. One thing we shall do forthwith is to drop the second place of decimals (which is misleading anyway) and say that on our calculation the gross income on the note issues in 1962 was about £2·6 million. Another way to express this, which is useful when we look at the cost side, is to say that the gross return was about 5d per £ of average annual circulation of notes.

To arrive at an exact figure of *net* income two sorts of cost should be deducted from the gross total: the cost of administering the assets held, and the operating costs of the note issues themselves. Administration of assets is likely to be significant only in the case of advances, but this is an unknown and unguessable item. Among the various items of operating costs two can be calculated, or estimated, reasonably closely: stamp duty and the cost of the licences required

101

under the 1845 Act.[1] What we neither know nor have any firm basis for estimating is the cost of clearing the notes between the banks.

The calculable costs of the note circulation of 1959 were rather more than £½ million. Deducting this from the gross return we are left with £2·1 million to cover the remaining costs—of manufacture and handling—and to provide profit. Let us express this, as before, as a ratio of average annual circulation: put this way it comes to about 4d per £, of this circulation. Next we deduct from this an informed— though not well-informed—guess of ½d as the cost per £ of annual circulation of manufacturing the notes. This leaves 3½d to cover handling costs and profits.

The banks themselves probably have no precise idea of handling costs. Much of the work involved—the sorting and counting of notes—forms part of the general duties of branch staffs and any attempt to calculate its cost would run into problems of definition and apportionment. Asked by the Radcliffe Committee how the cost of sorting notes compared with that of sorting cheques, one Scottish banker replied (Q. 4876) 'Much less', and the other added, 'Only at the very large offices does it mean an increase in staff: in the smaller offices it is a marginal operation, which can be undertaken without any addition to the staff'. A complication for any attempt to assess these costs is that the actual number of notes cleared during the course of the year greatly exceeds the annual average circulation. From the apparent holdings of the Scottish banks of one another's notes, which we can very roughly deduce from the monthly statements and the Bank Returns, it appears that the actual number of notes handled during the year is about nine times the number of pounds of annual average circulation. If this is so (and it is a very uncertain estimate) then for there to have been any profit at all on the circulation of 1962 the total cost of putting each bank note through the note exchanges would not have had to exceed about four-tenths of a penny.

Any comment on the relation of this figure to the actual cost of clearing a note would be entirely speculative. One may set it alongside estimates ranging from 9d to 1s 3d as the cost of clearing a cheque, but this is not particularly helpful as the two operations are hardly comparable in the work involved. At a guess I would say that the cost of clearing a note probably is less than four-tenths of a penny. If it is as low as three-tenths, which is not unlikely, the net

[1] One provision of the Act requires the banks to take out a licence, costing £30 for every place in which they have an office issuing notes, except that for all places in which they were issuing notes in 1845 they need only hold four licences.

profit on the total issue of 1962 may be put at about £500,000, or just under 1d per £ of average annual circulation.

Leaving the cost side of note issue and reverting to the calculation of gross income, one of the assumptions on which this rests requires a brief reconsideration. We have assumed that if Scottish banks ceased to issue notes their cash ratios would be reduced to 8 per cent and all earning assets would be increased in proportion. One consequence of this, however, would be that their liquidity ratios—the ratios to deposits of cash, bills and money at call—would be very much lower than those of the English banks (though not lower than the pre-war Scottish figures). In these circumstances the Scottish banks might feel obliged to increase their short assets, particularly Treasury bills, at the expense of investments and advances. This would cause the reduction in income, gross and net, to be larger than our estimate suggests. So far as this is what would happen it reinforces the conclusion that the banks at present derive a positive net income from their note issues.[1]

One final point to notice about the profits of note issue concerns their variability. The resources that the note issues place in the hands of the Scottish banks are free of interest costs. This means that, compared with deposits, the net income from note issues must be more sensitive to changes in interest rates.[2] As rates of interest rise the gross income from the note issues increases, but there is no accompanying increase in costs as there is with interest-bearing deposits. The net income from note issues will thus fluctuate more widely that that from deposits (taken as a whole) with movements of interest, and this effect will have been enhanced by the large-scale substitution of advances for investments since 1959. Before that year, as we have seen, the composition of deposits and the structure of assets were such as to depress short-run profits when interest rates were on the high side. The effect of the note issues was then to moderate this depression.

V. POSSIBLE CHANGES IN THE SYSTEM OF ISSUE

In what ways might the present system of issue be altered? The most obvious possibility is that the Scottish banks might cease to issue

[1] If, for example, we assume that in the absence of note issue the Scottish banks would have held £80 m. less in gilt-edged securities (about 10 per cent of deposits in 1962) and the corresponding amount more in Treasury bills, this would be equal to a decline in gross income (on the rates of return assumed here) of about £300,000.

[2] Cf. *Radcliffe Evidence*, QQ. 4871–2.

notes. With due regard to the manifest uncertainties of the estimate made here I think that the evidence weighs in favour of there being at least some positive income from the note issues.[1] Hence there is no reason why the banks should give up the right of note issue on this score.

A second possibility is that they might restrict the volume of their note circulation.[2] This would reduce their cover liability, and their cash holdings could be brought down to a level nearer to what they would maintain in the absence of the note issues. Up to this point the banks would simply be substituting Bank of England notes, now held as cover, for their own notes in circulation; the gain would come in the reduction of the costs of handling the issues. However, the restriction of the volume of Scottish notes in circulation would present the banks with some problems. To keep their issues below any given level they might well have to restrict the number of offices at which they issued their own notes.[3] This would increase the need for legal tender in tills since some branches would issue only English money, and this would amount to an increase in the level of non-cover cash, and so of their non-earning assets. This could be minimized by confining the issue of English money to their larger branches since these need to hold less till money in proportion to their deposits than the smaller branches, and if the banks did this the restriction of the note circulation would probably raise no questions of contracting the branch system. An important point however is that so long as the Scottish banks hold to their practice of clearing Scottish bank notes no single bank would gain much by restricting its own issue. This points to yet a third possible course of action.

It is clear that the main element of cost in the running of the note issues arises from the fact that the Scottish banks operate their issues as much like a cheque system as a currency; and this cost cannot be recouped by any system of charges. A partial answer to this situation is to attempt to reduce the costs of handling the note issues, and this the banks are doing by the introduction of machines to sort and count bank notes. But the complete answer would be to eliminate the clearing of notes altogether. This would mean that the Scottish banks would re-issue one another's notes, and it might be more acceptable to the banks if the issues were standardized. It is true that without the note exchanges the banks would probably find themselves holding

---

[1] Cf. *Radcliffe Evidence*, Q. 4871.

[2] The Northern Irish banks have clearly done this since 1945.

[3] This was how the English provincial banks of issue kept within the limits imposed on their issues by the Bank Charter Act of 1844.

more of one another's notes, and having higher individual circulation. This would reduce the gross yield of the note issues since it would amount to an increase in the non-earning assets held on account of the note issue. But the amount involved would be small compared with the saving in the costs of operating the issues.

THE PROFITS OF NOTE ISSUE: ESTIMATES AND ASSUMPTIONS

1. *Asset Yields*

The assumed rates of return on the various categories of earning assets used in the estimate of the profits of note issue, in section IV of this chapter, were arrived at in the following ways. For the average call-money rate I have simply taken the figure used in the estimate of the total profits of the Scottish banks during 1962 made in the June 1963 issue of *The Bankers' Magazine*. According to the writer this is 'based on information received from the money market'.[1] As this is a reasonable source for what is intrinsically a very difficult rate for an outsider to estimate, I am happy to use it. For the rate on bills and special deposits (these earn the allotment rate on Treasury bills) I have calculated a weighted average of the Treasury bill allotment rate and the average of the Scottish banks' published rate on four months Mercantile Bills (this being the middle of the three published bill rates). The rate on advances has been derived by averaging the Scottish banks' rates on secured and unsecured advances, over the whole year, and then combining them into a weighted average on the assumption that 60 per cent of advances were unsecured.[2]

To arrive at a feasible rate of return on investments presents more difficulties. There is a major unknown in the present structure of the banks' investment portfolios, Scottish or English. But even more, there is a conceptual problem as to what the current rate on a port-folio which has been built up in the past can be said to be. Is it, for example, the current market yield on the stocks held? Or is it the current yield on the original cost of the stocks?

To take these two problems in order, we have some fairly recent information on the maturity structure of the Scottish banks' port-folios. Figures published in the *Radcliffe Evidence*, and continued

---

[1] This statement is actually made in an earlier article on bank profits by the same writer in the August 1961 issue of the same journal.

[2] This was the proportion given by one Scottish witness to the Radcliffe Committee: *Radcliffe Evidence*, Q. 4814.

until mid-1960 in the monthly statements, give the broad division of their gilt-edged stocks into those of under, and those of over, five years maturity.[1] During the 'fifties this structure remained remarkably constant; despite considerable reductions in the total size of portfolios the proportion of short-dated stocks moved in the range of 26–28 per cent of the total. The latest figures showed a very slight rising trend in the short-dated stocks and I have assumed that in 1962 they formed 30 per cent of the total. After this I make two more assumptions. The first is that the longest maturities held are ten-year stocks; this is not completely true, but probably not far wrong. The second is that the banks buy no short-dated stocks at all but only ten-year stocks some of which they keep and some they sell when, with time, they pass into the short-dated bracket. These assumptions allow a crude dating of the different tranches of the portfolios. For example, those of shortest date, and about to be paid off, were bought ten years before; while the medium-dated stocks were all bought from one to five years ago. We now assume that each annual tranche was bought at a price that produced the average redemption yield of the year in which it was bought. From the series of annual redemption yields we calculate an average yield on the total of portfolios. Unfortunately for the 1962 calculation the series of average yields of medium-dated stocks in the *Annual Abstract of Statistics* only goes back eight years; so for the two most distant years I have used the short-dated yields. The lower yields on these stocks will bring the average down and help to reflect some very long-dated stocks bought at low interest rates in the 1940s.

After this description it would be superfluous to describe the resulting rate as rough and ready. But quite apart from the crudity of the method, it takes no account of two important points. First it ignores capital gains and losses on sales of securities before maturity; there have probably been considerable amounts of these in recent years. Secondly, so far as some capital gains enter into the redemption yields used, no account is taken of the fact that the banks are taxed *as dealers* on such gains. The rate which we obtain by this procedure probably errs in being too high.

2. *Costs of Issue*

The costs of issue which we can calculate exactly, or reasonably so, are the stamp duty and the cost of the licences which the legislation requires banks of issue to take out. Stamp duty is charged at 8s 4d per cent (i.e. 1d per £) of the annual circulation of each bank; the

[1] See Table XXI below, p. 138.

aggregate cost of this can therefore be calculated exactly. In 1962 it was £517,000. As for licences the position is that each bank must hold one, costing £30, for every place (i.e. town or village) in which its notes are issued, with the provision that four licences cover all places in which it was issuing notes in 1845. These original licences must now cost the banks, altogether, seventeen times £120, since the present five banks represent the consolidation of seventeen banks in 1845. The cost of the subsequent licences can only be guessed at. Let us assume that the 375 offices in existence in 1844 have come down to the existing banks in equal numbers, and that each of these seventy-five pre-1845 offices per bank was in a different place. By subtracting this figure from the number of places in which each bank is now represented we arrive at a total figure of 834 places for each of which the banks must take out £30 licences. On this reckoning the total cost of licences, including those for the 1845 offices, comes to £27,000. This brings the total of the calculable costs to £544,000.

Finally, a word about the estimate of the number of notes actually handled during the course of the year. I put this, for 1962, at about 1,100 million. This is arrived at by deducting the average holdings of Bank of England notes and coin as shown on the Bank Return (and relating to Saturday) from the average holdings of all notes and coin shown on the monthly statements (and relating to the third Wednesday in each month). Ignoring intra-weekly fluctuations, I assume that the difference between these two figures represents the average daily holding of the notes of other Scottish banks, and multiply it by the number of working days to give an annual total, by value, of the notes put through to exchanges. To convert this value total to numbers of notes I assume that it is made up of £1 and £5 notes in the proportions 3 :7.

CHAPTER 8

LIQUIDITY

We have examined the major items on the liabilities side of the Scottish banker's balance sheet and we must now look at his assets. The assets of a commercial bank are important from several points of view. To the bank itself they represent the employment of the resources which the public and its shareholders place at its disposal. The disposition of these assets must be made with more than one end in view: profitability is the general objective, but the ever-outstanding volume of short-term liabilities has traditionally forced banks to pay regard above all to the need for liquidity in their assets. For the economy at large the structure of the banking system's assets is also of the greatest importance. The banks are the most important of the financial intermediaries; in spite of the great growth of other types of financial intermediaries in recent years, as a body they still dispose of a larger quantity of the country's short-term capital than any comparable group of institutions. The asset structure of the banks is also of great importance for policy. The volume of bank advances at any time may be an explicit objective of policy and while it may be attacked directly, control is also exercised through the general level of deposits. But control over deposits brings in other assets, notably liquid assets. Some of the issues connected with the Scottish banks' assets will have to be discussed in later sections of this book and we will say correspondingly less about them at this juncture. In this chapter the liquid assets of the banks will be described and examined; in the following chapter we shall take a look at the so-called 'risk' assets. In both chapters we shall be considering the various elements from the viewpoint of their position within the total structure of bank assets. This total structure is shown, statistically, in Table XVIII; and we must first say a word or two about the figures assembled there.

Table XVIII shows the totals of the main assets of the Scottish banks in various years from 1928 to 1963, with (in the right-hand half) their ratios to the total of gross deposits and fiduciary note issues. With the exception of 1948 the figures are annual averages of

TABLE

The Main Assets of

ASSETS (£M.)

YEAR[1]	1. DEPOSITS (£M.)	2. CASH CURRENCY[6]	BALANCES WITH BANK OF ENGLAND	3. NON-COVER CASH[7]	4. CHEQUES, BALANCES WITH OTHER BANKS, ETC., AND TRANSIT ITEMS[9]	5. MONEY AT CALL AND SHORT NOTICE	6. BILLS TREASURY BILLS	OTHER BILLS[10]	7. INVESTMENTS GILT-EDGED	OTHER	8. TOTAL ADVANCES	9. TREASURY DEPOSIT RECEIPTS
1928[2]	171·4	17·3	0·9	..	..	13·9	8·1	8·8	69·9		92·6	—
1938[3]	244·9	19·1	1·3	4·8[8]	11·9	21·7	3·0	3·8	142·2		82·6	—
1948[4]	750·5	..	..	..	..	..	..		419·3		150·2	53·5
1951[5]	744·3	83·8	1·6	13·9	69·6	53·5	4·7	6·4	384·0	13·4	217·3	9·7
1953	740·3	100·0	1·6	14·3	73·5	65·0	13·8	2·2	383·1	12·0	205·3	—
1955	774·5	113·4	1·4	15·7	84·8	55·2	16·7	6·8	376·8	13·7	224·1	
1957	740·2	129·3	1·4	16·6	87·6	58·1	18·2	7·2	343·2	13·6	217·8	Special deposits
1959	776·4	134·2	1·3	17·7	86·6	68·7	21·1	6·3	302·4	23·0	271·3	—
1960	789·7	140·0	1·3	19·1	90·6	62·5	21·3	6·8	256·5	25·5	331·8	3·9
1961	805·9	144·8	1·6	21·1	105·6	66·3	22·0	8·3	223·7	25·5	361·1	9·5
1962	820·8	143·8	1·7	22·4	102·6	77·4	21·3	9·5	200·6	25·4	390·0	8·7
1963	846·0	144·7	1·6	23·2	..	81·7	25·1	9·8	193·8	26·9	414·9	—

Sources: 1928. *Macmillan Report*, Appendix I, Table 5.
1938 and 1951–7. *Radcliffe Memoranda*, Vol. 2, Statistical Appendix, Table 3.
1948. Annual balance sheets, various dates between September 1948 and April 1949.
1958–63 *Financial Statistics* (C.S.O.).

Notes: 1. With the exception of 1948, all figures are averages of monthly totals.
2. The figures for this year cover six of the eight banks then operating.
3. The figures for this year cover six of the eight banks, but not necessarily the same six as in 1928.
4. Absolute totals are shown only for those items which are defined in the same way on all balance sheets (some bills are included in the advances of one bank). The percentages in brackets are calculated from the figures of those banks which showed these items separately; they variously cover five to seven of the eight banks then operating.
5. The 1951 figures are averages of ten monthly statements.

the monthly totals drawn from various sources—the statistics published by the Macmillan and Radcliffe Committees, and the series now appearing regularly in the publications of the Central Statistical Office. No monthly totals are available for any of the immediate post-war years and rather than show nothing for these years the table includes figures drawn from the annual balance sheets appearing before, and shortly after, the end of 1948. At that time, such were the variations between the banks in how they presented the various asset items on their balance sheets that it was impossible to derive even moderately 'pure' figures for most assets. Consequently, for that

XVIII

Scottish Banks, 1928–63

ASSETS AS PERCENTAGES OF GROSS DEPOSITS PLUS FIDUCIARY NOTE ISSUES

	10.	11.	12.	13.	14.	15.	16.	17.	18.	19.
YEAR[1]	TOTAL CASH	NON-COVER CASH	CHEQUES, BALANCES, ETC.	TOTAL BILLS	MONEY AT CALL AND SHORT NOTICE	LIQUID ASSETS WITH TOTAL CASH: COLUMNS 10, 13, 14	LIQUID ASSETS WITH NON-COVER CASH: COLUMNS 8, 11, 13, 14	TOTAL INVEST-MENTS	TOTAL AD-VANCES	TREASURY DEPOSIT RECEIPTS
1928[3]	10·6	..	..	9·9	8·1	28·6	..	40·8	54·0	—
1938[3]	7·7	2·0[8]	4·8	2·7	8·9	19·3	13·6	57·4	33·4	—
1948[4]	(11·3)	(2·2)	(7·6)	(1·7)	(8·7)	..	..	54·5	20·2	7·1
1951[3]	11·4	1·7	9·3	1·4	7·3	20·1	10·4	53·1	29·1	1·0
1953	13·6	1·9	9·9	2·1	8·8	24·5	12·8	53·4	27·7	—
1955	14·8	2·1	10·9	3·0	7·1	24·8	12·2	51·1	28·8	—
1957	17·7	2·2	11·8	3·4	7·8	28·9	13·4	48·2	29·4	Special deposits
1959	17·4	2·6	11·1	3·5	8·8	29·7	14·9	42·2	34·8	—
1960	17·9	3·4	11·5	3·6	7·9	29·4	13·9	36·5	42·0	0·5
1961	18·1	3·3	13·1	3·7	8·2	30·0	15·2	30·8	44·8	1·2
1962	17·7	2·7	12·5	3·6	9·4	30·7	15·7	27·4	47·5	1·1
1963	17·3	2·7	..	3·9	9·7	30·9	16·3	26·1	49·0	—

6. 'Currency' comprises Bank of England notes (including those held as statutory cover for Scottish notes), coin and the notes of other Scottish banks.
7. Non-cover cash is total cash minus excess Scottish note issues. The note totals used are those given in the Statutory Bank Returns (i.e. Saturday figures) except for 1938 when an average of monthly figures relating to the date of each month's statement is used.
8. The 1938 figures exclude two banks, but which two is not stated. Non-cover cash for this year has been calculated on the assumption that the figures exclude the two banks with the largest fiduciary note issues. Were the excluded banks those with the two smallest issues, the figures would be £4·3 million and 1·8 per cent.
9. This item comprises balances with, and cheques in course of collection on, other banks *plus* items in course of collection between branches of the same bank (from *Annual Abstract of Statistics*).
10. Other bills include, and advances exclude, re-financeable export credits (under eighteen months to maturity) from 1961 onwards.

year, absolute totals are given only for those assets which are more or less uniformly defined on the balance sheets; however, ratios have been calculated for all the assets and where they do not relate to all the banks they are placed in brackets. Obviously, these balance sheet figures must be treated with reserve and it must also be borne in mind that they are subject to a seasonal factor in that most balance sheets appear in the last quarter of one year or the first quarter of the next; this causes deposit and liquid asset totals drawn from this source to be higher than annual averages.

For reasons which were touched on in the last chapter and which are discussed in the following section, assets are calculated as ratios of the total of deposits and fiduciary note issues: this removes the effect on these ratios of changes in the relative size of the note-issues. The ratio of *total* cash, which is shown in column 10 of Table XVIII, is determined almost wholly by the movements of the excess note issues which, in calculating the other ratios, we have excluded from the liabilities total. Consequently the movements of this total cash ratio occur for the most part independently of, and without effect on, the other ratios in the table. (A further consequence is that the ratios for any given year will add up to far more than 100 per cent if those in column 10 are included. But even if the total cash ratios are excluded the totals will come to more than this, due to the presence of proprietors' capital and reserves which enable the banks to hold assets in excess of their liabilities to the public.)

The 'liquid assets' of a bank in the modern British system are usually defined as cash, including currency and balances at the Bank of England, money lent 'at call or short notice' to the discount market, and bills. This definition has only crystallized in recent decades: before 1914, for example, bankers regarded their gilt-edged stocks as liquid assets. In the case of the Scottish banks the definition is extended both by the banks themselves and in official publications to include 'balances with, and cheques in course of collection on, other banks'; the validity of this extension is a question that will concern us later. The view of liquid assets that has come to be accepted is that they form a tiered structure of defence against the encashment of deposits. Cash is necessary to meet the daily outflow of funds either in the form of withdrawals of currency, or as claims against a bank at the clearing in which case balances with the central bank are called into play. Behind cash, money at call provides a well-nigh immediate source of replenishment, while bills provide a further reinforcement of assets which can be liquidated with very little risk of capital loss. The historical roots of this structure lie back in the final quarter of the nineteenth century when the banking system—or at least the English portion of it—was an atomized one made up for the most part of smallish banks; when the security of the system as a whole was by no means as removed from doubt as it is today; and when the role of the monetary authority was more restricted in scope than it has since become. As a consequence of later developments, what we have come to regard as the rationale of British banking practice in the holding of liquid assets is now to some extent unrealistic. For example, it is questionable if the English Clearing banks really do need to keep anything like one-third of their

112

deposits in liquid assets,[1] as they now do; and we need to bear this in mind when we are measuring the differentia of the Scottish position. However, while the risks against which liquid assets are the customary defence are smaller in scale in the modern banking system, they have not disappeared; and the size and composition of his liquid assets are by no means a negligible consideration for the present-day banker.

I. THE SCOTTISH BANKERS' CASH

When we look at the present-day liquid assets of the Scottish banks, the most striking thing about them is the size of the 'cash' item. At 17 per cent of deposits it is not only far and away above the corresponding English ratio, it is also very much higher than at any previous time in Scottish banking history. We have already found the explanation of this, in the last chapter, in the peculiar association between cash and note issue in Scottish banking. There is no legal requirement for the cash held as note cover to be separated in any way from other banking assets and it is therefore, quite properly, included in the cash item on a Scottish bank's balance sheet. Today, note cover forms well over four-fifths of the total cash held by the Scottish banks, and the cash ratio is almost wholly determined by the note ratio—the ratio of notes in circulation to deposits. When the note ratio changes, and it has changed very markedly during the last two decades, the Scottish cash ratio automatically changes with it. For this reason it is best to isolate the cash ratio when calculating and interpreting the other asset ratios in Scottish banking.

'Non-Cover Cash'
If we subtract from the total cash held by the Scottish banks the amount held as statutory cover, we are left with a comparatively small item which I have termed 'non-cover cash'. The movements of this, expressed as a ratio, are shown in column 11 of Table XVIII, and some comments are required on its derivation. To begin with, in the year for which we have to rely on annual balance sheets for our figures (1948) the content of the total cash item varied somewhat from bank to bank: some did, some did not, include holdings of the notes of other Scottish banks and balances with banks other than the Bank of England. Beginning with the Radcliffe statistics, and continuing in the monthly figures now published, we have a series of figures for total cash which is of uniform and constant definition.

[1] Cf. the remarks of Sir Oliver Franks in *Radcliffe Evidence*, QQ. 3755–6.

'Cash', as it is now recorded in official publications, is defined as total holdings of currency, including the notes of other Scottish banks, and balances with the Bank of England. Given such a uniform series it would seem to be a straightforward matter to calculate non-cover cash: merely deduct the amount of excess note issues—the amount that has to be 'covered'—from the cash total. But there is a problem even here. We have two figures for the average total note issues, a Wednesday figure and a Saturday figure, the latter always being the higher. Which should we use? On the face of it, the fact that the cash total is taken from the monthly statement seems to compel us to use the corresponding note total, i.e. the Wednesday figure. But the cover requirement is determined by the Saturday figure and if we assume that the banks do not vary their note cover much during the course of the week, then we should reckon the note cover on the Saturday circulation. There is no evidence that the Scottish banks do withdraw money from their cover funds on any scale during the course of the week and, say, place it in the discount market. There may well be a small movement of funds in that the banks, from purely precautionary motives, probably over-provide for estimated cover needs on a Saturday, withdrawing the excess on Monday when the exact figures of the Saturday circulation are known; but the amount involved is almost certainly slight. Wherever possible, therefore, the Saturday note total is used here to calculate non-cover cash.

The total of non-cover cash as we have isolated it is composed of three separate elements: legal tender held in excess of cover needs, notes of other Scottish banks and balances with the Bank of England. The last of these is the smallest: in 1962 out of our estimate of £22·4 million of non-cover cash it accounted for only £1·6 million. In the same year legal tender in excess of note-cover—mainly held in branch offices—amounted to £10·3 million, and if we subtract these two items from our total of non-cover cash we are left with £9·4 million of Scottish notes (the apparent precision of the last two figures is unwarranted, but they cannot be very far out).

But to define total 'cash' in such a way that non-cover cash comprises these three elements is open to the criticism that one of the elements included should not be there, while another is excluded which ought to be in. There are, among others, two important criteria by which a bank's liquid assets should be defined. One is that they should represent assets that are indeed available to meet unexpected outflows of resources. The other is that their scale within total assets should be both subject to control by the individual bank and an object of such control; in other words, the bank should be able to hold the asset in question at some definite level and should in fact try to do so. This latter criterion derives its importance from the fact that the techniques of control over the total volume of bank deposits used by the monetary authorities require predictable behaviour by the banks in the holding of liquid assets. We shall return to this point later in this chapter when considering the total liquidity picture in Scottish banking, and again in Chapter 13 in the wider context of monetary policy. What concerns us here is that 'notes of other Scottish banks' satisfy neither of these criteria, whereas 'balances with other banks' do. The notes of the other banks which each bank is holding can hardly be regarded as a freely available fund since they are more or less self-cancelling. Any bank must know that the Scottish notes which, at this moment, it is holding for the next note exchange, will be more or less exactly counterbalanced by the amount of its own notes in the hands of the other banks. Further, the quantity of such notes held by any bank is not under its own control, but is in fact determined by the actions of the other four. On quite a different footing are the balances which the Scottish banks hold with Clearing banks; on both these criteria these should be included in liquid assets and, indeed, in 'cash'.

All the Scottish banks hold free balances with correspondent banks in London. These balances are used to meet Scottish cheques which are paid into English banks and which are passed through the English clearing to the correspondents of the various Scottish banks or which, in certain circumstances,[1] are presented for payment at the London offices. This makes them basically the same in character and function as the balances held both by Scottish and English banks with the Bank of England. Scottish banks use their Bank of England balances for settling the indebtedness which arises between themselves, at the Scottish clearing. The two groups of balances together represent their working balances of London money. As net claims on banks entirely outside the Scottish system, balances with London correspondents satisfy the first of the two criteria, that of availability; but what can we say about their level?

At present the practice among Scottish banks is to include all 'balances with other banks' (except the Bank of England) with 'cheques in course of collection', so that we have no precise indication of their size and movements. Some banks have shown this item separately on their balance sheets in some of the post-war years. The Bank of Scotland did this regularly until recently; its ratio of such

[1] These are described in detail in Chapter 12, pp. 187-8.

balances to deposits was usually rather more than 2 per cent, but probably at least half of this represented balances with banks abroad which are different in character from London money. The National Bank of Scotland, before its union with the Commercial Bank, showed balances with its parent bank (Lloyds) of about $1\frac{1}{2}$ per cent, while the British Linen's balances with Barclays have normally been just over $\frac{1}{2}$ per cent of deposits.[1] Over the Scottish banks as a group these balances are probably not much above 1 per cent of deposits.[2] London balances, whether held with Clearing banks or with the Bank of England, are not held in a continuous, proportional relationship with deposits. They are determined, typically on the basis of agreed, minimum balances, or perhaps of average balances,[3] and at any time they are fixed in absolute terms. Balances with the Bank of England show an extraordinary constancy. In 1938 the total balance of six of the eight banks averaged £1·3 million; in 1962, in spite of the trebling of deposits in the interval, the figure for all the banks was £1·6 million, which presumably means that there has been no revision of these balances since the 1930s. There is some fragmentary evidence from annual balances sheets that balances with London correspondents are adjusted from time to time, probably in response to increases in the monetary volume of transactions flowing through the accounts; this volume, in turn, bears some relation to the level of deposits. Such adjustments however are probably spasmodic,[4] and in the short-to-medium run the rule is to maintain balances of a given absolute amount.

The total London balances of the Scottish banks thus amount to perhaps rather more than 1 per cent of deposits, which seems low compared with the 3·1 per cent ratio (in 1963) of Clearing banks' balances with the Bank of England. It is clear that the Scottish banks rely heavily on fluctuations in their money market loans to meet

[1] In both these cases these balances were partly offset by small reciprocal balances held by the parent banks.

[2] I am excluding here the balance which, on its annual balance sheet, the Clydesdale Bank invariably shows in account with its parent bank, the Midland. On the nature of this balance, see below, p. 123.

[3] Cf. F. S. Taylor, *Banking in Scotland*, 2nd ed. (Institute of Bankers in Scotland), p. 46.

[4] The only bank which showed 'balances with other banks' as a separate item both on pre-war and post-war balance sheets is the Bank of Scotland. Between 1937 and 1939, the amounts ranged from £434,000 to £753,000, and the ratios from 1·1 to 1·8 per cent. In 1951 the amount was £886,000 which suggests that it had not been adjusted since pre-war. In 1952 the amount jumped sharply, and it rose again in 1955. A similar sudden upward movement appeared in the annual balance sheet of the National Bank in 1956.

changes in their cash position. The timing of their payments in relation to their daily dealings with the market will be examined in detail later (in Chapter 12), but two features of it may be mentioned here. One is that settlements of indebtedness arising at the Scottish clearing are held over for two days thus giving ample warning of any outflow of funds on this score. The other is that some Scottish banks have special arrangements for withdrawing funds from the discount market after midday (which is unusual) and this helps to cover certain unpredictable claims that may be made against them. A relevant point made by some commentators is that the deposits of the Scottish banks may contain less of the more volatile London money than those of the Clearing banks, but others dispute this. It was possibly a consideration of this kind that lay behind the Radcliffe Committee's statement that Scottish banks ' . . . can safely operate with relatively lower working balances than the London clearing banks need to hold . . .' (para. 152). However, strong though the case may be for the greater predictability, and perhaps the lower volatility, of the Scottish banks' cash position compared with that of the English banks, the relevance of it seems to be undermined by the fact that the main settlements that the Clearing banks face—those arising from the afternoon clearing—do not have to be met until the following day, and this allows ample time for the recall of money from the discount market. The Scottish banks get along on what are probably rather low working balances, but it is difficult to resist the conclusion that most of the difference between them and the English banks is explained by the fact that the balances which the latter hold with the Bank of England contain a large conventional element and are well above their working needs in the present day.

The third component of non-cover cash is the legal tender held, over and above cover needs, in branch offices. One would expect this to be dictated by the volume of business; and one would also expect to find some relation, though a more flexible one, between the volume of business and the level of deposits. The figures roughly confirm this: in 1938 non-cover legal tender was $1 \cdot 1$ per cent of deposits; in 1951 it was $0 \cdot 8$ per cent, in 1955 $1 \cdot 2$ per cent, and in 1963 $1 \cdot 2$ per cent.

Thus a fairly complex picture emerges of the non-cover segment of the Scottish banks' cash. The three parts that comprise it have in common the fact that each is the object of positive decision and that, at least in the short-run, this takes the form of keeping them at certain absolute levels. Sooner or later legal tender in branch tills and balances with London correspondents will be adjusted roughly in proportion to deposits; balances with the Bank of England are

117

apparently revised, if at all, only on rare occasions. The fact that in total non-cover cash, as thus defined, is the object of positive decisions means that it is the group of assets the ratio of which, considered functionally in relation to monetary policy, corresponds most closely to the cash ratio in English banking; this has implications which we shall examine later. Meanwhile we should recall that non-cover cash as it should be defined in principle differs from non-cover cash as we have shown it in Table XVIII. However it so happens that the aggregate of balances with London correspondents, at present submerged in 'cheques etc.', is—if my views on it are right[1]—of roughly the same order as the amount of the banks holdings of one another's notes. Thus the figures shown in the Table may be taken as a reasonable, if rough, indication of the level of non-cover cash.

Note Cover and Cash Reserves

Do we now conclude from this analysis that the cash held as note cover may be completely disregarded in any review of the Scottish banks' cash position? Is it simply non-available for reserve purposes and is this all there is to say about it? In point of law there is no reason why it should be so regarded. The statutes do not require the hypothecation of legal tender cover to that function: it must simply be in the proper places (two offices per bank and the Bank of England), at the proper time (on Saturdays) and in the proper amount. One could argue that as a banker's cash reserve remains more or less intact through time, any depletions being quickly counterbalanced by inflows or made good by the liquidation of other assets, it should be perfectly possible for the note cover fund to serve a dual function. At first sight there might appear to be an important practical drawback in the limitation of the places at which cover may be held; but the fact that the Bank of England is one such location reduces the force of this, for the Bank is obviously a very useful place in which to have liquid funds. True, the Scottish banks appear to be able to operate on very low working balances, but they need other reserves behind these to bear the brunt of variations in their daily cash position. It is at any rate theoretically and legally possible for them to use the note cover funds as such fluctuating balances, provided they are up to strength on the average of four Saturdays. But however possible this may appear in principle, in practice it is not what happens. That part of cover cash that is held at the Bank of England, and it is the greater

---

[1] Cf. above, p. 68, note 1.

part, seems to be treated as an unusable fund.[1] The rest of it, which is held in one or other of the two authorized offices of each bank, is no doubt usable as a precautionary stock for the considerable number of branches within range of these offices (all but one of them are in Edinburgh or Glasgow). But this hardly amounts to more than a marginal use of cover cash for reserve purposes.

Does this mean that we dismiss the remark of the Scottish banker to the Radcliffe Committee,[2] repeated in the Report (para. 152), to the effect that the note cover fund 'performs a dual function as cover for note issue and as part of our general reserve'? The answer is no, in that it may well fulfil the psychological need to hold a precautionary reserve, and also in that it helps to give to the balance sheet an orthodox appearance in the matter of liquidity. As we argued in the previous chapter, were the Scottish banks to cease issuing their own notes they would probably embrace a cash ratio similar to that of the England banks. Working needs alone would probably not call for a ratio quite so as high as 8 per cent, but the emphasis that has been placed on this convention might well incline them to adopt it. They would certainly not be prepared to work with a ratio as low as the present ratio of non-cover cash, and this means that some part of the cash now held as note cover would be retained. In this rather peculiar sense therefore, one can say that the note cover fund—or part of it —fulfils a reserve function.

This is just a further reflection of the complication which the note-issues introduce into the Scottish cash position. They have the odd effect of reducing the working needs for legal tender, while increasing the actual amount held. A point to reiterate before we leave cash to look at the other liquid assets is that in any analysis of the credit effects of Scottish banking operations and the relation of these to policy measures, the note cover fund must be regarded as a passive element with no determining effects on the banks' actions.

II. OTHER LIQUID ASSETS

It is clear from the size of the non-cover elements of cash—and particularly their London balances—that the Scottish banks must rely to a considerable extent on their other liquid assets to meet

[1] See the statement by Ian W. Macdonald, Chairman of the National Commercial Bank, in his article, 'Scottish Banks under the Microscope', *The Banker*, April 1960, p. 257.
[2] *Radcliffe Evidence*, Q. 4869: compare this with the views of Macdonald, ibid., loc. cit.

short-term fluctuations in their resources. Free balances in London are no more than bare working needs dictate and any large outflows of resources must immediately be transmitted to their other liquid assets.[1] The important asset in this connection is the money lent 'at call' to the London discount market. The loans which the Scottish banks, like other banks, make on a day-to-day basis to the discount houses bring them into intimate contact with the central monetary mechanism and are an important reason for their having offices in the City of London: we shall look into this aspect of their activities more closely in Chapter 12. Here we shall look at their activities in the money market in terms of the effects on their asset structures.

'Other liquid assets' comprise 'money at call' and 'bills discounted'. Money at call is the larger of these two items. In recent years it has averaged between 8 and 9 per cent of deposits compared with a bill ratio of 3 to 4 per cent. Apart from a very small amount lent to the stock market for the period of the account, it is lent on a day-to-day basis to the discount houses.[2] In principle it is all recallable at any time of the working day; in practice much of it is continued from one day to the next and, with certain exceptions, it is not 'called' after midday. These exceptions, as well as the arrangements over interest rates, contain some complications which will be unravelled in Chapter 12. On the question of interest rates we can simplify the matter here by saying that a small proportion of this money is lent to the market at a 'basic' rate set at a fixed margin ($1\frac{5}{8}$ per cent) under Bank Rate, and the rest is lent at rates which fluctuate from day to day, and indeed during the course of the day, according to the supply and demand position in the market.

For a Scottish bank, as for any other bank, the discount market is the first resting place for any unexpected accretions of resources before other uses are decided upon. More, short loans to the market provide the Scottish banks with a means of coping with the various

[1] In this they are not so different from the present practice of English banks as one might suppose. Although a cash reserve of 8 per cent on the face of it offers more leeway, the fact that this ratio is more or less invariable means that fluctuations in reserves have to be met promptly by changes in other liquid assets.

[2] The proportion of the total 'money at call and short notice' of the Scottish banks which is lent to the discount market has averaged about 90 per cent since the end of 1961. Before then it seems to have been higher—about 95 per cent. Both these figures are higher than the corresponding figure for the Clearing banks. This is about 75 per cent; the remainder comprises a number of items such as loans to money brokers, stockbrokers, and some foreign currency balances: see C. W. Linton, 'The Commercial Banks and the London Discount Market', in *The London Discount Market Today*, The Institute of Bankers (London, 1962), p. 39.

predictable seasonal swings in their liabilities. We have observed them withdrawing market money to provide cover for the peak note issue in July. But the most important seasonal movement for any British bank is the annual fall in deposits in the first quarter of the year as tax payments flow into the Exchequer. The English banks meet this almost wholly by acquiring and relinquishing Treasury bills. The Scottish banks as a group meet the larger part of this movement by varying their 'money at call and short notice'. Bills—Treasury bills—also fluctuate with the ebb and flow of deposits and, with the increase in total bill holdings since 1950, this has tended to assume rather more importance. But this movement in bills is still normally smaller in absolute amount than that in money at call.

The surprising thing about the bill portfolios of the Scottish banks is that they are so small. This has not always been the case. Half a century ago the discounting of bills was a major form of lending to domestic borrowers, and 'discounts' were a considerable item among Scottish banking assets. By the 1920s, except in a few trades where it lingered on, the inland bill had given way to the bank advance, and the commercial bills held by the banking system were mainly bills of exchange arising from foreign trade. By this time too the Treasury bill had become an important feature of the short-term end of the capital market, and in some years the banks' holdings of these exceeded their commercial bills. In the late 1920s the bill portfolios of the Scottish banks accounted for 9 per cent of deposits, compared with 13 per cent in the English banks; and Treasury bills accounted for slightly more than half of the total.

The 1930s radically altered this picture. The supply of commercial bills shrank with the onset of the slump: the foreign trade of Scotland probably fell more than the average and the Scottish banks' holdings of commercial bills correspondingly declined.[1] But what is surprising is that their Treasury bills also declined. In 1938 their bill ratio was under 3 per cent, with commercial bills still accounting for rather more than half the total. This was in sharp contrast to the English Clearing banks which managed practically to maintain their bill ratios, making up for the decline in commercial bills by holding more Treasury bills. The increased demand for Treasury bills in the 1930s, coupled with some drop in their supply, drove the bill rate down to very low levels, and this was clearly responsible for the Scottish lack of enthusiasm for Treasury bills. This movement in their bill portfolios illustrates an attitude to the holding of bills—and more

[1] Cf. 'Scottish Banking and Cheap Money', *The Banker*, November 1938, p. 168.

particularly Treasury bills—which contrasts markedly with that of the English banks and which persists in great measure to the present day. For all banks bills rank behind money at call in point of liquidity; but this has more practical effects on the actions of the Scottish banks, than on those of the English banks. For the Scottish banks bills are a marginal asset: the amount of them held, apart from seasonal holdings (and even these provide only a partial exception), is influenced by the attractiveness of the bill rate. This is, of course, also tied up with their practices in the holding of all liquid assets and we shall take this up again shortly.

During the Second World War the Scottish banks' bills fell to even lower levels than before it. There was, however, remarkably little disturbance of their asset structure during these years. Due apparently to their disposition to absorb longer-term securities the Scottish banks were not involved to anything like the same extent as the English banks in the holding of Treasury Deposit Receipts, the non-marketable short-term asset introduced by the authorities as a means of compulsory wartime borrowing from the banking system. Within the Scottish banks' assets T.D.R.s more or less counterbalanced the fall in advances; at their peak in 1945 they were only about 11 per cent of deposits compared with 40 per cent in the English banks; and as their issue was tapered off in succeeding years, the resources freed were used by the Scottish banks to re-expand advances. The important consequence of this was that the Scottish banks entirely escaped the very high post-war liquidity which affected the English banks, whose T.D.R.s were largely replaced by Treasury bills. A further result of this was that the Scottish banks were not involved in the compulsory funding operation of November 1951, by which part of the swollen bill portfolios of the Clearing banks were replaced by securities of somewhat longer-term.

Since 1951 the Scottish banks have increased their holding of Treasury bills as well as their money at call. For the banks as a group ratios of both assets have only gone up by about 1 per cent, but in the case of bills, starting from a much lower level, this represents quite a big relative increase. Individually there have almost certainly been some deviations from this average picture. Unfortunately the only detailed figures we have for the individual banks are those contained in the annual balance sheets. As the seasonal influence is most strongly felt in liquid assets, these annual figures are of limited value for tracing individual differences of policy. The percentages for individual banks over the three-year period 1960–2 are shown in Table XIX; that they are almost all higher than the aggregate percentages shown in Table XVIII springs from the fact that all but one of the balance sheets relate to dates in the final quarter of the calendar year. There are some divergences to be seen even in these seasonally distorted figures. There is an obvious contrast between the Royal Bank and the Clydesdale in the amount of bills they hold—at any rate on the last day of the year. The Royal probably does tend to hold a relatively high proportion of bills at all times and, possibly with the National Commercial, it may make greater use of bills to meet the seasonal movement of deposits than some of the other banks. The Clydesdale's bill ratio, which is very low for the time of the year, is partly explained by the fact that in its balance sheet it invariably shows a very substantial balance—of the order of 6 per cent of deposits —in account with its parent the Midland. This balance must be in the nature of a short loan, enabling the parent bank itself to hold more liquid assets; in fact the view in banking circles is that it represents a transfer of the seasonal inflow of funds to the Midland to swell its deposit total in the end-year balance sheet.

TABLE XIX

Scottish Banks' Ratios of Liquid Assets, 1960–2[1]
Per cent of Deposits plus Fiduciary Note Issues

	1 TOTAL CASH[2]	2 NON- COVER CASH[3]	3 MONEY AT CALL AND SHORT NOTICE	4 TOTAL BILLS	5 LIQUID ASSETS WITH TOTAL COST (COLS. 1, 3, 4)	6 LIQUID ASSETS WITH NON- COVER CASH (COLS. 2, 3, 4)
Bank of Scotland (February 28th)	16·1	1·9	11·3	2·5	29·9	15·7
Royal Bank (December 31st)	15·4	2·7	10·9	9·7	36·0	23·3
British Linen (September 30th)	17·4	1·8	11·0	3·2	31·6	16·0
National Commercial (October 27th–29th)	19·4	1·9	10·7	6·8	36·9	19·4
Clydesdale (December 31st)	14·7	2·3	11·3	3·0	29·0	16·6

[1] All figures are averages of three annual balance sheets the dates of which are shown against each bank. The Bank of Scotland figures refer to the balance sheets of February 28th in the years 1961–3.

[2] In every case cash is defined as currency (including notes of other Scottish banks) and Bank of England balances.

[3] This is derived by subtracting the excess portion of the note totals shown on the balance sheet (and relating to the date of the balance) from the cash figure.

As the Radcliffe Committee's statistics show, the Scottish banks began to hold more Treasury bills from the middle of 1952. At first it was probably the uncertainties introduced by the revival of monetary policy after November 1951 which was responsible for the rise. But as the decade wore on two other factors came into play. One was simply the rise in short-term rates of interest which made bills much more attractive assets to hold than they were before 1951. The other was the increasing public emphasis, after 1955, on the 'liquidity ratio' of the banking system, that is the ratio to deposits of the total of cash, money at call and bills. As a result of changes in the scale of the Treasury bill issue and of the way in which it is taken up by the banking system, together with closely related changes in the techniques of monetary management, the liquidity ratio, since the war, has replaced the cash ratio as the important ratio for credit control.[1] This led during the 'fifties to an increasing emphasis on maintaining a stable liquidity ratio, at first informally and in private by the Bank of England, and then more publicly as the significance of the change became a topic of discussion in the financial press.[2] Then, sometime during 1955, the rule regarding the liquidity ratio was made rigid in that the English banks were requested to observe a 30 per cent minimum.

The figure of 30 per cent was not, of course, taken out of the blue. There was a convention in English banking of maintaining an overall proportion of quick assets of about this level; and the pre-war figure was usually near it.[3] There is, however, no evidence of such a convention in Scottish banking. In the 1920s the Scottish banks' average ratio of *total* cash, money at call and bills was near to 30 per cent; but there was no attempt in the 'thirties to maintain it, and with the drop in bills and an accompanying decline in cash due to note circulation changes, it fell almost to 20 per cent where it remained until the early 1950s. After 1951 it began to rise and it has gone on doing so until it has now reached an annual average of 31 per cent, where it is more or less comparable with the English ratio. This rise, however, is due almost wholly to an increased holding of cash, both absolutely and relative to deposits, consequent upon the rise in the note issues. There has, as we have seen, been a slight rise in 'other liquid assets', and

---

[1] This change is discussed more fully, and in the context of monetary policy, in Chapter 13 below, pp. 194–6. Some commentators place the date of the change further back, in the interwar period, but I do not accept this.

[2] The Bank of England has now given an account of this development in its *Quarterly Bulletin*, December 1962, p. 252.

[3] *Radcliffe Evidence*, QQ. 3735–60.

this has been perhaps partly stimulated by the propaganda for 30 per cent. According to one of the Scottish bankers appearing before the Radcliffe Committee,[1] 'It started as what I might describe as a journalistic fetish in the City', but he went on to admit: 'In recent years we have seen fit to step up our liquidity ratios, partly perhaps even out of regard for this convention in the City . . .'[2]

The rule of a 30 per cent minimum ratio was only applied rigidly to the Clearing banks. The actual percentage is now in process of being reduced. In the spring of 1963 the banks were told that they might go below the minimum by as much as 1 per cent. In October of the same year the Governor of the Bank of England intimated that their liquidity ratios might be allowed to fall as low as 28 per cent in the seasonal period of low liquidity in the following spring and, although this relaxation was occasioned by special circumstances, it was linked by the Governor with a proposal emanating from the banks, and accepted in principle by him, of a gradual reduction of the Clearing banks' liquidity ratio to a new minimum at an even lower figure. The English Clearing banks are known to have been seeking such a reduction on the grounds that in modern conditions a 30 per cent reserve is higher than they need; and a figure of 25 per cent is thought to be in their minds. The intention on the part of the Bank appears to be that, if and when this reduction is achieved, the new ratio will be a fixed minimum in the same way as the earlier 30 per cent—a 'fulcrum against which special deposits . . . could be applied . . .'[3]

British banks other than the Clearers have not been subjected to a stated minimum ratio. Instead they were asked, individually (and at a later date), to observe their 'usual' minima. In their evidence to the Radcliffe Committee[4] the Scottish banks' witnesses made it clear that there was no tradition of a 30 per cent minimum in Scottish banking, but one of them did concede, under questioning, that if the ratio fell to 26 per cent in February, before the seasonal inflow of taxes had run its full course, 'it would be definitely too low'. In the Radcliffe Report itself rather too much was built on this admission[5]; at least, the modernity of it was insufficiently recognized (a glance at

[1] *Radcliffe Evidence*, Q. 5023. There was actually more to it than this as the account in the *Bank of England Quarterly Bulletin*, December 1952, shows.

[2] Ibid. Q. 5024. This statement presumably referred to an earlier period of the 1950s, before the Scottish note issues had reached their present high ratios to deposits.

[3] See the speech of the Governor of the Bank of England at the Mansion House, on October 16, 1963.

[4] *Radcliffe Evidence*, QQ. 5022–37.   [5] *Radcliffe Report*, para 155.

125

the Committee's own figures would have shown that as late as 1955 the February ratio was as low as 22 per cent). Furthermore, neither in the questioning of witnesses, nor in the Report itself, was there any attempt to clarify what the 'liquidity ratio' either did or should mean in the context of Scottish banking. Indeed the questions and answers on this matter suggest most strongly that the Committee and the witnesses were talking about two different things.

In the statements of Scottish bankers, as well as in the statistics now published, two items of assets are invariably included in 'liquid assets'. These are 'balances with, and cheques in course of collection on, other banks' and *total* cash; the appropriateness of both inclusions must be examined. Take the former first. 'Balances with other banks and cheques in course of collection' from a single aggregated item in all the statistical sources available to us. There is no question that the free, net balances held by Scottish banks with other domestic banks are legitimately to be regarded as forming part of their total liquid assets. But the inclusion of claims (cheques etc.) 'in the pipeline' is another matter entirely. These items make up about three-quarters of the total of 'balances and cheques', amounting in 1962 to between 3 and 4 per cent of deposits. The inclusion of them thus has a noticeable effect on the total liquidity ratio.

In an article on bank liquidity, in the Bank of England's *Quarterly Bulletin*,[1] it is stated that in the case of the Scottish banks these items are included 'because a large proportion of the funds are held by, or being collected from, banks outside the Scottish banking system'. Now whether or not these items should be included in the Scottish banks' liquidity ratios raises two quite separate sets of issues, which stem from the two functions of liquid assets. One of these functions—the older one—is simply to ensure the liquidity of the bank in the face of demands for cash. For the individual banker, such claims on other banks as cheques are liquid assets in the sense that they are in process of being converted into cash. There is a certain case for regarding them as 'liquid' in this sense, but it is not, in my opinion, a very strong case. Every banker must know that the claims which he is pushing into the pipeline at any moment are almost equally counter-balanced by similar claims on him, moving along the same channel. One might say: given that there is bound to be a certain volume of claims outstanding against him, the claims on other bankers in his own hands allow him to meet these obligations; but even this is an odd argument, However, if we grant that there is a slight ground for the *individual* banker taking this view of his claims in course of

[1] December 1962, p. 252.

collection, there is certainly no case for regarding the aggregate of them as contributing to the liquidity of the banks *as a whole*. Furthermore, even if it is true that 'a large proportion of the funds are being collected from banks outside the Scottish banking system', this makes no difference to the position. The flow of bank claims between Scotland and England is a two-way flow and as largely self-cancelling as that which flows between the individual banks of the Scottish system. (To add these claims to the London balances held by the Scottish banks, for purposes of reckoning the liquidity of the system as a whole, would be equivalent to a country reckoning its international reserves by adding the value of unpaid exports to its gold reserves and ignoring the imports not yet paid for.)

The second function of liquid assets is to act as a fulcrum against which the authorities can operate in such a way as to control the volume of bank deposits. This is a function of comparatively modern growth, and it is the more important one today. The policy actions of the monetary authorities in Britain today require that the banks should observe a more or less constant ratio of total liquid assets to deposits. If they do this then the authorities can operate on the volume of bank deposits by varying the quantity of liquid assets in banking hands.[1] The essential thing is that the ratio should be the object of purposive action by the banks themselves, while the assets which are included should be those which the authorities are manipulating. Under modern conditions the authorities control the banks by manipulating the volume of cash and short-term assets;[2] and on this basis the liquidity ratio of the banks is appropriately defined as the total of cash, money at call and bills.[3] The 'claims in transit' of the Scottish banks satisfy neither of the two conditions above. First, they are not the object of any purposive action by the banks themselves since there is nothing that any single bank can do to affect the volume of them: their ratio to deposits is a purely passive quantity. Secondly they are not, obviously, part of the volume of short-term assets which the authorities manipulate. If one could count on the ratio of these claims remaining constant over time, then practically speaking it would not matter if they were included in liquid assets for reckoning the total ratio. But there is no reason to expect that they do or will show such constancy.

[1] For a fuller account of this see below, Chapter 13, pp. 202–3.

[2] Cash, *per se*, is not limited in any way: it is freely interchangeable with Treasury bills. But the overall total of cash and bills is the object of policy control.

[3] There are some loose ends here: e.g. commercial bills form part of liquid assets but are not fully under the control of the authorities; but this does not affect the argument presented here.

The other item which is normally included in the liquid assets of the Scottish banks when calculating their liquidity ratios, and which we must query, is *total* cash. We have seen that more than four-fifths of the cash holdings of the Scottish banks is the legal tender held as cover against their own note issues. We have also seen that, as the banks exert no positive control over the extent of their note circulation, the size of this note-cover fund—both absolutely and in relation to deposits—is a passive quantity determined by the demand for Scottish notes in circulation. As such, the note-cover fund plays no direct part in determining the actions of the banks in lending or investment, and hence it has no direct influence on the credit effects of these actions. It is therefore inappropriate to include this element in defining the 'operative' liquidity ratio of the Scottish banks. This ratio is to be defined as the ratio of their non-cover cash (including their balances with London banks and excluding holdings of one another's notes) money at call and bills.[1] The full implications of this will have to be considered when (in Chapter 13) we look at the Scottish banks in the wider monetary setting.

[1] One must include in bills certain medium-term export credits. By an arrangement dating from early 1961 the banks may re-finance (i.e. re-discount) credits, or parts of them, which fall due for repayment within the following eighteen months. Such credits are obviously every bit as liquid as bills and the inclusion of them in the liquidity ratio is recognized by the Bank.

CHAPTER 9

RISK ASSETS

The term 'risk assets' is no more than a rough label for those assets that fall outside what, by today's convention, are referred to as liquid assets. The two principal assets involved are 'loans and advances' and 'investments'. Loans and advances may be said, unequivocally, to be more risky than liquid assets. As funds lent almost wholly to the private sector they carry less security than if they were lent to the state which, for the most part, is the case with liquid assets; while they are comparatively illiquid in that, although technically recallable on demand, in practice they can rarely be liquidated quickly. But to describe 'investments' as risk assets is more questionable. They consist today almost wholly of gilt-edged securities so that risk of default is absent. At one time—in the pre-1914 era —gilt-edged securities were normally classed as liquid assets; a combined total of government securities and money at call was frequently shown on balance sheets and the securities were regarded equally as a reinforcing of the cash position. At that time the liquidity of bonds was considered to reside in their ready marketability. Today, with a vastly increased volume of debt of all kinds, a separate element of 'liquidity' has come to be stressed more and more: this is freedom from risk of fluctuation in capital values. Gilt-edged securities with more than the shortest span of life to run are clearly subject to instability of value, and this, coupled with the high levels to which bank portfolios have climbed since the early 1930s, has caused them to be banished from the fold of liquid assets—at any rate by those who comment on financial affairs. The banks themselves have not departed quite so far from their traditional attitudes.[1] They still regard gilt-edged securities as reinforcing their liquid position although now such reinforcement is regarded as proceeding to an important extent from a timed succession of maturities. Also, as far as the selling of securities before maturity is concerned, they would presumably admit that unless there was official support of the gilt-

[1] See *Radcliffe Evidence*, QQ. 3744, 5039.

edged market, they could not divest themselves of large amounts of investments without seriously depressing the prices of these assets, and hence involving themselves in capital losses.

But whatever label one chooses to apply to them, there is a cogent reason for classing advances and investment together in that they are more closely competitive than any other groups of assets. Granted that the banks must, for reasons prudential and conventional, hold certain quantities of short-term assets, and that on profit grounds they will not want to go much beyond this point, and given the general range of assets which British banks are prepared to hold then the remaining portion of their resources must be invested either in advances or in securities.[1] The more the banks put into the one asset, the less they can put into the other; and similarly, if for some reason funds are released from one of the uses these resources will normally be moved into the other. Hence the well-known scissors movement of advances and investments—the tendency for the levels of the two assets to move contrariwise.

But the two assets are far from being perfect substitutes for one another. They differ, as we have seen, in liquidity. They also differ in profitability: advances normally yield a higher return than securities, and even though the costs of managing them are higher, they are the more profitable asset. Investments are, to an extent, a residual asset in the banker's eyes: when insufficient borrowers of the required standing present themselves, the funds which he would otherwise have lent to private borrowers will probably be placed in gilt-edged to be re-liquefied when the expansion of advances becomes possible. But investments are only a residual asset beyond a certain point. The liquidity of gilt-edged securities is still important and all British banks like to preserve a cushion of them between their liquid assets, which are vulnerable to official policy, and their advances. This attitude gains more force today when open-market policy is directed against the whole liquidity position, and not simply against the cash ratio. If the bankers are to live with the risk of at times being forced below their minimum liquidity ratio, in the interests of a restrictive monetary policy, they need an asset which can be discarded in order to give time for the reduction of advances. A certain minimum level of investments is therefore as important to them as their liquid assets, and this puts a definite, though undefined, limit on the substitutability of investments and advances.

[1] I am ignoring here various items of assets such as 'trade investments' and 'bank premises, etc.'—items which from a balance sheet point of view are of minor importance.

I. LOANS AND ADVANCES

'Loans and advances' are the balance sheet result of the greater part of banks' activities as lenders to the private sector. In the following chapter we shall be looking at the actual conduct of the Scottish banks as lenders of money: here we shall confine ourselves to the broader balance sheet aspect of the matter. The totals of Scottish bank advances have described very large movements during the last few decades. After a decline in the First World War, the ratio of advances to deposits recovered during the 1920s to reach a level of 54 per cent at the end of that decade. Then came a drastic fall with the depression of the 'thirties; and it was not until 1936 that the total of Scottish advances turned upwards again, by which time their ratio to deposits had dipped below 30 per cent. In 1938—the only year of the 'thirties for which we have really satisfactory figures—the advances ratio of six of the eight Scottish banks was 33 per cent, compared with an English figure of 41 per cent. As both groups of banks had had similar ratios in 1928, the decline in Scottish advances had been much sharper and the reason, of course, was the greater severity of depression in Scotland compared with England and Wales as a whole. Indeed, as an index of the fall in demand for bank finance on the part of Scottish industry and trade this comparison almost certainly understates the matter in that during the interwar period a substantial fraction of Scottish banks' advances—probably a bigger fraction than with the English banks—went to finance the holding of stock exchange securities; but more of this later.[1] During the Second World War Scottish bank advances, following a general movement, fell to even lower levels than in the depression. In the war years the borrowing of many industries was restricted in the interests of the war economy, while the war industries themselves received much of their finance directly from the Government. The Government, of course, had to obtain a large part of this finance from the banking system, but in the balance sheets of the banks, Scottish and English alike, this appeared as Government securities of one kind or another.

By 1945 Scottish advances had fallen to 18 per cent of deposits. In the immediate post-war years they rose comparatively quickly, to reach 30 per cent of deposits in 1951. With the first of the restrictive phases of post-war monetary policy, in 1951–2, the Scottish advances ratio fell back to around 27 per cent and there, except for an up-and-down movement in 1954–5, it remained until the release of the banks,

[1] Below, pp. 157–8.

131

in 1958, from all the informal restraints which had lain on them since the beginning of the war. This release was followed, in the Scottish as in the English system, by a remarkable upsurge in advances which, by July 1961, when the sterling crisis of that year caused a reimposition of restraints, had carried the Scottish advances ratio to 45 per cent—just two points behind the English figure.

How have the post-war movements in Scottish advances been financed? The recovery of advances immediately after the war was made possible partly by a run-down of T.D.R.s; but Scottish holdings of these were never large—they were only 11 per cent of deposits at their peak—and by 1948 the Scottish banks had begun to liquidate investments, providing a foretaste of what was to come ten years later. Between July 1958 and July 1961, Scottish advances rose by £167 million, or 77 per cent; rather less than two-thirds of this increase was financed by the liquidation of securities, and the rest by a rise in deposits. The path followed by this expansion in Scotland was broadly the same as in England, although the increase in Scottish advances was somewhat less than in the South where the corresponding total rose by 87 per cent. The most notable difference between the two systems was in the 1961 pause itself. In Scotland it was remarkably short-lived. Scottish advances fell back in the late summer of that year, but probably as much for seasonal reasons as any other. In November 1961 they resumed their upward trend; and by April 1962 they had passed their previous peak. When they levelled off in mid-1962 they were 5 per cent higher than in mid-1961. In England, on the other hand, a longer pause was observed and bank advances only began to rise again in the spring of 1962. This contrast of movement is interesting: it suggests that the Scottish banks were exempted from the 1961 pause. If so, it represented an important step towards co-ordinating monetary policy with regional needs.

In February 1958, one general manager of a Scottish bank giving evidence to the Radcliffe Committee stated (Q.4851): 'I do not visualize in my lifetime seeing our advances even 40 per cent of our deposits.' Five years later, in February 1963, the aggregate advances ratio of the Scottish banks stood at just under 52 per cent, that of the English banks at 49 per cent. This Scottish banker was not in the least exceptional at the time, in the view he took; the point of quoting him is to underline the extreme difficulty of predicting the future demand for bank finance. In the late 1930s the hypothesis was advanced that the demand for bank finance was declining secularly.[1]

[1] See R. S. Sayers, *Modern Banking*, 1st ed. (Oxford 1938), pp. 237–45.

The recent expansion of advances by no means disproves this, since bank loans in the aggregate remain smaller in relation to the national income than in the mid-1920s. But the future trend of demand is not now so clear as it seemed a few years ago. Assuming that it continues to grow will the banks be able to meet it?

If bank deposits rise, with official help, then clearly the absolute total of bank advances can go up also though, as recent years have shown, a rising level of bank deposits overall need not entail a proportionate degree of buoyancy in Scottish deposits. What is less certain is how far further increases in advances ratios can contribute to increased bank lending. In their evidence to the Radcliffe Committee the Scottish bankers, speaking as they were before the recent transformation of their balance sheets, were unable to put a firm maximum value on their advances ratios, and the English banks were equally uncertain.[1] This uncertainty is understandable: looking back from the present phase, at the time when advances ratios were anywhere near a point where the question of a limit could arise, the present generation of leading bankers were young men; the only guidance they can now call upon are memories of the attitudes of their seniors in the 1920s. One of the Scottish bankers felt that the 1912 level of 62 per cent of deposits in advances was too high for today.[2] Presumably, somewhere not far ahead now, between 50 and 60 per cent, lies the ceiling. Already, as the ratio has risen through the 40 per cents, there have been warning cries from the bankers themselves; but when they have acclimatized themselves to the change the ultimate limit may be found to lie nearer 60 than 50 per cent.

The Scottish banker just referred to gave as his reason for regarding the 1912 ratio as too high in present conditions, the fact that in the intervening years the contingency reserves had been whittled away by inflation. Another conditioning influence would be the minimum level to which the banks are prepared to allow their investments ratios to sink. How big a cushion of gilt-edged do they want to preserve between liquid assets and advances? The English banks with investments running, on average, at 15 per cent of deposits (in early 1964) may not have far to go; but the Scottish banks with an investments ratio still around 27 per cent appear to have greater scope, even taking account of such other factors as a smaller effective holding of liquid assets.

So far we have been discussing advances in terms of aggregates and before we turn to look at investments we should glance at the

[1] *Radcliffe Evidence*, QQ. 4850–8, 3744–7.
[2] Ibid., QQ. 4852–3.

figures for individual banks. In any banking system there are variations of policy and conduct which are concealed by aggregates, and the Scottish banks are no exception to this. As regards advances one or two banks have diverged from the mean figure. In the 'thirties the Royal had a very high advances ratio, while the Bank of Scotland, the British Linen and the North Bank had lowish ratios; and these differences were reflected in investments. The present-day figures for the individual banks bring out one notable variation from the average; this appears in Table XX where the various individual changes in advances, investments and deposits are shown for the period 1958–62.

TABLE XX

Changes in Advances, Investments and Deposits, 1958–62[1]

	ADVANCES	INVESTMENTS [2]	DEPOSITS	ADVANCES IN 1962 1958=100	ADVANCES RATIOS[3] 1962 PER CENT	INVESTMENTS RATIOS[4] 1962 PER CENT
	£ m.	£ m.	£ m.			
Bank of Scotland	+47·4	−36·5 (−36·1)	+20·1	217	46·5	24·1 (21·0)
Royal Bank	+28·5	−17·0 (−18·5)	+ 9·1	162	51·5	21·8 (13·8)
British Linen	+24·6	−14·7 (−15·5)	+13·5	196	52·5	27·6 (24·7)
National Commercial	+50·9	−48·8 (−51·0)	+ 5·4	175	51·0	22·6 (20·0)
Clydesdale	+21·7	−11·5 (−11·7)	+20·4	145	35·6	37·8 (34·0)

[1] Calculated from totals on the annual balance sheets appearing in these two years.

[2] Changes in total investments with, in brackets, changes in Government and Government-guaranteed securities.

[3] Ratios of advances to the totals of deposits and fiduciary note issues.

[4] Ratios of total investments to deposits and fiduciary note issues with, in brackets, the corresponding ratios of Government and Government-guaranteed securities.

The Bank of Scotland's advances as a proportion of deposits are still below the average but this bank has shown the biggest relative increase since 1958 and this has brought it nearer to the mean figure. The surprise in these figures is the small rise recorded by the Clydesdale,[1] the more so as its advances ratio was not significantly lower

[1] By the end of 1963 the Clydesdale's ratio had risen to 38·1 per cent—still well below the average.

than the average in 1958. As we have seen in Chapter 3 the Clydesdale is the most regionally orientated of the banks, with twin foci in the West Lowlands and the North East; the explanation of the slow increase of this bank's lending may lie in particularly strong connections with those Scottish industries, such as shipbuilding, which have been meeting increasing difficulties during these years. But this is a doubtful conjecture and on the evidence that we have we can really make no suggestions.

II. INVESTMENTS

When asked by the Radcliffe Committee about the higher investments ratio of the Scottish banks, and whether it was to be regarded as temporary, one of the Scottish bankers replied:[1] 'I would hope so, but it has been temporary for a long time.' He went on to date the beginning of this 'more heavily invested' condition from the inflation of the 1914–18 period; but there is evidence of the condition further back than that. In the final quarter of the nineteenth century, during what, before 1930, was called the 'Great Depression', Scottish banking showed a striking combination of stagnant advances and rising deposits.[2] The inadequacy of the figures prevents a reliable comparison with English banking trends during this period, but—using the figures we have—by the end of it the Scottish ratio of advances and discounts was 51 per cent while that of the English joint-stock banks was 65 per cent. Scottish banks' investments, if we include loans made on the security of stock, were proportionately higher than those of the English joint-stock banks. Coming forward to 1912 we have rather firmer figures: the Scottish investments ratio then stood at 30 per cent compared with 18 per cent for the English joint-stock banks.[3]

The Scottish banks, like the English banks, emerged from the First World War with much higher investments than they had had before it; but, unlike the English banks, they saw little fall in their investments ratios during the 1920s. In the 1930s the British banking system as a whole ran into a period of falling advances resulting from economic depression, and rising deposits caused by expansionary

[1] *Radcliffe Evidence*, Q. 4861.
[2] Between 1876–7 and 1896–7 advances and discounts rose from £57 million to £64 million, while deposits rose from £64 million to £96 million (in each case the earlier figure excludes the City of Glasgow Bank which failed in 1878).
[3] It was lower than this for some of the larger English banks: see Balogh, op. cit., p. 71.

monetary policy. The decline in Scottish bank advances was, as we have seen, relatively much greater and more prolonged than in England; it was also coupled with a sharp fall in bills. The consequences of all these movements was a particularly marked rise in investments. In 1938 they stood at 57 per cent of Scottish banks' deposits compared with an English figure of 28 per cent.

During the Second World War the position of investments within total Scottish banks' assets remained unchanged. The absolute amount of securities held increased in step with the war-induced inflation of the banks' resources. But with bills and advances already so heavily reduced by economic depression the effect of war finance on the asset structure of the Scottish banks was comparatively slight. Two consequences followed from this in the post-war period. One was that the Scottish banks had to begin to liquidate investments earlier than the English banks, as their advances recovered. The other, mentioned earlier, was that they escaped the high liquidity which affected the English banks following the liquidation of T.D.R.s, and consequently were not involved in the compulsory funding operation which accompanied the re-activation of monetary policy in late 1951.

During the 'fifties and early 'sixties the Scottish banks' investments have for the most part moved inversely with advances. But not wholly so: there was a phase in 1954 when advances and investments increased together on a rising tide of deposits, but this was followed in 1955 by a drop in investments when the authorities put the squeeze on deposits. In that phase advances declined only after the famous July request by the Chancellor. But the movements of the early 'fifties, though interestingly interwoven with the financial history of those years, have been completely overshadowed by the events of 1958–61. Between July 1958 and July 1961, the Scottish banks liquidated £95 million of gilt-edged securities, and there has been a further, though smaller, decline since then. This phase, however, has left the Scottish banks still with a considerably higher ratio of investments than the English banks, and the question is, will they be prepared to go correspondingly further, in shedding securities, if the demand for bank finance continues to rise? Will they, for example, be prepared to see their investments ratios go down to something like the English level? The answer is: probably not, and for two reasons. The higher Scottish investments ratio is now the reflection not of a lower advances ratio, but of a lower 'true' liquidity ratio (that is, eliminating note-cover cash from assets). A further marked fall in the investments ratios of the Scottish banks would entail their advances ratios going well above those of the English banks, and they might feel inhibited from going as far as this. Secondly, with a lower level of effective liquid reserves, the reserve aspect of investments is possibly more important for the Scottish banker. Taking these factors into account, and assuming a growing demand for advances, I think that we can expect eventually to see Scottish investments come down to something like 18 per cent of deposits, and advances rise to just short of 60 per cent.

The Composition of Investments

The composition of the Scottish banks' investments has some important features that call for comment. These investments today consist predominantly of gilt-edged securities. At the end of 1962 'British Government and Government-guaranteed securities' formed 88 per cent of the total investments of the Scottish banks as a group. The remainder consisted of 'trade investments', that is holdings in bodies like the Industrial and Commercial Finance Corporation and the Scottish Agriculture Securities Corporation; holdings in subsidiary companies, which are mainly hire purchase finance companies, but, in the case of the Royal Bank,[1] include two English banks; and, finally, 'corporation mortgages', which are short- and medium-term securities issued by local authorities. The concentration of portfolios on government securities is a development of the last fifty years. Before the First World War the balance sheets of most Scottish banks showed smaller amounts of British Government securities than other securities, the others being a mixed bag of Indian and Colonial, municipal, bank and railway stocks.

The most interesting and important aspect of the present gilt-edged portfolios of the Scottish banks is their maturity structure, and on this evidence presented to the Radcliffe Committee has thrown valuable light. The figures published by the Committee, and continued for a short time by the Scottish banks, made a division of securities into those of up to five years maturity, and those of over five years. These figures, covering the period 1951–60, are given in Table XXI.

Two remarkable facts emerge from this table. The first and more obvious one is the shape of the maturity structure itself. Throughout this decade securities with more than five years to run were never less

---

[1] In the holding of 'investments' other than gilt-edged securities the Royal Bank diverges markedly from the Scottish average with 36 per cent of its total investments in this form at the end of 1962. This is largely accounted for by its holdings in its subsidiaries.

TABLE XXI

The Scottish Banks' Gilt-Edged, 1951–60

	TOTALS[1] £ m.		PROPORTIONS PERCENT OF TOTAL HOLDINGS	
	0–5 YEARS	OVER 5 YEARS AND UNDATED	0–5 YEARS	OVER 5 YEARS AND UNDATED
			%	%
1951	80·4	303·6	21·6	78·4
1952	96·7	259·4	27·2	72·8
1953	109·3	273·3	28·0	71·4
1954	94·0	316·4	22·9	77·1
1955	81·6	225·9	26·5	73·5
1956	89·0	253·5	26·0	74·0
1957	96·0	247·2	28·0	72·0
1958	94·4	243·4	27·9	72·1
1959	82·2	220·2	27·2	72·8
1960 (June)	75·5	186·6	28·8	71·2

Sources: 1951–8, *Radcliffe Memoranda*, vol. 2, Statistical Appendix, Table 3; 1959–60, Monthly Statements, *Financial Statistics* (C.S.O.).

[1] Annual figures are averages of quarterly totals.

than seven-tenths of the aggregate holdings of gilt-edged of the Scottish banks. The second is the apparent stability of this maturity structure during a decade in which sentiment swung strongly against fixed-interest securities, and the more strongly against the longer maturities. The proportion of short-dated stocks took a jump in 1952, but this may well be explained by a permanent change of policy on the part of one or two banks since, with the exception of the drop in 1954, it then remained steady for the rest of the period. But these figures conceal an important change which took place during these years, and of which the half-yearly statutory statements provide evidence. The statements show[1] that whereas in the early 'fifties the Scottish banks were holding some undated or very long-

---

[1] These statements, published by all except the Bank of Scotland, carry an abbreviated list of the various government stocks held. In 1954, of the four banks who are still now publishing them, three held War Loan and the fourth held Conversion Loan, all four held Victory Bonds (redeemable by drawings up to 1976) and two held Funding Stock (1999–2004). In 1959 no banks held War Loan or Conversion Stock and three held Victory Bonds (it is not possible to deduce anything from 'Funding Stocks', as there were two more issues by that year). The *Radcliffe Report* speaking (para. 153) of the 'appreciable amount of undated stocks' which the Scottish banks held until a few years earlier, stated: 'these are believed to have been largely sold, and certainly the tendency has been to shorten the average life of the portfolios.'

dated stocks, by 1959 most of these had been shed. Thus although the proportion of securities of over five years maturity remained very stable during these years there was almost certainly a marked shortening of the maturity structure within this class. In spite of this change however the Scottish banks' portfolios are probably, still, longer in average maturity than those of the English banks. The two Scottish bankers who gave evidence to the Radcliffe Committee indicated that their banks held stocks of up to fifteen years life;[1] and it is probable that as a group they do not keep as much of their portfolios under ten years maturity as the English banks.

One thing is quite certain: the Scottish banks do not subscribe to the English practice of keeping half or more of their investments in stocks with less than five years to run. The purpose behind this latter policy is twofold. On the one hand it ensures a continuous flow of maturities which can be relied upon automatically to reinforce liquidity; while, on the other, if securities have to be sold before they mature the risk of capital loss is less than with the longer-dated stocks. The Scottish banks must subscribe to these desiderata, but compared with their English counterparts they put more store by a higher average yield than by a higher average liquidity. There is an obvious reason for this is the very scale of their investments; for decades, now, the Scottish investments ratio has been in the region of twice the level of the corresponding English ratio. But there is yet another interesting fact to remark. The ratio to deposits of the Scottish banks' short-dated stocks has actually not been so much less than the corresponding ratio of the English banks. In 1958 this ratio was 13 per cent for the Scottish banks compared with an English ratio of 16 per cent. In June 1960 the Scottish ratio, at just below 10 per cent, was only about one percentage point below the English ratio, if we assume that one-half of the English banks' gilt-edged were short-dated stocks. In other words, for the five years immediately ahead of any one year, the Scottish banks have been able to provide for annual reinforcements of liquidity from maturing stocks on pretty much the same relative scale as the English banks, even though their portfolios leaned so much more heavily to medium- and longer-dated stocks.

But the Scottish banks' portfolios as a whole were—and probably still are—more vulnerable to the effects of falls in market values.

---

[1] *Radcliffe Evidence*, Q. 5049. Practice will, of course, vary: a note on the 1962 balance sheet of the Clydesdale Bank states that the majority of the stocks held matured within ten years, and a past statement by the Bank's Chairman indicates that this has been the practice for some time.

These made their mark in the mid-'fifties. At that time the depreciation of investments due to the continuing fall in gilt-edged prices presented all banks with an accounting problem. Most banks wrote down the book value of their securities, and made corresponding reductions in their hidden reserves. Others, including four of the Scottish banks, continued to show their securities 'under cost and below redemption value', with a note showing the market valuation of their portfolios at the balance sheet date. The four Scottish banks which recorded a discrepancy between book and market values, showed an average depreciation of their portfolios of 5·8 per cent in 1955 and 7·1 per cent in 1956—markedly higher figures than those shown by three of the English 'Big Five' which also adopted this procedure. By 1958 only three of the Scottish banks recorded any depreciation and the average was then down to 2 per cent; in the following year none was shown.

It used to be argued in the 1950s that banks are rarely compelled to liquidate securities and that consequently the depreciation of market values below the price originally paid makes little difference to them : they can normally hold on for the redemption price. The wholesale liquidations of 1958–62 have rather weakened this argument. The banks were not, of course, then compelled to sell off their securities, and presumably they only did so because they were convinced that any losses on this score would be counterbalanced by higher earnings on advances. But there may well have been some losses, and the presumption is that the Scottish banks with their larger portfolios were more exposed to them. One mitigating factor, not often mentioned, is that the banks are classed as dealers in securities for tax purposes ; as a consequence any capital gains they make on the sale of securities are taxable, while losses reduce their tax liability. This means that in effect losses are practically halved by the operation of taxation. The Scottish banks, as we have seen, have shortened their portfolios since the mid-'fifties, and this will have reduced their sensitivity to the 'Roosa effect'.[1] The remark in the Radcliffe Report (para. 153) that : 'The Scottish banks' protection against open market operations is therefore less strong than that of the English banks' is probably still true, but to a smaller extent than when it was written.

A final comment on the Scottish banks' investments is prompted by a remark in the Radcliffe Report. The Committee, noting (in para.

---

[1] This is the effect of a rise in interest rates on the willingness of banks and other holders of securities to sell them in order to expand loans or finance expenditures. It is so called after Robert V. Roosa, of the U.S. Treasury, who has been a strong protagonist of its importance.

153) that the Scottish banks have 'committed themselves more deeply in their investment portfolios' by maintaining higher investment ratios and holding longer bonds than the English banks, connected this (and a willingness to make longer-term advances) with the bigger savings element in Scottish deposits. The implication was that a higher proportion of 'time' deposits within the total has made their deposits more stable and induced a greater readiness to 'go long' in their acquisition of assets. Our analysis of the Scottish banks' holdings of the various assets, in the past and in the present, throws doubt on this account of the matter. The high bond holdings of the past seem to have resulted mainly from a comparatively weak demand for advances which in turn had its roots in a long-standing lack of buoyancy in the Scottish economy. But considerations of income have also played their part: in the 1930s they sustained a preference for bonds rather than bills, and throughout they have probably been the main reason for the longer maturities favoured by the Scottish banks.[1] At the same time, by a reverse interconnection, larger port-folios make it possible to hold longer maturities without impairing the function which securities still fulfil in the liquidity structure of the banks.

*   *   *   *   *   *

The dramatic changes in the Scottish banker's assets since 1959 have, of course, brought their structure into what he regards as a much more desirable shape that it has actually had for nearly three decades. The wholesale substitution of advances for investment has gone far to restore what the banker regards as a 'normal' distribution of his loanable resources between the public and the private sectors of the economy. It has also, as we have seen, had effects on profits: advances are the most highly yielding of the banker's assets and the rise in them has stirred banking profits from their earlier stagnation. In these developments the experience of the Scottish banks has been closely parallel with that of the English banks, but one consequence of the change has been of peculiar significance to them. The higher proportion of advances within total assets has made the income which the banker derives from his assets more sensitive to short-run changes of interest rates. This is particularly important to the Scottish banker since the interest costs of his deposits are also

[1] Income considerations are closely tied up with the high proportion of interest-bearing deposits in Scotland, but this is a different sort of connection, involving a different motivation, from that implied in the Radcliffe Report.

relatively sensitive to interest rate changes because of their heavy weighting with interest-bearing deposits. The asset changes of recent years have therefore not only increased Scottish bank profits: they have done something to reduce their variability in the face of fluctuations in the short-term rate of interest.

CHAPTER 10

THE SCOTTISH BANKS AS LENDERS

One effect of the upsurge of bank advances since 1958 has been to place the banks back in the traditional position where a substantial fraction of their resources is lent to the private sector of the economy. The depressed conditions of the interwar years had carried the Scottish banks to a point where more than two-thirds of their resources were invested, in one form or another, in obligations of the State, and the financial upheaval of the Second World War increased this proportion still further. Today, their resources are divided more or less equally between the public and private sectors, and the balance will probably swing still further yet in favour of the latter. As a group the commercial banks are probably still the most important of the financial intermediaries, although in terms of aggregate resources other groups, notably the insurance companies, are overhauling them rapidly. The banks however have always occupied a unique place as providers of finance. In the words of the Radcliffe Report (para. 138), 'from the point of view of most borrowers [they] are much the most accessible institutional source of credit'. Through their branch systems and their willingness to lend to all who meet their requirements of creditworthiness, the banks have played an all-important role in the financial structure and the chances are that they will go on doing so for some time yet. This is as true of the Scottish banks as of any other British banks, and it is important therefore to review their activities as providers of finance to private borrowers.

Historically, large claims have been made for the part played by the Scottish banks in the economic development of Scotland. They seem to have played a particularly vital role in the eighteenth century when, following the union with England, wider trading prospects were opening up and industrial and agricultural developments were beginning but the country was still much poorer than its southern partner.[1] At this time a method of lending was devised—the cash

[1] For an account of the growth of Scottish banking within the context of the economic development of the country, see H. Hamilton, *The Industrial Revolution in Scotland* (Oxford, 1932), Ch. XII.

credit—which was peculiarly well-adapted to the needs of the country and which carried the seeds of important future developments. The cash credit, which was introduced by the Royal Bank in 1729, in the first year of its operation, was a system of lending on character backed by personal guarantee. A borrower of promising ability who could get two or more people to act as personal guarantors was granted what today we would call an overdraft right: an account was opened for him which he was empowered to overdraw up to a certain limit. Interest was charged only on the actual debit balance of any day, and if the account moved into credit interest was paid on the credit balance.

The cash credit has many interesting and important facets. In its early days it was an instrument of economic development: it overcame the dearth of material assets which could be pledged as security for loans, to place finance in the hands of would-be entrepreneurs. A good example of this is The British Linen Company, which later became the bank and which was started with a £3,000 cash credit from the Royal Bank.[1] In its security aspect the cash credit was an important extension of the concept of personal guarantee. But, equally if not more important, it was a prime innovation in banking technique: the idea of the overdraft as a fluctuating advance descends directly from the Scottish cash credit. For its full development the overdraft system required the growth of the cheque-using habit; but the running account, which could move on either side of the line dividing debits and credits, was a necessary first stage, and the cash credit was the first distinctly modern form of this.

In terms of the amount of lending that it accounted for, the cash credit in its original form was at its zenith in the eighteenth century. The discounted bill, which was always important as an instrument of finance, was almost certainly surpassing it by the beginning of the nineteenth century. By the middle of the last century the old cash credit had declined considerably and the discounting of bills was the dominant form of Scottish bank lending. But by this time the granting of overdraft rights against other forms of security than the personal guarantee had arisen in Scotland and this—essentially a development of the cash credit idea—increased steadily through the second half of the century.[2] The discounting of bills continued to be

---

[1] See Neil Munro, *The History of the Royal Bank of Scotland, 1727–1927* (Edinburgh, 1928), p. 109.

[2] We have the complete set of annual balance sheets of the Dundee Banking Company, from its founding in 1764 until its absorption by the Royal Bank in 1864, in *A Century of Banking in Dundee* by C. W. Boase (Dundee, 1864). These

a significant part of the Scottish banks' lending; however, by the end of the century the inland bill was declining rapidly although the process had not gone so far in Scotland as in England.[1] By the 1920s the inland bill had become a rarity in Scotland, as in England, confined to one or two trades like timber and whisky blending, or to remote parts of the country.[2] Then, as now, the overdraft was the prime vehicle of bank advances in Scotland.[3] Today the cash credit in its old form is a very minor element of lending: from the banks' point of view it has disadvantages compared with other forms of guarantee and these are generally preferred.[4]

The modern position is that the overdraft is much the most important way in which the Scottish banks lend. The straight loan has probably declined in importance since before the Second World

show the following breakdown of lending:

	Per cent of total lending		
	1764	1810	1864
Cash accounts	63	25	12
Personal bonds	7	nil	nil
Bills	30	75	50
Overdrawn accounts	nil	nil	6
Heritable bonds	nil	nil	28

Here, 'cash accounts' means cash credits, 'heritable bonds' means advances on the security of land and buildings, while 'overdrawn accounts' presumably signifies advances without security. 'Heritable bonds' first appear in 1811 but only begin to rise after 1819; 'overdrawn accounts' first appear in 1839; 'life policies' also appear on balance sheets between 1852 and 1863. It is impossible to say how typical the Dundee Banking Company was. Before 1800, as a provincial bank, its business and the character of its lending would be somewhat different from the three senior banks, and figures of the Bank of Scotland which I have seen confirm this. In 1764, for example, while cash accounts accounted for a similar proportion—59 per cent—of the Bank's lending, its bills discounted appear to have been nil. Lending on personal and heritable bonds, on the other hand, accounted for 33 per cent of the total. But bills appeared on the balance sheet in 1766 and became a sizeable amount in the 1770s.

[1] For the English trend see Balogh, op. cit., p. 77. By 1895 the discounts of those Scottish banks which showed them separately were generally exceeded by their advances, but compared with English banks like the Midland and Lloyds the ratio of discounts was still comparatively high.

[2] A banker whose experience goes back to these years tells me that one could still come across little enclaves of bill financing in the Highlands.

[3] See *Macmillan Evidence*, Q. 2735: the exception noted there was in the London offices where loans were customary, but even this has probably changed now.

[4] See J. J. Gordon and W. A. Mitchell, *Securities for Advances* (Institute of Bankers in Scotland, Edinburgh, 1955), 2nd edition, p. 60.

War, when loans for the speculative holding of stock exchange securities, restricted between 1940 and 1958, were a significant element of total advances;[1] but the advent of the 'personal' and 'term' loans (which are described later) may eventually reverse this trend. On the agreed list of interest rates which, until late 1964, the Scottish banks published (and which we examine in the next chapter) three types of lending were distinguished: 'cash accounts', 'overdrafts' and 'short loans'. 'Cash accounts' were overdrafts granted against first-class security, and they were charged ½ per cent less than so-called 'overdrafts' which were overdrafts granted without security or against security of less than first-class status. A short loan was a fixed loan for a period of one to three months made against marketable securities and normally charged ¼ per cent less than cash accounts. In November 1964, the terms 'cash account' and 'overdraft' were dropped, though how far the distinction in types of lending which they signified would be affected was not known at the time of writing.[2] But to describe the forms of lending, necessary though it is, does not take us far towards answering the questions which, these days, are asked about bank lending. To these we must now turn.

I. THE CHARACTER OF SCOTTISH BANK LENDING

As providers of finance the Scottish banks have always regarded themselves essentially as short-term lenders, as financing circulating capital, such as stocks or goods undergoing process, and not fixed capital in the shape of buildings and durable plant. In this they are, of course, in the long-standing tradition of British banking. Indeed they helped to form this tradition. They developed originally under the same conditions as English banks—conditions of a predominantly agrarian and mercantile economy. There grew up a practical emphasis on short-term lending which experience gradually and painfully established as the most appropriate type of lending for note-issuing and deposit banks. This practice was not altered by the growth of manufacturing industry; and it was confirmed by the development of branch-banking and the need to rely 'on the judgement of branch managers [who might] reasonably be expected to assess the capacity of a borrower to repay in a short time, though they could have no assurance in estimating long-term profitability'.[3] But in the present day this account of the matters must be immediately qualified by the known fact that in recent decades British banks have

---

[1] *Macmillan Evidence*, Q.2768.
[2] *Radcliffe Report*, para. 136.
[3] This and subsequent comments on this recent change (in pp. 166–74) were incorporated when this book was in proof.

increasingly provided some finance for medium- and long-term purposes. In the interwar period, particularly in the 1920s, the English banks were heavily and painfully involved in providing reconstruction capital for such industries as cotton and steel. There is no firm evidence that the Scottish banks were drawn into this, though the state of Scottish industry in those years certainly left them with some frozen assets.[1] But, leaving aside that unfortunate passage in British banking, it is generally recognized that the banks have departed considerably from their classical maxim of only making 'self-liquidating' loans.

The Radcliffe Committee remarked on this fact with particular reference to the provision of finance for small concerns. In a passage where it considered and made recommendations about the financial facilities for small firms, it said (para. 941), 'It is evident, too, that, though the bank advance is conventionally a short-term loan, the banks do in fact lend on a large scale to such customers to finance medium-term and long-term requirements.' It went on, however, to observe that the fact that bank overdrafts are subject to annual review caused some borrowers to regard them as 'too unreliable a form of credit for medium- or longer-term purposes', and to recommend that the banks should either give stronger assurances that such loans would not be prematurely recalled, or formally embrace the American system of term loans, that is loans granted for fixed periods (usually up to five years), repayable by regular instalments, and not recallable before the agreed term. The thinking behind these views and recommendations derives very strongly from the modern emphasis on the development of the economy: financial institutions, like other organs of the economy, are judged these days by the extent to which they are thought to aid or retard the forces of growth and change. An important part of the process of development is the birth and subsequent growth of the small firm, and the Radcliffe Committee following a line of criticism of the financial system started by the Macmillan Committee, were obviously interested in this question.

How does the lending policy of the Scottish banks appear in the light of this strong, modern concern with the encouragement of growth and new developments in industry? In one respect the Radcliffe Committee found in their favour: 'the Scottish banks', it said (para. 153), 'have traditionally been more willing to acknowledge the long-term nature of some of their advances and have not been reluctant to act accordingly'. When one turns to the oral evidence this willingness to accept the fact that some lending is inevitably long-

[1] *Macmillan Evidence*, QQ. 2781–2.

term comes out particularly in regard to agriculture. It appears for example that the Scottish banks, official restrictions apart, are willing to make a loan to a man in whom they have confidence to enable him to purchase a farm, even though the repayment of the money might take several years and even as long as twenty-one years.[1] The witnesses were asked if their attitude towards a small industrialist would be the same, to which the reply was, 'Broadly speaking, yes.' Thereupon the following question was asked by Professor Sayers and answered by the Treasurer (i.e. General Manager) of the Bank of Scotland:

Q. 4808   You would be prepared to lend for a quite considerable period to enable him to extend his factory, to put in new machinery, and so on? Provided we had faith in him, and had reason to believe that he was likely to succeed and that this would help him to do so.

Furthermore the witness agreed that they might be prepared to take repayment at so much per year (Q. 4809), though here the same proviso would probably apply as in the case of the loan to the farmer to buy his farm, namely that the bank would retain 'in theory the right to repayment at demand' (Q. 4804). Elsewhere, the other witness (the General Manager of the British Linen Bank) agreed that the Scottish banks probably allow their loans 'to stand for a longer period than the English banks normally do' (Q. 4839). He also stated: 'A small proportion of our advances have taken broadly the form of an advance entered into to achieve a specific purpose, which would take a number of years and which would be built up towards a maximum and then gradually paid off. . . . In making that advance the bank automatically gives up its right to call for repayment at any time.' (Q. 4841). He had however already said (Q. 4839) that 'we could not afford to make exceptions too generously' to the principle of short-term lending.

There is no question that the replies of the two Scottish witnesses *read* better than those of the English bankers who appeared before the Committee, in the sense that they do evince *some* readiness to depart from the hallowed principle of short-term lending. The English bankers admitted that their advances although reviewed annually are frequently renewed repeatedly and run over many years; they also admitted that many such loans although recallable in theory, in practice could not be called in quickly. But they were generally

[1] *Radcliffe Evidence*, QQ. 4801–5, 4810–13.

148

inflexible on the question of whether they could offer something like the American term loan;[1] on this point the comparison certainly favoured the Scottish banks.[2]

When one speaks to businessmen in Scotland either on the question of term loans, or simply on the general character of the Scottish banks as lenders as it strikes them, one can be presented with a less rosy view of the matter. For example, in the course of an investigation made into finance, as part of the inquiries conducted by the Toothill Committee,[3] the desirability of term loans was specifically mentioned by one or two businessmen who had had difficulty in raising finance. One finds two threads running through modern comment on the Scottish banks. On the one hand it is said that the Scottish banks are more flexible than the English banks, more ready to lend without security, 'on character'; this accords with the verdict of the Radcliffe Committee. On the other hand one frequently meets the view —especially in Scotland—that the Scottish banks are too conservative in their attitude to lending, and certainly more rigid than their English counterparts. There is, in fact, a long tradition of criticism of the banks in Scotland. It began in the 1850s,[4] when it had become obvious that the Peel Bank Acts had effectively put a stop to the formation of any new banks, and it fastened vociferously on the 'monopoly' which was thus said to have been conferred on the existing banks. Echoes of this old agitation are still heard today, mingling with modern instances of 'stickiness' and unhelpfulness on the part of the Scottish banks, to constitute a definite body of dissent from the favourable verdict on them. It is very difficult for anybody, whether he is closely involved or not, to decide which of

[1] *Radcliffe Evidence*, QQ. 3948–58.
[2] I have reservations about the Radcliffe Committee's association of this disposition to recognize the long-term nature of some of their loans with the greater proportion of savings deposits within the Scottish banks' deposits (para. 153). I should have thought that it descends most strongly from the old cash-credit tradition. The cash-credit was not a long-term loan but it was a 'long prescription': it explicitly recognized the continuing character of the banker's relation with his borrowing customer.
[3] The Committee of Inquiry into the Scottish Economy, 1960–1, appointed by the Scottish Council (Development and Industry) under the chairmanship of Mr J. N. Toothill. The Committee's Report appeared towards the end of 1961. An inquiry into Scottish finance and into reported cases of difficulty in obtaining finance was carried out by the author, for the Committee.
[4] The leader in this agitation was the Glasgow Chamber of Commerce, and the movement can be more or less dated from 1856, when the first of a dozen petitions against the Bank Acts and the Scottish 'banking monopoly' was sent by the Chamber to Westminster.

149

these two conflicting opinions carries the greater weight. For what it is worth my conclusion is that the consensus of view is in favour of the Scottish banks on this point; it is impossible to present this as more than a subjective impression of the extent and weight of opinion behind each view, but it is supported by the results of the investigations into finance for the Toothill Committee, which will be discussed later.

One Scottish bank has now formally embraced the term loan. This is the Clydesdale Bank: its scheme, modelled on that of its parent, the Midland, is stated to be 'intended primarily for the smaller type of industrial and commercial undertaking . . . for such purposes as purchasing or improving business premises or for buying plant, machinery and equipment'. The loans are repayable by half-yearly instalments spread over ten years in the case of buildings, and three to five years in the case of plant; and, provided the loans are fully secured, the rate of interest is 2 per cent over Bank Rate, with a minimum of 6 per cent. There have, however, been clear signals that support for the term loan idea is by no means confined to the Clydesdale. Indeed the most striking advocacy of it, in Scotland, has come from the chief officer of another bank. In his presidential address to the Institute of Bankers in Scotland, in June 1959, W. R. Ballantyne,[1] General Manager of the Royal Bank, called into question the whole traditional credo of bankers on the nature of their lending. Of overdrafts, technically recallable on demand, he said: 'We delude ourselves if we regard them all as being essentially short-term by nature'; and he went on to advocate term loans made at less 'unrealistic' rates of interest than those customary in banking and conjoined, eventually, with fixed-term deposits. Ballantyne's views were re-echoed by a spokesman of the National Commercial Bank on the occasion of its birth in September of the same year.[2] According to the statement made then, the new bank, though not convinced of the need for personal loans, regarded term loans as 'another matter'. The Bank apparently looked forward to these—and flexible interest rates on variable-term deposits—developing quickly in Scotland. But four years later neither the Royal Bank nor the National Commercial had done anything about term loans. The reason may simply be that the great expansion of advances between 1959 and 1962 has removed worries about the buoyancy of demand for bank loans on the traditional pattern, and so relaxed the pressure to find new outlets. Possibly, too, the unfortunate experiences of the

[1] *Scottish Bankers' Magazine*, August 1959, pp. 68–74.
[2] Reported in *Financial Times*, September 6, 1959.

banks in hire purchase and personal loans, in the boom of 1959–61, has for the time being strengthened the forces opposed to new experiments in lending. In one particular field of finance—export credits—the English and Scottish banks have formally embraced medium-term lending. Since January 1962 they have been prepared to provide finance for the export of capital goods for periods of three to five years at fixed rates of interest. Where finance is required for longer periods the scheme is operated in conjunction with insurance companies who take up the longer maturities.

Another aspect of development which attracted the attention of the Radcliffe Committee was the finance of 'new inventions and innovations of technique' by small businesses.[1] The Committee considered that there was a problem here but conceded that the risks were especially high; and it concluded that the commercial development of innovations of this kind called for the setting up of an 'Industrial Guarantee Corporation'. The Scottish banks do enjoy a long-standing reputation of helpfulness towards the man starting up in business, and the cash-credit was the traditional vehicle of this help. In the early days the cash-credit was the means by which new enterprises—in the full sense of the term—were launched; later, it seems mainly to have been the means of establishing new men in existing, traditional trades and professions. It is by no means unimportant that the man of promise should be able to establish himself in a trade, however ancient it may be. But backing a man who wishes to break out of existing grooves is a different undertaking altogether, and while there is no evidence to suggest that the Scottish banks have been any less helpful than the English banks in this, there is a suspicion that this level of performance might be bettered. The position is difficult—as the Radcliffe Committee recognized; it is easy to criticize, but not so easy to find examples of would-be entrepreneurs frustrated for want of financial backing. In the investigation conducted by the author into alleged cases of difficulty in securing finance by firms in Scotland,[2] a high proportion of the difficulties—of which comparatively few were reported—concerned bank finance. But this largely reflected the fact that the banks are the most important and most accessible lenders to the small- and medium-sized firms, and it is only fair to state that it was from the banks that most of the firms concerned got accommodation in the end.[3] All these cases, of course,

[1] *Radcliffe Report*, paras. 932–52.
[2] See above, p. 149, note 3.
[3] Lord Piercy, Chairman of I.C.F.C. (in which the Scottish banks, along with the English banks, are shareholders), told the Radcliffe Committee: 'Rather

concerned firms that were in existence; in the very nature of the thing it is very difficult to establish just how far completely new ventures fail to get started for want of finance.

On the results of the inquiry referred to, and within the limitation that it only took in established firms, the author concluded that one could not support any major indictment of the Scottish banks on the score of their general attitude towards borrowers. But there is room for a plea for a more positive attitude on the part of the Scottish banks towards anything in the nature of a new development or a new departure. The problem of a region like Scotland, whose economy is lagging behind that of other parts of the country, is essentially one of growth. One part of it is that existing firms within the region are not participating in beneficial changes in the size and character of their output: they may—they frequently do—belong to traditional industries whose markets are static or growing only slowly, and they may find it difficult to branch out into products with fast growing markets. Another part of the problem is that such a region does not get a proportionate share of new men and new plants: on the one hand initiators and innovators may not be arising with sufficient frequency within the area; and on the other hand, the region may not be attracting its due share of the new plants of large national and international enterprises. Development, in all these senses, is vitally important for the country as a whole, but it is particularly important for lagging regions such as Scotland.

The Scottish banks, as the most important—though not the only —financial institutions involved, carry a definite weight of responsibility in this matter. We quoted a Scottish banker[1] as saying that the banks would lend money if 'they had reason to believe that the borrower was likely to succeed'. This idea that there is a more or less distinct line which separates men and their projects into two groups— those that are 'likely to succeed' and therefore creditworthy, and those that are not—is an ancient and widely-held view among bankers. It is so firmly held that the outsider must question it with diffidence, but it is necessary to ask whether in this field the pattern of probability does not take a more normal shape than bankers seem willing

---

little gets through to us in Scotland because the bankers intercept most of it.' (Q. 12,666). I think that this rather overstates things: a comparison of I.C.F.C. lending in Scotland with, say, Wales, or the North East of England, does not show an unduly low figure. Indeed in the next question Lord Piercy seemed to agree that the low Scottish figure was largely accounted for by structural factors producing a low demand for development finance.

[1] Above, p. 148.

to recognize. Creditworthiness, in the sense of the likely success of projects, is surely a spectrum which reaches by gradations all the way from the lunatic to the point where certainty of success is as predictable as it ever can be in an uncertain world. Whether or not a given borrower will succeed is not determinable by a yes or no: it is a matter of relative risk, and the decision to lend to this or that borrower will depend on how far a bank is willing to push its margin of risk. If this view of the matter is right then I think that one may reasonably expect that the Scottish banks should always be considering, searchingly, the point at which they place this margin, to see whether in some cases at any rate it could not be pushed out rather further. The amount of finance involved, and the increase in their overall risk, might be quite small; but the effects for the Scottish economy in the end might be disproportionately significant. Along with this I think that they might adopt a more positive attitude of encouragement to borrowers in the field of small manufacturing business—encouragement, that is, of development and experiment, coupled with a willingness to inform them about all possible avenues of financing their business. This requires more than a change of sentiment at the head office: it must be transmitted to the branch manager on whom everything of this kind depends. On their side however the banks have a right to expect that in view of the national importance of industrial innovation something like an Industrial Guarantee Corporation should be set up to bear some of the heavy risk attaching to the more revolutionary propositions that may come before them.

Until very recently lending in Scotland, whether by the banks or by other institutions and individuals, has been subject to a peculiar condition resulting from Scottish law. Before the passing of the Companies (Floating Charges) (Scotland) Act in 1961 it was impossible under Scottish law to take a floating charge over the movable assets of a business. In effect, Scottish law recognized no rights of security unless the security subjects had actually been delivered to the party taking the security. In the case of heritable assets, like land or buildings, or marketable securities, transfer or disposition of title is possible without their use, or the benefits of ownership, being denied to the borrower. But in the case of movable assets like plant or stocks, in the nature of the thing this is not possible. In England, on the other hand, it has been possible for incorporated companies to grant security over movables. Thus a creditor could take a security over assets which remained in the use of the borrower, and of which the component items were continually changing. This difficulty over security in Scotland has been partly circumvented as far as bank lending is concerned by the readiness of the Scottish banks to grant unsecured loans. One Scottish witness before the Radcliffe Committee put the proportion of unsecured loans for his bank at about 60 per cent;[1] and it is believed that the average proportion is higher in Scotland than in England.[2] This has meant a correspondingly high placing of reliance on personal integrity and in this connection the greater frequency of changes of ownership in companies, in recent years, is said to have made it more difficult to make unsecured loans.

The question of the floating charge was investigated by the Scottish Law Reform Committee and in 1960 they reported in favour of a change in the law to make this possible.[3] This has now been done, by the passage of the Companies (Floating Charges) (Scotland) Act, and it remains to see what effect it will have. Before the passage of the Act informed opinion seemed to think that it would certainly have some effect, and that it was an important matter, but that the amount of extra lending that would become possible would not be quantitatively large.[4] Among the beneficiaries of the change will certainly be the small and medium-sized firm. The Scottish banker who told the Radcliffe Committee that his proportion of unsecured loans was 60 per cent, also said that the proportion of the total number of loans that was given without security was smaller than this, implying that on average the unsecured loans were larger in amount than the secured loans. It is also significant that an English banker asked the question, 'The floating change is a sign of getting towards the margin?', replied 'Yes'.[5] It is very probable that the inability of the smaller Scottish firm to borrow on the security of its plant or its trade debtors may, in the past, have impeded its growth. It is also possible—this has been alleged—that outside firms have been deterred from coming to Scotland because of this difficulty of raising finance on a floating charge.

A matter in which the Macmillan Committee showed greater interest than the Radcliffe Committee was the effect on the lending

---

[1] *Radcliffe Evidence*, Q. 4814.

[2] *Eighth Report of the Law Reform Committee for Scotland*, Cmnd. 1017, para. 7.

[3] Ibid., para. 55.

[4] One opinion since the Act is that its main value may prove to be in the public issue of debenture stock: see D. G. Antonio, 'Companies (Floating Charges) (Scotland) Act, 1961', *Scottish Bankers' Magazine*, November 1961, p. 173.

[5] *Radcliffe Evidence*, Q. 3702.

efficiency of the Scottish banks of their relatively small size.[1] The earlier committee was very much concerned with industrial reconstruction and rationalization, and the question of bank size in the context of an increasing scale of industrial enterprise was raised by them. Since then the process of industrial and commercial concentration has gone a good deal further and the question is an even more pressing one today. At the present time only one Scottish bank has advances of more than £100 million, and in two cases the totals are substantially below that figure. In an age when the bank borrowings of numerous companies can run, individually, into millions of pounds it is obvious that the Scottish banks are at a severe disadvantage compared with the big English banks. It is not simply that no bank can afford to commit a significant fraction of its resources to one borrower, though this is important enough; there is the added fact that the swings of payments through a big account can be an embarrassment to a small bank. The problem may be overcome to some extent by the sharing of accounts between banks. The Macmillan Committee was, indeed, assured that this was the answer to the problem. The present-day Scottish bankers, if pressed, would probably be less sanguine. Not that the English banks are exempt from this difficulty; even they have to share the accounts of the very largest firms. But for the Scottish banks the problem obviously arises at a much lower level of size of customer. The mitigation of it has been one of the greatest advantages accruing from the recent round of mergers, but it is doubtful if these have kept pace with the growth of the problem during the last decade, Short of an extreme consolidation into one or perhaps two banks, this is a disadvantage under which the Scottish banking system must continue to labour.

II. TYPES OF BORROWERS

An analysis of bank advances is, of course, published quarterly by the British Bankers' Association. This includes the advances of the Scottish banks but, unfortunately for our knowledge both of Scottish banking and the Scottish economy, the analysis of Scottish advances is not published on its own. With the exception of loans to two classes of borrowers, farmers and nationalized industries, we have no separate figures of this kind for the present day. A separate analysis of Scottish bank advances has been published once, by the Macmillan Committee. It is worth showing this analysis alongside that for the English banks, and along with an analysis for all British

[1] *Macmillan Evidence*, QQ. 2815-19, 2845-6.

TABLE XXII

Classification of Bank Advances, 1929–30 and 1962

	1929–30¹		1962²	
	ENGLISH BANKS	SCOTTISH BANKS	ALL BANKS	
Textiles	8·3	4·7	4·3	
Heavy industries (iron, steel, engineering and shipbuilding)	6·4	7·3	16·5	Iron, steel, non-ferrous metals and engineering
Agriculture and Fishing	6·9	7·2	10·0	
Mining and Quarrying	3·0	2·3	0·3	
Food, drink, tobacco	6·4	5·7	5·4	
Leather, rubber, chemicals	2·2	1·4	2·7	
Shipping and transport (incl. railways)	2·5	3·3	3·6	Shipping and shipbuilding, transport and communication
Building trades	4·8	1·5	5·3	
Miscellaneous trades (incl. retail trades)	14·8	8·6	16·8	Retail trade and unclassifiable industry and trade
Local Government and public utilities	5·3	6·3	3·9	
Amusements, clubs, churches, charities, etc.	2·7	0·7	1·2	(incl. hospitals)
Financial (incl. banks and discount houses, stock exchange and building societies)	14·4	23·8	11·9	Finance (stockbrokers, hire purchase, other financial)
Other advances	22·1	27·1	17·9	Personal and professional
	99·8	99·9	99·8	

Sources: *Macmillan Report*, Appendix 1, Table 8.
Financial Statistics (H.M.S.O.), October 1963, Table 20.

¹ The figures relate to 'various dates from October 22, 1929, to March 19, 1930'.
² Averages of four quarterly figures and relating to all advances made by member banks of the British Bankers' Association through their offices in this country. (See *Financial Statistics*, October 1963, p. 95.)

banks in a recent year, and this is done in Table XXII. The classification of borrowers used in the present-day analysis differs at some points from that in the Macmillan Report; where there is such a difference, or where the comparability of a category is in doubt, the description used in both classifications is given.

The differences between the English and Scottish figures for 1929–30 are for the most part unremarkable, but they contain some points of interest, and one of major significance. The higher percentage of English advances to the textile industry probably reflected the embroilment of these banks in the misfortunes of the cotton industry at that time. The low ratio of Scottish advances to the building trades must reflect the stagnation of building activity in interwar Scotland. But far and away the most striking and significant difference was between the English and Scottish ratios of 'financial' advances. (Here the Macmillan figures appear to include short money loans to the discount market and the stock exchange; these are not treated as 'advances' in the modern statistics.) The very high proportion of Scottish loans in this category must be explained by what a witness before the Macmillan Committee referred to as the 'very substantial amount of their advances against Stock Exchange securities'.[1] These loans were made to borrowers who wished to hold stock for speculative purposes. The relative importance of them varied between the banks but just how substantial they could be is shown by the figures of those banks which distinguished them on their balance sheets.

TABLE XXIII

Loans against Stock Exchange Securities, 1928 and 1938
Percentage of Total Loans and Advances

	1928	1938
Royal Bank of Scotland	8·3	3·7
Union Bank of Scotland	27·3	.. [1]
National Bank of Scotland	17·7	15·1

Source: Annual balance sheets.

[1] Not shown separately in this year.

This is a type of lending on which the restrictions in force during most of the post-war period laid a complete veto; and it is unlikely

[1] *Macmillan Evidence*, Q. 2768. Like other features of Scottish bank lending these loans first became significant in the final quarter of the last century: in 1896–7, for five banks showing them separately they formed 27 per cent of the total of loans, advances and discounts.

that the relaxations of 1958 have led to any major revival. Compared with the pre-war position the decline in what were loans for largely speculative purposes represents a change of major proportions in the composition of Scottish bank lending. It has meant that, since the pre-war years, the volume of financing of expenditures on goods and services by the Scottish banks has increased more than in proportion to the rise in total advances.

The broad similarity between the lending patterns of the Scottish and English banks, shown in the 1929–30 figures, probably holds today, and we may take the quarterly analyses by the British Bankers' Association as a rough likeness of the present-day Scottish position. But a regular, separate analysis of Scottish bank advances is a much-required improvement of modern Scottish statistics.

The Department of Agriculture for Scotland provides us with one of the only two indications which we have of Scottish banks' lending to particular sectors of industry. It obtains, and eventually publishes, the total of bank advances to Scottish farmers which are outstanding at the end of May in each year.[1] In May 1960 the proportion of Scottish bank advances lent to farmers was 12 per cent; this compared with a figure of 10 per cent for British banks as a whole.[2] In 1938 the Scottish figure was around 7 per cent so that farmers now get a bigger proportion of bank loans than they did then. One interesting fact is that four-fifths of the total advances by the Scottish banks to farmers is lent to owner-occupiers although there are fewer of these than tenants in Scotland. The explanation is said to lie 'partly in the fact that advances to owner-occupiers include some money required for the purchase of farms', but the possession of more acceptable security by farm owners may also have something to do with it.[3] If security has been important then this may mean that Scottish tenant-farmers have not been so well provided with bank credit as they might. Between May 1958 and May 1960, Scottish bank advances to owner-occupiers increased by 50 per cent compared with a 40 per cent increase in advances to tenant farmers. The proportion of bank advances going to agriculture whether for Scotland or the country as a whole, is high in relation to the relative importance of agriculture

[1] The figures appear in *Scottish Agricultural Economics* (annually, HMSO), though not regularly in every issue.

[2] The difference may be slightly wider than this in that the figure of aggregate Scottish advances used here may not be so 'clean' as the figure used for calculating the British percentage.

[3] See G. F. Hendry, 'Bank Advance to Scottish Agriculture', *Scottish Agricultural Economics*, vol. VI (HMSO, 1955), p. 41: this ties in with the evidence to the Radcliffe Committee cited above, p. 148, note 1.

in the total economy; but this is a recognized feature of bank lending in this country. While on the subject of agriculture it may be mentioned that in 1933 four of the Scottish banks subscribed to the capital of the Scottish Agricultural Securities Corporation Ltd., a body set up as part of a policy to improve agricultural credit facilities. The Corporation actually draws its funds from three sources: a Government loan, the share-capital subscribed by the banks, and a public issue of debenture stock[1] (the first and third are quantitatively the most important); and its function is to make long-term loans to farmers to buy and to improve farms.

The monthly figures for the Scottish banks, as for the English banks, show their advances to the nationalized industries separately. There is nothing remarkable about these advances which in recent years have averaged between 2 and 3 per cent of total advances.

III. THE FINANCE OF THE CONSUMER

One particular channel into which the commercial banks feed funds, hire purchase finance, has shown a remarkable development in recent years and the banks' relations with it have undergone a spectacular change. In 1958, following the monetary relaxations of that year, and in a great rush led by Barclays, almost all British banks invaded the field of consumers' credit. The banks have, since before the last war, lent funds for the finance of hire purchase, although since 1945 this form of lending has been one of those most subject to official restraint. The 1958 movement however was a much more direct grasping at the fruits apparently to be won by financing the consumer. It took two forms: first, the banks acquired capital holdings, carrying varying degrees of control, in existing hire purchase finance companies; secondly, many of them instituted schemes of 'personal loans', that is unsecured loans to personal borrowers at fixed rates of interest and repayable by instalments over periods of up to two years.

The Scottish banks as a whole partook very fully in these developments. As we saw in Chapter 2, they have all acquired direct interests in hire purchase finance companies. The Commercial Bank of Scotland was in fact the first British bank to take this step with its purchase, as early as 1954, of Scottish Midland Guarantee Trust Ltd. That it was not followed by other Scottish banks until the general movement started four years later may—in some cases certainly will

[1] See E. Thomas, *An Introduction to Agricultural Economics* (London, 1949), pp. 51–2.

—have been due to sheer conservatism; but it is highly likely that after the Commercial's coup the authorities indicated disapproval of any further moves of the kind at that time. In addition to their direct participations in hire purchase companies four of the Scottish banks instituted personal loans. These are designed to meet the needs of the borrower wishing, typically, to finance the purchase of durable consumer goods. The rate of interest charged (mid-1964) is 5 per cent; but as this is calculated as a fixed charge on the initial loan the real rate of interest is roughly twice the nominal rate.[1] This makes personal loans very much more expensive than other types of bank finance; but even so they are cheaper than most hire purchase finance, with which they compete, and as the interest paid qualifies for tax remission the net cost to the average taxpayer is not very much more than the nominal rate of interest. The two banks that stood out against adopting the personal loan at the time were the National and Commercial Banks, then unmerged. When they came together it was stated that the new bank was not convinced of the need for personal loans and there has been no change of heart since then, which is perhaps to be expected in view of what followed the banks' plunge into these new waters.

For the phase of close association between the banks and consumers' finance has had a most inauspicious beginning. The new links between the banks and hire purchase finance were followed by a remarkable boom : during the two years 1959 and 1960 hire purchase debt and other instalment credit in Britain rose from £556 million to £935 million, and this hot-house growth produced some unpleasant blooms. It is clear now that the banks pumped more finance into their new associates than these could properly administer. A spate of frauds in the second-hand car trade coupled with other bad debts (due, for example, to hirers defaulting on contracts when the value of second-hand cars fell sharply) led to losses running into millions and involving the whole group of hire purchase companies.[2] Furthermore, in the banks' personal loans the expansion was more exuberant than wise, and it is believed that there were considerable losses here too.

In spite of these severe reverses, in which they have shared, there can be no question about the future significance for the Scottish banks of their closer embracing of consumers' credit. There are two

[1] This is because, with regular repayments, the average outstanding debt of the borrower over the life of the loan is only about half the initial amount.

[2] There is a useful account of this phase in 'Hire Purchase: What Went Wrong?', *Scottish Bankers' Magazine*, February 1962, pp. 227–31.

important potential results for them. The first is that the future expansion of consumers' credit will do much to ensure buoyancy in their advances should anything be needed to do this. In the present phase, with advances ratios within striking distance of their probable maxima, there is not much point in speculating about the existence of a secular decline in demand for bank finance and how it may affect the banks in the future. But we have remarked the historical vulnerability of the Scottish banks' lending totals to general depression and to the retarding forces which beset the economy of Scotland. The finance of consumers' credit will give them insurance against this in two ways. First it provides them with a new and expanding outlet for advances. Secondly, the wider geographical spread of the interests which the new acquisitions have brought may do something to mitigate the economic vulnerability and slower expansion of the home base. But neither of these potential advantages will mean anything unless solutions are found to the problems of credit control (and crime control) revealed in the recent débacle.

The second main consequence of these acquisitions is that they give the banks a means of participating in the expansion of this (so to speak) secondary layer of financial institutions. The relatively more rapid growth of the *non-bank* financial intermediaries, compared with the commercial banking sector, in mature financial systems, has been established most clearly in the case of the USA;[1] but there is not much doubt that it is also true of Britain. By owning firms in this sector of the financial system the banks gain a share in the fruits of its more rapid rate of expansion. To participate in this development is in some way even more necessary to the Scottish banks than their English counterparts. It has recently been demonstrated, what had previously been questioned, that the competition of the non-bank intermediaries for deposits may in fact reduce the level of deposits in the commercial banking system.[2] But there has never been any question about the vulnerability of a regional group of banks like the Scottish system to losses of deposits resulting from the activities of other financial intermediaries. It is therefore particularly important for the Scottish banks to participate in non-bank financial intermediation as a safeguard of their long-run profitability.

[1] See Raymond W. Goldsmith, *Financial Intermediaries in the American Economy since 1900* (Princeton and the National Bureau of Economic Research, 1958).

[2] See A. N. McLeod, 'Credit Expansion in an Open Economy', *Economic Journal*, September 1962, pp. 611–40. A shortened version of McLeod's argument may be found in A. B. Cramp's 'Banks and their Competitors', *The Banker*, February 1963, pp. 89–96.

IV. ACCEPTANCES

There is one item on the Scottish banks' balance sheets about which we should say a little here, although *per se* it does not involve the lending of funds. This is the item, variously described, which we shall call 'acceptances and engagements'. This item comprises certain undertakings by a bank on behalf of customers which involve no outflow of funds and which are exactly matched by reverse obligations on the part of the customers; hence they appear as an identical total on both sides of the balance sheet.[1] The undertakings, (which amount to contingent liabilities) include guarantees given on behalf of customers for example in connection with shipbuilding contracts,[2] acceptances, confirmed credits, and engagements involving forward exchange.[3] For the Scottish banks the most important of these is acceptances: in December 1958 they accounted for some four-fifths of the total.

'Acceptances' signify bills of exchange which have been 'accepted' by a bank, that is to say the bank has agreed to its name appearing on the bill as liable for it in the event of the party on whom the bill is drawn failing to meet it. A bill which has been accepted by a bank is known as a 'bank bill' and as such commands the finest rates in the London discount market; and for adding its guarantee the accepting bank collects a commission. The most important acceptors are the Accepting Houses—merchant banking firms in London for whom acceptance is a major activity—but the commercial banks also do a certain amount of this business. The Scottish banks have long engaged in it. They seem first to have gone into it on a large scale in the late 1860s and the 1870s, following the opening of the London offices. At that time the London joint-stock banks regarded acceptance as an altogether inappropriate form of business for a domestic bank, and the Scottish banks' heavy engagement in it contributed to the hostility of the London bankers towards their presence in the capital.[4] The English view that acceptance business should be left to merchants and overseas banks may have derived from the abuses of acceptance credit in the 1850s and 60s,[5] but it was also probably

[1] One Scottish bank, the National Commercial, does not include the item in the main balance, but shows it in a footnote.

[2] See F. S. Taylor, *Banking in Scotland* (Institute of Bankers in Scotland), 1955, p. 31.　　　　[3] See *Radcliffe Memoranda*, vol. 3, p. 7.

[4] See *Select Committee on Banks of Issue, 1875, Minutes of Evidence*, QQ. 6205–6211, 6886–90, 7515–27.

[5] W. T. C. King, *History of the London Discount Market* (London, 1936), Chs. VI, VII.

connected with the fact that the English bankers, almost up to 1914, had very little to do with overseas banking business.

The Scottish bankers found acceptance business a profitable activity of their London offices, although some acceptances would normally arise in the course of their domestic Scottish business. It is interesting to see from the figures published by the Radcliffe Committee[1] that the acceptances of the Scottish banks today actually exceed those of the London Clearing banks. In December 1958 Scottish banks' acceptances were £46·8 million compared with £32·0 million for the English banks. Other 'engagements' however were very much smaller in the Scottish banks: £12·1 million compared with £482·6 million. The large English figure for this item may result from a greater activity in confirmed credits and foreign exchange dealings. The acceptances of the Scottish banks exceed by many times their holdings of commercial bills indicating that they do not absorb their own acceptances to any extent, as the English banks do.

The Scottish banks engage in all forms of foreign business. They all have foreign departments, located in Glasgow and most of them dating from shortly after the First World War. This was the period when the British commercial banks undertook foreign banking business on a large scale: before 1914 it had been left largely to the merchant banks and to the London offices of foreign banks.[2] We have already seen that the prospect of sharing in this expansion of foreign business was a motive in the affiliation of some of the Scottish banks to English banks, at that time. One Scottish bank, the Union, took another course: in 1919 it joined with seven London banks to form the British Overseas Bank. This institution was founded specifically to undertake all types of foreign banking business—acceptance, foreign exchange and even some issuing and underwriting of securities. In 1924 the control of it passed entirely to the Union Bank, Williams Deacons and the Prudential Assurance Company. The bank operated throughout the interwar period; but it was weakened by the political disorder of the 1930s, and in 1938 the three controlling institutions surrendered their participation in favour of the general shareholders.[3]

[1] *Radcliffe Memoranda*, vol. 2, statistical appendix, Table 1, pp. 202–3.

[2] See A. S. J. Baster, *The International Banks* (London, 1935).

[3] See *Economist*, December 17, 1938, p. 607. The Union Bank and its two partners held the 'B' stock which carried control; the 'A' stock was held by the general shareholders.

CHAPTER 11

INTEREST RATES AND CHARGES

It is not usually possible to say a great deal about the interest rates and other charges of commercial banks because of a lack of really precise information about them. The Scottish banks, however, have for long been accustomed to agree on a common schedule of interest rates and of commission and charges, to apply in their Scottish business, and this is published. This gives us some definite facts about the structure of Scottish banks' interest rates and their movement over time, although it would be untrue to suggest that the published information tells us everything that we would like to know about their practices in these matters. For the most part, here, we shall concentrate on interest rates, though in a final section the most important of the other charges—that on current accounts—will be examined.

The agreements on rates and charges between the Scottish banks go back to 1836 when the Edinburgh and Glasgow banks first managed to see eye to eye on a common set of interest rates. They were joined by the Dundee banks in 1838. Both these dates are significant in that they were years of economic difficulty and financial crisis, and there is no doubt that the original purpose of the agreements was to protect the profits of the banks from the tendency of the margin between lending and deposit rates to shrink in years of depressed trade.[1] The power of the banks in combination was enhanced by the 1845 Act which prevented the setting up of new banks at a time when it was still a feasible proposition to do so; and although there were occasional lapses from the rules in the early decades, the agreements have remained a central element in Scottish banking policy. They are comprehensive, covering all but the newest types of business (e.g. personal and term loans are excluded); they by no means preclude flexibility; but like all price agreements they are

[1] This emerges from an interesting letter written in 1836 by the General Manager of the British Linen Company and quoted in J. D. C. Dick's *Interest Commission and Charges* (Institute of Bankers in Scotland, 1953), pp. 6–8.

vulnerable to outside competition. One important limitation on the agreements is that they apply only to Scotland; they do not bind the banks in their London business.

I. INTEREST RATES

The broad policy governing the Scottish banks' interest rates is the same, in essentials, as that of the English banks. It embodies three major principles. The first is that interest rates as such are not used as a means of limiting the demand for bank finance: if the demands of those borrowers whom the banks regard as creditworthy exceeds what the banks can supply (until recently this situation had not existed for a long time) then credit is rationed—perhaps by raising the standard of creditworthiness itself. The second principle is that while there is some discrimination between borrowers in the rates charged according to the security given and the risk involved, the range of differences is very narrow. And third, the interest rates of the Scottish banks, like those of the English banks, are altered in step with Bank Rate, though their relationship with the Rate is not a rigid one.

Until November 1964, the list of bank rates published by the Scottish banks contained eight rates. Three of these were rates of discount on mercantile bills and of the remaining five three were lending rates—on 'cash accounts', 'overdrafts' and 'short loans'[1]—and two were borrowing rates—on deposit receipts and savings accounts (now re-named deposit accounts). Table XXIV shows the movement of these five more important rates during 1945–59, a period which included the full range of Bank Rates that we have had since the Second War.

It was always stressed that the published rates were minimum rates 'applicable only to the best cases in each category',[2] and while Scottish bankers have claimed that there has been little discrimination between customers,[3] there has been some variation in the rates charged. The Radcliffe Committee was told[4] that 'in some banks it is customary to charge $\frac{1}{2}$ per cent over the minimum when there is a little doubt as to the safety of the advance'. Then, in 1961, the agreements were actually amended to allow banks to lend at $\frac{1}{2}$ per cent below the cash account rate 'in approved cases'. But other sources of flexibility have always been present. For example the agreements have always left the definition of security to the individual banks

---

[1] For the definition of these various types of lending, see above, p. 146.
[2] Dick, op. cit., p. 25.   [3] See *Macmillan Evidence*, QQ. 2728–9.
[4] *Radcliffe Evidence*, Q.5020.

TABLE XXIV

Interest Rates of the Scottish Banks 1945–59: Published Minima

RATE	31/12/45	8/11/51	12/3/52	17/9/53	13/5/54	27/1/55	24/2/55	16/2/56	7/2/57	19/9/57	20/3/58	22/5/58	19/6/58	14/8/58	20/11/58
Cash Accounts	4	4½	5½	5	4½	5	6	7	6½	8½	7½	7	6½	6	5½
Overdrafts	4½	5	6	5½	5½	5½	6½	7½	7	9	8	7½	7	6½	6
Short Loans	3¾	4¼	5¼	4¾	4¼	4¾	5¾	6¾	6¼	8¼	7¼	6¾	6¾	5¾	5¼
Deposit Receipts	½	¾	1½	1¼	1	1¼	2	3	2½	4½	3½	3	2½	2	1½
Savings Accounts[1]	1½	1½	2	1¾	1½	1¾	2	3	2½	4½	3½	3	2½	2	2
Bank Rate	2	2½	4	3½	3	3½	4½	5½	5	7	6	5½	5	4½	4

[1] This rate is applicable up to a maximum of £500; above that the deposit receipt rate is applied.

and it has been acknowledged that some borrowers might obtain an unsecured advance at the secured rate.[1] More importantly, the practice of allowing some customers—the large ones—to borrow through the London offices where the Scottish agreements have never applied has constituted a major form of discrimination.[2]

The effect of these various elements of flexibility has been to bring Scottish practice nearer to that in England—where such discrimination as there is favours the big borrower—than has appeared on the surface. The changes introduced in late 1964 now seem to foreshadow an even closer move towards English practice. In the November 1964 issue of the *Scottish Bankers Magazine* (pp. 113–14) the following statement appeared: 'The Scottish Banks have agreed that the terms "Cash Account" and "Overdraft" will no longer be used to signify the rates of interest to be applied to overdrawn accounts. In future rates will bear a stated relationship to Bank rate—e.g. "1 per cent over Bank", "2 per cent over Bank", etc. and there will be a minimum rate for each class.' The list of rates published on November 24, 1964, following the raising of Bank Rate to 7 per cent, departed even more significantly from the traditional pattern than the statement in the *Scottish Bankers Magazine* would have led one to expect. It omitted any reference to lending rates, and merely stated the change in the rate on deposit receipts and deposit accounts. According to the *Scottish Bankers Magazine* the dropping of the old titles of rates 'may presage a closer examination of the term of each overdraft and the degree of risk attaching to it and perhaps closer bargaining on rates'. Actually even more than this seems to be foreshadowed—nothing less than the removal of lending rates from the scope of the agreements. However, at the time of writing these changes are less than a month old and their implications, and even their precise meaning, are obscure.

Scottish Interest Rates and Bank Rate
The level of Scottish bank rates is closely, though not rigidly, geared to Bank Rate. The close following of Bank Rate dates from 1863. Before that year Scottish bank rates were subject to the influence of the Bank of England's Rate, but they were not kept continuously in touch with it, and they were changed only about half as frequently.

[1] *Macmillan Evidence*, QQ.2729–30; *Radcliffe Evidence*, Q.5020.
[2] Local authorities are explicitly favoured: they get loans, with or without security, for periods of not less than fifteen days, at Bank Rate; and they may have overdrafts at only ½ per cent over the Rate. The nationalised industries presumably get the same treatment.

Since then the relationship between the Scottish rate structure and Bank Rate has altered from time to time, although with one exception the changes have been slight. An indication of the varying relation between the Scottish rates and Bank Rate is given in Table XXV: this shows the level of three of the Scottish rates at times of high, 'normal' and low Bank Rates, in three different historical periods since 1900.

TABLE XXV

Scottish Bank Rates in Three Periods

		PRE-1914			INTERWAR			POST-1945		
	FROM	27/4/04	16/8/07	7/11/07	31/6/22	6/8/25	15/4/20	13/5/54	21/1/60	26/7/61
DATES	TO	11/3/05	30/10/07	11/1/08	4/7/22	30/9/25	27/4/21	26/1/55	22/6/60	4/10/61
Cash Accounts		5	6	7	$4\frac{1}{2}$	$5\frac{1}{2}$	7	$4\frac{1}{2}$	6	$8\frac{1}{2}$
Overdrafts		$5\frac{1}{2}$	$6\frac{1}{2}$	$7\frac{1}{2}$	$5\frac{1}{2}$	6	$7\frac{1}{2}$	$5\frac{1}{2}$	$6\frac{1}{2}$	9
Deposit Receipts		$1\frac{1}{2}$	3	4	$1\frac{1}{2}$	$2\frac{1}{2}$	4	1	2	$4\frac{1}{2}$
Bank Rate		3	$4\frac{1}{2}$	7	3	$4\frac{1}{2}$	7	3	$4\frac{1}{2}$	7

In the interwar years when Bank Rate was 'normal' (i.e. 4 or $4\frac{1}{2}$ per cent) the Scottish rate on secured overdrafts was 1 per cent over, and on unsecured overdrafts $1\frac{1}{2}$ per cent over, the Rate. However, certain minima and maxima were observed: the secured rate never went below $4\frac{1}{2}$ per cent nor the unsecured rate below $5\frac{1}{2}$ per cent, while they never went above 7 and $7\frac{1}{2}$ per cent respectively. The upper limit on the rates meant that when Bank Rate rose to 7 per cent there was no margin between it and the Scottish secured rate. The deposit receipt rate was normally 2 per cent below Bank Rate, but there was an effective minimum of 1 per cent and a maximum of 4 per cent (reached at Bank Rates of 2 and 6 per cent respectively).

Before 1914 the position had been slightly different. Then, the margin between Bank Rate and the Scottish secured rate was normally $1\frac{1}{2}$ per cent, or $\frac{1}{2}$ per cent wider than in the 1920s. On the other side, the deposit receipt rate was normally only $1\frac{1}{2}$ per cent under the Rate. Thus at normal levels the spread between the deposit and lending rates was the same before 1914 as in the interwar period, but in a higher relationship with Bank Rate.

There have been three changes of note in the levels of the various Scottish rates since the end of the Second War. First, two traditional minima were breached when, in 1945, the secured rate went down to 4 per cent and, in response to the request of the first post-war Chancellor, the deposit rate was lowered to ½ per cent. Secondly, and more importantly, since the re-activation of interest rate policy in 1951 the margins between the Scottish rates and Bank Rate have been wider than they were before 1939. The secured rate is back to its pre-1914 margin of 1½ per cent over, while the deposit receipt rate is now 2½ per cent under (narrowing to 2 per cent when Bank Rate is 3 per cent). This second change has caused the spread between the deposit and lending rates to be wider than in any previous period. Thirdly, and most important of all, the traditional maxima are no longer observed. When Bank Rate is high there is no narrowing of the margin between the Rate and the Scottish lending rates; in 1959 and 1961, when Bank Rate was 7 per cent, the Scottish secured and unsecured rates were 8½ and 9 per cent. Also, the former upper limit of 4 per cent on the deposit rate has gone. One rate which has been constant since the beginning of the century is the minimum rate on unsecured overdrafts. This has remained at 5½ per cent and this is noteworthy in view of the fact that the majority of advances are unsecured.[1]

These variations in the structure of Scottish bank rates seem to show that here, as in other aspects of banking, practices which appear static and conventional to a degree do alter from time to time with major changes in the financial environment. For example, the lowering of the Scottish rate structure in the interwar period may well have been a response to the depressed conditions of those years. We are on firmer ground in assigning the wider spread between deposit and lending rates, after 1945, to such features of the post-war scene as rising costs due to inflation, and portfolio losses caused by the transition from cheap to dear money. The raising of the deposit rate above its traditional maximum is a symptom of the weakness of the Scottish position in regard to deposits: the comparatively wide margin between this rate and Bank Rate simply cannot be allowed to become even wider in times of dear money when the competitive power of other institutions appears to get stronger anyway.

---

[1] A further change which amounted to an increase in the interest charges on some accounts was introduced in 1961. It was then agreed by the banks to defer giving credit for cheques paid into overdrawn accounts for three days instead of, as formerly, giving immediate credit. This applies also to accounts running 'concealed overdrafts'—accounts which by skilful timing of drawings and lodgements are kept nominally in credit but which, because of the time taken to clear paid-in cheques, are actually in debit.

Scottish Rates and English Rates

How do the Scottish rates compare with those of the English banks? In view of the monetary integration of the two countries and the presumed mobility of funds between them, one would expect there to be no substantial differences between the interest rates of the two systems. This is indeed what one finds, but there are nevertheless some divergences. The position in England and Wales has, of course, been less clear than in Scotland. This is not simply due to the fact that the London Clearing banks have only two agreed and published rates—the deposit rate and the call money rate.[1] There is the added difficulty that uniformity of interest rate structures in English banking is a recent growth; as we go back in time we quickly run into periods when geographical variations of practice greatly complicate comparisons.[2] Such evidence as we have about English rates confirms the commonly expressed view that the Scottish lending rates are higher and that this has been true for some time. The *Macmillan Report* (para. 70) gave the rates charged by the English banks on advances as varying from ½ to 1 per cent above Bank Rate, with a minimum ranging from 4 to 5 per cent. This compared with a Scottish range of 1 and 1½ per cent over Bank Rate, with minima of 4½ and 5½ per cent; but it should be noted that at that time a bigger proportion of Scottish advances were overdrafts with interest chargeable only on debit balance; the fixed loan was less common than in England (and in any case of a somewhat special character).

The position in the English banks as it appeared when the Radcliffe Committee examined it is summarized thus in the Report (para. 137): 'Most customers pay 1 per cent over Bank Rate subject to a minimum of 5 per cent; exceptionally creditworthy private borrowers pay only ½ per cent above Bank Rate, while the nationalized industries, whose overdrafts are guaranteed by the Government, pay Bank Rate or 4 per cent,[3] whichever is the greater.' There was a previous impression that some borrowers might be charged as much as 1½ to 2 per cent over Bank Rate,[4] but these were probably exceptional cases. Leaving aside such marginal borrowers, the levels of these rates appeared formally to be about the same as those given to the Macmillan Committee, though, of course, one could not be certain about the average level due to possible shifts of borrowers between cate-

[1] This is the minimum rate at which they lend money to the discount market: see below, p. 188.

[2] See 'What Pattern for Money Rates', *The Banker*, September 1954, pp. 141–8.

[3] One of the witnesses of the English Clearing banks gave this minimum as 3 per cent: *Radcliffe Evidence*, Q. 3691.

[4] See 'No Epitaph for Freedom', *The Banker*, March 1956, p. 133.

gories (perhaps more getting the 'blue-chip' rate of $\frac{1}{2}$ per cent over Bank Rate). Ignoring this, we may conclude that with the widening of the margin between Bank Rate and the Scottish lending rates, the gap between Scottish and English lending rates was wider in 1959 than it was before 1939. But is the position today (1964) the same as it was five years ago? According to *The Times* (June 22, 1964): 'Over the past two years the range of rates charged on [English] advances has widened considerably and now 2 per cent over Bank Rate is common while 3 per cent is not unknown.' Even more recently, *The Banker*[1] has discerned three current developments in English banking: a moderate increase in interest rates applied gradually to marginal borrowers; the charging of a committment fee on certain (large) overdraft facilities; and a move to raise the point at which rates on advances cease to fall with a lowering of Bank Rate. These developments in themselves would seem to foreshadow a narrowing, if not an elimination, of the former disparities between English and Scottish lending rates. But the changes introduced by the Scottish banks in November 1964 have created a new major uncertainty on the Scottish side of this comparison. It is unlikely that the changes on either side have yet gone far enough to invalidate what we have said about the relationship between the two interest rate structures; but it is impossible to say how long this position will continue or how it will develop.

A comparison of English and Scottish deposit rates is straightforward in the post-war period, but for pre-1939 years it is complicated by the fact that there were then two English rates—a London rate and a country rate. The country rate was normally a flat $2\frac{1}{2}$ per cent, although it is said that there were attempts to go below this level after 1932.[2] The London rate was $1\frac{1}{2}$ per cent under Bank Rate from the late 'eighties to 1914; during the First World War the margin widened, and in 1919 it was fixed at 2 per cent under the Rate. There it stayed until 1932 when, with a 2 per cent Bank Rate, it narrowed again to $1\frac{1}{2}$ per cent. The Scottish deposit rate at $1\frac{1}{2}$ per cent under before the First World War, and 2 per cent under in the 1920s, was thus usually the same as the London rate before 1932, but $\frac{1}{2}$ per cent above it after that date since, until 1945, it never went below 1 per cent. Before 1932 the Scottish deposit rate was sometimes above and sometimes below the English country rate, but it was below it after 1932 until, in 1940, the English rate was brought down to 1 per cent.

[1] See 'Levering up Bank Lending Charges', *The Banker*, September 1964, pp. 551–4.
[2] See 'What Pattern for Money Rates', ibid., September 1954, pp. 142–3.

Since 1951 the English deposit rate—now a single rate—has been 2 per cent under Bank Rate, narrowing to 1¾ per cent when the Rate falls below 4 per cent; this means that it is usually ½ per cent higher than the Scottish deposit rate.[1]

The differences between the levels of English and Scottish bank rates, small though they are, are surprising in view of the proximity of the two systems and the ease with which funds can be moved between them. In practice they have always been qualified in important ways. The nationalized industries and other public authorities, for example, borrow as cheaply in Scotland as they do in England. But, more important than this, it is clear that some firms that borrow from Scottish banks are, and for long have been, in a position to borrow from English banks. If they are very large then, even if they are Scottish-based, it is unlikely that one Scottish bank, or even two, could meet their needs, and they will have to go to England for some of their short-term funds. But even firms that are not among the largest, if they are well-known or have English connections, will be able to raise bank loans in England. As the position of good borrowers *vis-à-vis* the banks has for long been a strong one the Scottish banks have not been able to charge higher rates to borrowers like these than they could obtain in England. But how have the Scottish banks been able to compete with English rates and yet remain within their own agreements? The answer, before the changes made in the last three years, was that such firms might borrow through accounts at the London offices of the Scottish banks. Here, the Scottish agreements do not apply and the Scottish banks observe the London deposit rate and charge lending rates which are competitive with those of the English banks. The Radcliffe Committee was indeed told by one Scottish banker: 'Some of our larger customers have been borrowers at our London offices for many years, and get the benefit of lower borrowing rates from our London offices'; and the same was implied in the evidence to the Macmillan Committee.[2] The

---

[1] The Scottish rate on deposit (savings) accounts, payable on balances up to a certain maximum (at present £500), is usually ½ per cent higher than the deposit receipt rate when Bank Rate is 4 per cent or under. Above that the two rates are the same. After the stabilization of Bank Rate at 2 per cent in 1932, the deposit account rate was 2½ per cent.

[2] *Radcliffe Evidence*, Q. 5016. See also *Radcliffe Report*, para. 160 and *Macmillan Evidence*, QQ. 2754–60. This point came up as early as 1875 when a Scottish witness before the Select Committee on Banks of Issue, questioned on the opening of London offices by the Scottish banks, admitted that no individual bank could ignore the possibilities that this offered for doing business at rates below those on the agreed list: *Select Committee on Banks of Issue, 1875, Minutes of Evidence*, QQ. 1702–3.

majority of those who borrow from Scottish banks do not have access to English banks and they must pay, and always have paid, the Scottish rates. In 1961 the banks agreed that they might charge $\frac{1}{2}$ per cent under the Cash Account rate 'in approved cases'. Who were these approved cases? Clearly not the 'blue-chip' borrowers since even with a reduction of $\frac{1}{2}$ per cent, the Scottish secured rate was still 1 per cent over Bank Rate and these firms could get their loans at only $\frac{1}{2}$ per cent over the Rate from English banks. Such firms would presumably still negotiate their Scottish bank loans through the London offices.[1] The main class of customers to which this measure seems to have been directed is that of good, medium-sized firms who could, if they wished, borrow in England at rates which even with the recent loosening up are probably still about the same as they were when the Radcliffe Committee looked at them. Prominent among these firms will be the subsidiaries and branches of firms with headquarters in England, or even abroad, which have ready access to non-Scottish banks. These now form an important segment of Scottish manufacturing business and one that is bound to grow under the influence of two forces: the increasing integration of ownership of English and Scottish businesses, and the attraction of firms to Scottish locations under the regional economic policies of recent years. Indeed, it may well have been these trends which determined the banks on their decision to allow a lending rate below the Cash Account rate. Coupled with the introduction of the floating charge, this change increased the competitive power of the Scottish banks and the most recent changes appear to do so even more.

The differences that have subsisted between English and Scottish bank rates, amounting perhaps to a 1 per cent wider spread between lending and deposit rates, have not escaped attention. Scottish bankers have justified them on the ground of a less favourable cost position in Scottish than in English banking. The costs of the Scottish banks are—or have been in the past—higher because of the greater proportion of interest-bearing accounts and the lower level of fees

---

[1] An interesting recent event was the much publicized transfer of the account of the House of Fraser from the National Commercial Bank of Scotland to the Midland Bank in 1961. The reason given by Sir Hugh Fraser (quoted in *The Times*, July 29, 1961) was that the National Commercial 'could not see their way to offer us terms comparable to those which our associates were receiving from other banks. The terms obtained from the Midland Bank represent a substantial saving to the company.' As the House of Fraser was presumably enjoying relatively favourable terms already, this must have been a straight case of one bank outbidding another in the terms it was prepared to offer to an important customer.

and charges, particularly for chequeing accounts; because of the more extended branch system; and because of the need to accumulate higher reserves to offset the risks of depreciation on very large security portfolios.[1] The position has of course taken a big change for the better over the last few years with the emergence of a much more favourable asset structure. There has also been a series of changes, over a longer period, in the system of charging for current accounts. These developments may so improve the revenue position as eventually to allow some reduction of the wider spread of Scottish rates. If this is not done the interest rate structure of the Scottish banks will be a source of weakness to them on two counts. First, on the deposit side of their business, the lower level of the Scottish rate will continue to add to their admitted vulnerability to competition for deposits. We need not repeat the reasons why the Scottish banks are particularly exposed to the competition of other financial institutions for deposits;[2] but their low deposit rate is clearly one of them. On the lending side a persistently higher level of Scottish interest rates might prove a weakness depending on how British bank lending develops in the future. Following the recent rise in their advances ratios all the banks are much happier with their asset structures than they were. But should a declining dependence on bank finance lead eventually to a return of lower advances ratios the Scottish banks may meet stronger competition in lending from the English banks. As we have seen, the opportunities for this are increasing with the growing integration of ownership of English and Scottish industry; and the Scottish banks, on their side, have taken steps to improve their ability to meet it. Difficult though it is, at the present time, to interpret the significance of the most recent changes in the interest rate policy of the Scottish banks, these developments do seem to imply a major step towards that 'more flexible price list . . . for money in and money out' for which the Chairman of the National Commercial Bank called in November 1963.[3]

II. CHARGING FOR CURRENT ACCOUNTS

The agreements between the Scottish banks are not confined to interest rates, but extend to the whole schedule of fees and commissions charged for such services as issuing drafts and letters of credit, for accepting bills, and for maintaining current accounts with all the facilities that go with them. The last of these services is far

[1] Alexander, op. cit., pp. 542–4.   [2] See above, pp. 73–4.
[3] See above, p. 75.

174

and away the most important, both for the banks themselves, and for the economy which they serve. For the economy at large the facilities of the current account invest the banks with a monetary role, charged with the bulk of the monetary settlements of the system. For the banks themselves the business of providing this service is the largest single claim on the efforts of their staff and the use of their premises and equipment, and hence the largest single item of their costs. The means by which they attempt to recoup these costs are therefore of the greatest importance to them.

The banks' current accounts do, of course, make a contribution to income quite apart from the commissions charged on them. The deposits held on current account enable the banks to hold an equal quantity of assets. It is arguable that these assets must be regarded as heavily weighted with liquid assets of low, or even no, yield, because of the presumed mobility of current account balances. Granting this, it is nevertheless certain that some of the income flowing in from the earning assets is imputable to the resources derived from current accounts. The presumption these days is that this income is insufficient to cover the costs of servicing current accounts and all British banks now make a charge for this service. In Scotland the present system and scale of charges dates only from 1961. It lays down a minimum charge of 6d per debit entry in an account, but with the stipulation that accounts which involve more work than is covered by this charge are to be costed and charged individually. In effect, the 6d per cheque applies to personal and perhaps small business accounts; the larger business accounts and those with a heavy turnover are charged on the individual system which is general in England—though the tone of Scottish bankers' comments on what they are doing implies a more rational costing process than the English banks have ever admitted to.

The revision of the Scottish system of charging for current accounts, which brings them nearer to the English pattern than they have been before, is merely the latest change in a process of development which reaches back 100 years and of which the final stage has not yet been reached. Until 1892 the Scottish banks paid interest on balances held on current accounts—a practice which also prevailed in some provincial areas of England and, indeed, lingered on there until 1945.[1] Until 1863 this interest was paid at the deposit receipt rate on daily balances, but in that year a reduction was made in this rate and the current account holder was offered the alternative of receiving interest on his daily balance at 2 per cent below the deposit rate, or on his minimum monthly balances at 1 per cent below. In 1885 the payment

[1] See *The Banker*, September 1954, p. 144.

175

of interest on daily balances was discontinued and the rate on monthly balances was reduced to $1\frac{1}{2}$ per cent below deposit rate; in 1892 this too was stopped. The timing of these two last changes is significant: this was the period when extremely low rates of interest and a stagnant demand for advances in Scotland were making inroads into banking profits.

Throughout this period, and until 1952, charges were made for the collection of cheques but on a system individual to Scotland. The charge was laid not on the drawer (as in England) but on the payee; but if the accounts of the drawer and the payee were in banks in the same place no charge was made.[1] Commissions were charged on the negotiation of documents and cheques drawn on England (though not on London). However, the exemption of local cheques, and the absence of any standing charge, made the charges on the smaller personal and business accounts more or less negligible; and even where the collection of cheques did attract a charge it was not high.[2] This system remained in force for sixty years, during which time the use of cheques increased greatly and it became increasingly clear that the current account holder would have to make a greater contribution to the costs incurred in operating the chequeing system. In 1952 the system was completely reformed and the English principle of laying the charge on the drawing instead of the receiving of cheques was introduced. A charge of 6d was made for each debit entry in an account, with a minimum of 10s per half-year, but there was a small offset to this in an allowance of 6d for every £100 of minimum credit balance per month. At the same time the principle of individually negotiated charges for especially costly accounts—e.g. wages accounts—was introduced.

The 1952 reforms marked the major step in the modernization of the Scottish banks' practices in the matter of current account charges; for the most part the subsequent changes have been in the amount of the charges themselves. In 1958 these were raised: a standard charge of 30s per ledger page of forty entries (i.e. 9d per debit *or* credit entry) was imposed, with a minimum of 12s 6d per half-year. At the same time the monthly allowance on minimum credit balances were raised from 6d to 9d per £100. The effect of this was to raise the

---

[1] This difference in the system of charging led to friction between the Scottish banks and the English country banks, in the 1860s and 1870s. The Scottish banks were then charging the English banks for Scottish cheques passed to them for collection—just as they charged one another, on the understanding that this was passed on to the payee. At the same time, however, they were obtaining collection of English cheques through the country clearing without any charge.

[2] The charge was 1s per cent, with a minimum of 3d.

cost of personal accounts, with relatively few credit entries, by rather more than 50 per cent; on business accounts with as many credits as debits the total charges were more than doubled. The revisions of 1961, by putting a charge of 6d on debit entries only, are a step back to the pre-1958 position, and they reverse the previous trend towards a higher level of charges on current account.[1] Why have the Scottish banks done this? The answer is that it followed inevitably on the adoption by the Scottish banks of the same charge as the English banks—6d per transaction—in the credit transfer system instituted in 1961. A credit transfer is a method of making a payment by ordering a bank to transfer funds directly to a specified account. It is a more direct method of settlement than a cheque (where the order to the banker is sent in the first place to the ultimate recipient who then collects through his own bank); but it also has the advantage that it can be made easily available to people who are not bank customers. Anybody can make a payment by credit transfer at any bank office in Britain at the standard charge of 6d. This charge is well below the figures usually quoted as the cost of collecting a cheque, which range from 9d to 1s 3d. On the face of it the credit transfer does not seem to be substantially cheaper in terms of the use of banking resources than the cheque system. The banks themselves give as their reason for the lowness of the charge their hopes that, with the spreading use of the service, the cost will fall; and also that it will be the means of introducing the banking habit to classes—particularly the wage-earning classes—who have not yet embraced it.[2] One may surmise that the desire to spike the guns of those who, following the Radcliffe Committee,[3] favour the establishment of a giro system of payments on the continental model (possibly run by the Post Office) is not entirely absent. Whatever the reasons, the 6d charge was agreed on by all the banks including the Scottish banks.

Having accepted this charge the Scottish banks found themselves under a disadvantage which did not lie upon the English banks.[4] The Scottish banks' charge for handling cheques is a published rate,

[1] There was an offset in the deferring of credits to overdrawn accounts which we have already noticed (above, p. 169, note 1), but this is best regarded as an increase in the interest charged on overdrafts.

[2] See B. C. Sharp, 'The New Credit Transfer Service', *The Banker*, March 1961, p. 184.

[3] *Radcliffe Report*, paras. 960–4.

[4] In all these remarks about the English current account system I am excluding the Midland Bank's 'Personal Account' scheme. This scheme offers a minimal current account service at an announced charge of 4d per cheque (plus stamp duty).

M

and it could not be maintained at an amount higher than for the credit transfer which performs exactly the same function. The reduction of the charge on cheques therefore followed inevitably on the institution of a cheap system of credit transfer.[1] Because of the obscurity which surrounds the English banks' charges it will not be known, except to the individual customer, if the charge for handling cheques has been reduced; and even the customer himself may not know since the basis on which he is charged is often as much a mystery to him as to anyone else. The English banks are thus not under the same compulsion to reduce these charges although pressure from some customers may make them do so, and in the end commissions on cheques may, even for them, have to come into line with those on credit transfers.[2] At the moment, however, it is probable that the cost of keeping a current account is less in Scotland than in England.

But the Scottish banks have gone rather further than the 6d charge on credit transfers would seem to require. The 1961 revision removed both the charge on lodgements and the minimum charge on the keeping of current accounts, neither of which was really affected by the competition of credit transfers. This seems to point to a calculated policy of cheapening the current account in order to attract the non-banking classes. With their poor showing in the growth of deposits the Scottish banks are under greater pressure than the English banks to tap new sources of deposits. Also, these changes, which will have appreciably reduced the earnings from commissions, came towards the end of the phase of expansion of loans and advances, when the prospect of an augmented income from their lending was clearly before them. Nevertheless, this reduction in current account charges reversed what previously was thought to be an inevitable upward trend in the cost of this service to the customer and it may have repercussions on the future interest rate policy of the Scottish banks.

Among the reasons given for the wider spread between the Scottish lending and deposit rates has been the contention that the charges on current accounts do not cover the cost.[3] It may be argued that the burden of the costs of banking (including profits) is broadly divisible between borrowers, current account holders, and holders of time deposits; the more that is carried by one type of customer, the less need fall on the others. Given the quasi-monopolistic position of the

[1] Cf. 'Scots Banks Cut Charges', *The Banker*, March 1961, pp. 152–3.
[2] Cf. ibid., p. 152. For a more radical bit of prophecy see 'How Much do the Banks Want the "Little Men"?', *The Banker*, June 1963, pp. 407–8.
[3] See Alexander, op. cit., p. 543.

banks and the fact that they do not, as far as borrowers and current account holders are concerned, charge the highest price that the market will bear, there is some truth in this view. But it is true only within limits which are set, in the case of each group of customers, by the possibilities of competition from other institutions. These possibilities are strongest in the case of holders of interest-bearing deposits, and here the limits of free action in setting the price are so much the narrower. For the Scottish banks the limits are narrowed even on the lending side since, if they get too far out of line with English bank rates, they will begin to lose their better borrowing customers to these banks. There is undoubtedly some room for manoeuvre in determining the relative burdens to be borne by interest charges and commissions, but it is not wide. Furthermore, as we have argued earlier, it may be that the Scottish banks will find it becoming even narrower in the future because of increasing competition from other financial intermediaries, and possibly also from the English banks themselves, if advances do not in the long-run prove as buoyant as they have been since 1958. It is this consideration that places a question mark over the recent reduction in current account charges. If the present moves to attract new banking customers succeed in capturing the large untapped market of the wage-earning classes, and if the hopes now pinned on the automation of banking operations are realized, the costs of operating the cheque system may fall sufficiently to justify the present charges.[1] If these things do not happen, the eventual narrowing of the interest rate spread of the Scottish banks will be that much the more difficult to achieve, and this will react on the position of the banks both as lenders and borrowers.

III. 'MONOPOLY' IN SCOTTISH BANKING

The relative fewness of banks in Scotland, the apparent protection given them by the Peel Bank Acts, and the obvious fact of their common agreement on rates and charges have for more than a century exposed the Scottish banks to the accusation of constituting a 'monopoly'. At times, in the last century, there was a very considerable agitation, particularly in the West of Scotland and with the Glasgow Chamber of Commerce in the van. The most recent comment on the Scottish banks in this vein has proceeded from no less a body than the Radcliffe Committee. The Committee did not mince matters when it stated (para. 59): 'In fixing the terms on which they

[1] Cf. 'The New Charges and Interest Rates', *Scottish Bankers' Magazine*, May 1961, p. 33.

do business the Scottish banks act as a tight cartel'; but it went on to add 'to a higher degree even than the English'. Both clauses are necessary to a proper perspective of this matter. The Scottish agreements on interest rates and charges do constitute a 'cartel' arrangement by the usual definition of that term; but the English banks, quite apart from the fact that they agree on some of their interest rates, are not noted for competition in the prices of their loans. There is, of course, always room for differences of view on the creditworthiness of individual borrowers, so that a firm may get a finer rate from one English bank than from another. But this is by no means excluded with the Scottish banks either; the kind of firm that can get this treatment in England can almost certainly get it in Scotland too. Whether or not the English banks compete with one another in the matter of current account charges is obscure, as is everything connected with this aspect of their business. It is presumed that the powerful customer can get some reductions which are denied to the weaker ones, and he might not get this in Scotland. This hardly adds up to much of a difference in degree of monopoly between the two systems. English banking is an oligopolistic industry and, as is frequently the case, the resulting situation approximates to that of monopoly. Given the basic similarity of banking between Scotland and England there is indeed something to be said for the Scottish system of publishing an agreed set of rates and charges. The consumer, while always having an interest in low prices, does attach some merit to prices that are announced and known to all; the apparent irrationality and arbitrariness of English banking charges are a long-standing source of irritation to English banking customers. The disadvantage of the Scottish system lies in a possibly greater power of resisting pressure to reduce costs and improve efficiency. But the ever-present threat of competition from the English banks, the developing competition of other institutions, and the constant pressure on the profits of the banks exerted by inflation on the one hand and their position as a service industry on the other, place very narrow limits on the operation of this power.

The General Managers' Committee
In conclusion we should say a word about the body through which the Scottish banks formally agree on questions of interest rates and charges. This is the Scottish banks' General Managers' Committee. At one time the business of this Committee was indeed largely confined to the agreements on rates and charges, and to matters concerned with the note exchanges and the cheque clearing. But in

recent years there has been an increasing flow of matters in which the banks have had at the very least to consult together, and more often than not to take some sort of joint action. The agreement, together with the English banks, on a common coding of cheques in magnetic ink, for use in the new electronic sorting and recording equipment is a matter domestic to the banking system. But most of the occasions for joint action arise from official actions such as restrictive credit policies or proposals for legislation, or from official or quasi-official inquiries such as those of the Radcliffe and Toothill Committees. The demands now being made and met for fuller and better statistics is another example. In this trend, the position of the Scottish banks is on all fours with that of the English banks. The Scottish Committee has been in existence longer than the Committee of London Clearing Bankers but its present scope and activities are very much the same.

There is evidence that the consultations between bankers, Scottish and English alike, extend beyond matters of a technical and statistical kind. The recent re-naming of their 'savings accounts' as 'deposit accounts' by all the Scottish banks is an example of this (though arguably this was bound up with the agreements on rates). It certainly cannot be excluded that the habit of agreeing together on one set of questions leads to consultation and a desire for unanimous action on others. These other questions may include departures in banking practice of more than technical significance and the effect may be some dampening down of innovation. But until Scottish general managers take to writing their memoirs this remains pure speculation.

CHAPTER 12

THE SCOTTISH BANKS AND LONDON

The Scottish banks form a sub-group within the British monetary and banking system and as London is the centre of that system their relationship with the City is very important. This has long been the case. In the eighteenth and early nineteenth centuries the financial separation between Scotland and England was more pronounced, and Edinburgh enjoyed some position as a financial centre within Scotland. But the importance of London was asserting itself as early as the second half of the eighteenth century. We remarked that the Bank of Scotland and the Royal Bank, in the 1760s and 1770s, took steps to stabilize the bill exchange rate between Edinburgh and London by means of a stabilization reserve held in London[1]—a pattern for the development of the Sterling Area mechanism in later days. In the 1780s and 1790s they took to holding a reserve of government securities which in time of stress could be sold for gold in London and this marks the beginning of the Scottish banks' reliance on London as a reserve centre. Finally, with the great expansion of domestic and overseas trade during the middle decades of the nineteenth century London came to be a centre for the finance of trade; the London bill became an instrument both for financing the period of shipment and of effecting international payments; and the Scottish banks found that this was affecting Scottish trade as much as any other.

It was this last development that seems finally to have decided the Scottish banks to establish themselves in London in the 1860s and 1870s, though the other reasons reinforced it. By then the banks were handling a large volume of payments between Scotland and London; the English bills coming into the hands of Scottish customers were largely payable in London, while increasingly the bills drawn on the

---

[1] For an account of this action see 'The Royal Bank of Scotland and the London–Edinburgh Exchange Rate in the Eighteenth Century', *The Three Banks Review*, June 1958, pp. 27–36.

larger Scottish mercantile houses were payable there too, and their bankers had to make the necessary arrangements. Added to this, the development of the London discount market was now making it possible to lend money both profitably and with high liquidity, and it was becoming necessary to be on the spot to reap the maximum benefit.

The possibilities of capturing some of the ordinary banking business of London, which was then expanding rapidly, were by no means absent from the calculations of the banks, but financial convenience was probably the major factor which impelled them to set up their original branches in the City of London. Today the relative importance of these different reasons for being in London has changed. For one thing the commercial bill is no longer the dominating instrument of finance and payments that it was a hundred years ago. It is true that the ultimate settlements in most of Britain's overseas trade, and in the monetary exchange between the various regions of the country, take place in London. But the institutional mechanisms have changed, and the need for direct representation is no longer so pressing. Access to the London money market remains an important *raison d'être* of the City offices of the Scottish banks. But today the majority of them have very close links with English banks, and it is not inconceivable that in these cases the funds they place in the market could be channelled through their English associates. (At least one bank delegates its foreign exchange dealing to its English connection.)

The reason for a London office that has grown in importance relative to the others, in this century, is the general business one. The London offices do a great deal of ordinary banking business and, furthermore, they give services which they could not provide efficiently were they not in close physical contact with the multifarious financial institutions of the City. One important aspect of their London business has somewhat artificial roots in the agreements on rates of interest and charges. As we have seen, the rates of interest maintained under these agreements are less favourable than many of the larger Scottish firms could get in England; in order to retain this business the banks agree to the transfer of such accounts to the London offices where London rates apply. Another source of London business lies in the migration of Scottish business to the South. The shift of the head offices of some Scottish firms to London has exerted a long-term dampening influence on the growth of the Scottish banks, but its effects are to some extent mitigated by the London offices. When Scottish firms move South they can—and some in fact do—

maintain their connection with their Scottish bankers through the London offices.[1]

But Scottish bankers stress that their London offices are also successful in capturing business in competition with English banks. Their success here is perhaps of the kind enjoyed by small organizations which are competing with much larger rivals; it rests on a certain individuality of service, helped in this case by the greater independence of the London offices of the Scottish banks; and it is probably self-limiting in that it would begin to erode the conditions which make it possible if it went beyond a certain point. However, this point has clearly not yet been reached. The establishment of City offices in the 'sixties and 'seventies met with some hostility from England and at the time this deterred the Scottish banks from planting more than a single office apiece in the capital. It was not until the interwar years that this bridgehead was extended; then, all the banks opened one or two more London offices, mostly in the West End. Since 1945 further offices have been opened while, following the union of the National and Commercial Banks, three have been closed.

I. THE SCOTTISH BANKS IN THE MONEY MARKET[2]

Of all the Scottish banks' activities in the capital it is their dealings with the money market that are most peculiarly associated with their presence in London. Access to the London money market is very important to a Scottish banker. We have seen that the free cash balances which the Scottish banks maintain with the Bank of England and with their English correspondents are low working balances offering very little margin against unforeseen withdrawals. This fact invests their money at call—the second-line reserve behind their cash—with particular importance. In the terminology of the money market the Scottish banks are 'outside institutions', which means that they belong to that large group of institutions which operate in the market but which do not belong to the circle of the London Clearing banks. In recent years as a group they have been placing £70–90 million of funds in the market, or roughly 7–8 per cent of the

---

[1] One important group of migrants have been the branches of Scottish accountancy firms which have later become independent partnerships. These have often kept their connections with Scottish banks and have been an important source of new business.

[2] In writing this section I have been greatly helped by the relevant chapters of an unpublished manuscript on the Discount Market by Mr Roger Alford.

funds borrowed by the discount houses. Obviously they are only a small element in the market, but as individuals they rank among the more important of the outside institutions. The day-to-day management of their liquid assets is conducted by the London City offices, and 'a large measure of discretion' is necessarily given to the London managers.[1]

The relations of the Scottish banks with the money market show a certain ambivalence. They are 'outside institutions' whose history and development have been separate from those of the English banks; at the same time they are domestic banks, in some cases enjoying close links with one or other of the English Clearing banks. The result is a certain mixed quality in their dealings with the market. This comes out in their practices in the buying of Treasury bills. The Scottish banks were not parties to the agreement, dating back to 1934, between the Clearing banks and the discount houses, by which the former refrain from tendering directly for Treasury bills (other than those obtained for customers), but buy them from the discount houses. However, in spite of their not being bound by the agreement, some of the Scottish banks adhere to the principle of it. Expectably, the two affiliated banks buy their bills from the market, although one of them departs from the rule by which the English banks do not buy bills which are less than one week old. One of the independents also gets its Treasury bills from the market, but at least two banks—one of them before it was involved in a merger—have been accustomed to tender directly for bills. A bank like the Royal Bank of Scotland may well follow both practices—tendering directly at one time, buying from the market through one of its English affiliates at another.[2]

The bill holdings of the Scottish banks are not large and much the more important aspect of their money market dealings—for themselves and for the market—is their lending of money, 'at call', to the discount houses. Representatives of the discount houses call each morning on the Scottish banks, as they do on their other City lenders. At that time some, probably the bulk, of the funds previously on loan will be continued, or possibly re-lent at different rates; but some may be 'called' (i.e. recalled) or new money lent, according to the position of the bank at that stage of the day. As the money position of a bank evolves during the day funds will be called or lent by phone. Normally the commercial banks do not call funds from the market after midday—at least this is the practice of the Clearing banks and

---

[1] *Radcliffe Evidence*, Q. 4893.

[2] I have been told by one discount house that occasional purchases by Williams Deacons Bank are thought to be destined for its parent, the Royal Bank.

the Scottish banks seem generally to adhere to it but with a marginal, though not insignificant, difference. Balogh in his *Studies in Financial Organization* (p. 127) states that the Scottish banks retain the right to call after midday, but what this seems to refer to is agreements between at least some of the Scottish banks and some discount houses allowing for the recall—in exceptional circumstances, and towards three o'clock—of moderate funds. This is perhaps best regarded as a kind of 'reverse privilege money'[1] and we should at this point digress for a moment to say something about 'privilege money' itself.

The commercial banks, English and Scottish, have agreements with particular discount houses for the granting of 'privilege money'. These are essentially overdraft facilities on which a discount house can draw at the very end of the working day (i.e. at 3 p.m.) if it needs a smallish amount of money to balance its books without going to the Bank of England.[2] Unless a discount house obtains enough loans to cover the whole of its portfolio of bills and short bonds, by the end of the day, its only recourse is to go to the Bank of England and either rediscount bills or borrow on the security of bills and bonds,[3] at Bank Rate. As Bank Rate is a penal rate they naturally wish to avoid this but in any case they have to go to the Bank by 2.30 p.m.[4]: privilege money allows them to cover any small shortfall in their funds which may develop after this time. Privilege money is said to have originated in the 1920s when the discount houses stayed open until 3.30 p.m. and there was a risk of late parcels of bills arriving from New York for them to take up. The granting of it is usually coupled with an agreement on the part of the discount house concerned to maintain a rather higher cash balance with the granting bank than they otherwise might.

The facilities to withdraw funds from the market in the afternoon, which some Scottish banks enjoy with some discount houses—in common it may be said with some of the overseas banks in London —are a kind of privilege money in reverse. Why is it necessary for the Scottish banks to have such an arrangement? The reason must lie in the smallness of their free cash resources coupled with the risks of withdrawals of money to which their position outside the English

[1] I am indebted to Roger Alford for this term.

[2] C. W. Linton, in *The London Discount Market Today*, The Institute of Bankers (London, 1962), p. 43. According to this total privilege money facilities are thought to be in the region of £5 million.

[3] Nowadays they normally borrow on the security of bills and bonds.

[4] This is the latest time at which the Bank of England will lend at its 'front door' —i.e. at Bank Rate.

clearing system exposes them. The ability of the Scottish banks to operate on such slender cash balances depends on the maximum possible foreknowledge of prospective outflows of cash coupled with the ability to withdraw money from the market. Reverse privilege money gives them an extra safeguard against certain demands to which they are exposed.

During the course of the banking day the London money position of a Scottish bank is exposed to a number of outflows of cash. The daily Scottish cheque clearings and note-exchanges give rise to indebtedness between the banks which is met by drawing on Bank of England accounts. But these create no uncertainties of cash provision since the final settlement of the balance on any day's clearing is delayed for two days. Another potential demand on a Scottish banks cash is the need to meet cheques drawn upon them but paid into English banks.[1] These must be divided into two groups: those which are drawn on the City office, and those drawn on all other branches. Take the latter group first: these are posted by the branches of the English banks concerned to their head offices, and they are presented for payment on the spot at the City offices of the Scottish banks very shortly after the opening of business. The Scottish City offices will, by the same morning's post, have received from Scotland all the English cheques paid in there the previous day; these will be sent to their English correspondents for collection and for crediting to their accounts. Any difference between these two amounts will be known almost at the outset of business and the opening call from the money market will take account of this position.

The cheques drawn on the City offices of the Scottish banks and paid into English bank accounts are collected by the English banks on what are known as the 'Walks' collections[2]: that is to say they are presented directly for payment by each of the 'big Five' separately, and in an 'amalgamated Walks' by the other six Clearing banks. The Walks collections take place in the morning, around 11 o'clock, so that the cash liabilities which they create can be met by morning calls from the market. However, large cheques drawn on the City offices of Scottish banks may be presented for payment, by special messenger, any time up to 3 o'clock, and the possibility of these (coupled

---

[1] This passage draws on the 'London Bankers' Clearing House', in R. S. Sayers, *Modern Banking*, 5th Edition (Oxford, 1960), Appendix, pp. 279–87. This appendix has been revised in the recent Sixth Edition of Professor Sayers' book but the revisions do not appear to affect the above account which is based partly on the author's own enquiries made in 1962.

[2] Ibid., pp. 285–6.

187

with late transfers of money by cable or telex) give rise to un-certainties in the money position in the later part of the day; it is against these that the facilities of reverse privilege money exist. These uncertainties can be, and are, reduced by the 'education' of customers in the habit of notifying the banks of any large cheques impending. They cannot be entirely eliminated and occasionally a Scottish bank can be embarrassed by the late presentation of a large cheque; this is one other disadvantage of smallness of size. But for the most part skilled and careful management of their London money allows the Scottish banks to operate successfully on a very slender cash reserve.

The 'outside' character of the Scottish banks in the money market appears also in the arrangements under which they lend money to the discount houses. Since 1954 the system under which the Clearing banks operate has been to lend a proportion—about one-half—of their market money at a 'basic' rate which is now fixed at 1⅜ per cent below Bank Rate, and the remainder at a 'free' rate which fluctuates according to the supply of money on offer.[1] The general principle which, originally at any rate, lay behind the division between 'basic' and 'non-basic' money was that the former should roughly cover the amount of Treasury bills which the discount houses needed to carry in order to supply the banks with their needs; that is to say, it tied in with the agreement between the market and the Clearing banks on the Bill tender. Since 1954 the practical operation of the system has diverged from the original conception, but the principle of basic and non-basic money remains.

The Scottish banks engage in a modified version of this arrange-ment. Like the English banks they have agreements with the indivi-dual member of the discount market on lending rates. Under these all the Scottish banks lend a certain amount of money at the Clearing banks' 'basic' rate, but the proportion of their total call money which they lend at this rate is much lower than in the case of the English banks.[2] The rest of the Scottish bankers' call money is lent at the

[1] The rate is only free within certain limits. It cannot for example rise above Bank Rate, since it would then pay the market to resort to Bank of England. But more pervasively, the whole management of the market by the Bank of England—mopping up surplus money, relieving stringency, and adjusting the size of the weekly offer of bills—has a fundamental influence on the general level of the rates.

[2] An exact comparison is not possible but figures which one Scottish bank quoted to me show less than one-sixth of its call money lent at the basic rate, and this tallies broadly with other figures obtained from a discount house.

One of the Scottish banks' witnesses told the Radcliffe Committee that the Scottish banks got 'slightly less' than the Clearing banks for their basic money (*Evidence*: QQ. 4883–4). This does not accord with my own information on this

fluctuating market rates, but it is not all lent at a single rate. The banks—and this applies with odd exceptions to all the commercial banks—do not re-lend the whole of their non-basic money each day at the going rate. In fact at the end of each day a bank will normally have lines of money lent to each discount house at a number of rates. This number may be as many as five although some banks try to limit it to, say, three. What happens is that each day, in considering its lending policy, a bank will continue lines of money at the rates at which they were previously lent if these do not diverge too widely from the current market rate, and their existing rates will be taken into account in the bargains which they strike with discount houses for any new money they have to offer. The aim is to get a certain average return over all of a bank's call money, including that lent at the basic rate. This average will be affected by any marked movement of the day-to-day market rate: for example, if the current rate hardens and lenders think that this trend will persist they will begin to call the lines of money which are running at comparatively low rates and re-lend them at the higher rates now ruling.

Finally, yet another index of the 'outside' character of the Scottish banks, though one that they may share with the smaller Clearing banks, is their non-participation in the Bank of England's 'back door' mechanism. When the Bank operates on its own initiative to relieve pressure or to remove an excess of money in the market it does so by buying or selling Treasury bills, at the market rate; and it commonly does this through the big Clearing banks. For example when the Bank wishes to relieve pressure due to an inflow of tax payments into public accounts it may do so by buying near-maturity Treasury bills from the big Clearers: the money released is immediately passed to the market by the banks concerned. The method of doing this is one more example of the informal, but well-understood, mechanism of monetary management, depending above all on the close relations that exist between the Bank of England and the Clearing banks. The fact that the Scottish banks are not used in this way springs in the first place from their smallness of size, and also their low holdings of Treasury bills; but it does to some extent reflect their rather more distant relations with the Bank of England.

point but it may be true of some banks. Before the Second War, according to Balogh, op. cit., pp. 127 and 129 n. 1, the Scottish banks received ¼ per cent below normal rates for their 'fixtures' (money left with discount houses for comparatively long periods). This was said to be an offset to the right to call money in the afternoon; if so it may only have applied to amounts equal to the reverse privilege facilities.

II. THE SCOTTISH BANKS AND THE STERLING SYSTEM

At the outset of this book we remarked that the Scottish banks had 'their own place within the wider family of sterling area institutions'. Because of the position of this country at the centre of a web of international monetary connections the British money and banking system has no clearly defined boundary. The Scottish banks may be viewed as being situated, financially speaking, where the domestic banking institutions begin to shade into those of the overseas sterling area. What we have seen in this and the intervening chapters throws more light on this view of them, and before we move on to consider the involvement of the Scottish banks with monetary policy we should take a brief look at it.

The many countries and territories which make up the monetary area functionally based on the use of the pound sterling and centred on London, present a wide variety of institutional financial links with this country. All of them are involved in some degree in the status of sterling as an international currency, but for some—countries like Australia and New Zealand, for example—this involvement goes with a very high degree of monetary autonomy. For others, for example the territories still administered as colonies and even for some of the newly-independent countries, the monetary link with this country is so close as to make their monetary systems little more than extensions of the British system.[1] The interdependence of their economies with that of this country is frequently close but distance and the interposition of political obstacles like tariffs usually impose some discontinuity in the underlying economic relationships with Britain.

The Scottish banking system is obviously part and parcel of the domestic monetary system of this country, and this is matched by a complete integration of the Scottish economy with that of Britain as a whole. But some aspects of Scottish banking, and the nature of the relation with London, invest it with a character more closely resembling certain institutions of the outer sterling area than the other banks of this country. A Scottish bank, in fact, suggests a cross between an overseas sterling bank—say, a colonial bank, or an Australian trading bank of the pre-1939 era—and a colonial currency board. The note issuing right is similar in principle to that of a colonial currency board; the note-cover fund likewise resembles the fund of sterling assets which a currency board must hold, one for one, against

[1] See P. W. Bell, *The Sterling Area in the Post-war World* (Oxford, 1956), pp. 6–7; A. C. L. Day, *Outline of Monetary Economics* (Oxford, 1957), Ch. 34.

the issue of currency in its own territory and which it exchanges either way against its own notes. The main difference is that a Scottish bank may hold only one type of sterling asset against its note issues—Bank of England notes. (Another difference is that Bank of England notes circulate side by side with Scottish bank notes in Scotland; but even this is a matter of degree since at times British money has circulated in some British colonies alongside colonial currency.) The position of the Scottish banks themselves in London is similar to that of some of the overseas banks. This goes beyond their formally being classified as 'outside' banks and affects their liquidity structure. If we put on one side the note cover fund—regard it as unusable fund— then we are left with a small stock of working balances in London, buttressed by funds placed in the money market and this is very much more like the pattern of the overseas banks than that of the London Clearing banks. In this connection it is interesting to notice that some of the overseas banks have reverse privilege money arrangements with discount houses, similar to those of the Scottish banks. This is all, of course, a matter of financial forms and in the field of finance the all-pervasiveness of underlying principles is such that one can exaggerate the significance of forms. But, nevertheless, it is interesting to notice that, among banking institutions, the Scottish banks are an individual species of the genus sterling.

CHAPTER 13

THE SCOTTISH BANKS AND MONETARY POLICY

The ties of the Scottish banks with London are one aspect—an institutional one—of their relation to the wider monetary system of the United Kingdom. We must now consider other, and broader, aspects of this relation. In particular, we must look at how they stand as vehicles of those policies by which the monetary authorities pursue internal and external stability. But before we see how the various instruments of monetary policy impinge on the Scottish banks we must first probe into a question which is a central one in all discussion of monetary policy: the determination of the volume of bank credit. What we have to consider is whether and in what ways the peculiarities of the Scottish banks influence the processes by which the quantity of bank credit is determined. To answer this we must make a journey along a difficult and, at times, obscure trail, through regions of theory which have yet to be completely mapped out.

I. THE SCOTTISH BANKS AND THE QUANTITY OF CREDIT

Banks are monetary institutions: the deposit liabilities which they create and maintain are the dominant form of money in our economy, and the transfer of them by cheque provides the major machinery for settling payments. The Scottish banks as an integral part of the British banking system are involved in this monetary function and play some part in determining the level of bank deposits in the system as a whole. The Radcliffe Committee in its Report has, of course, challenged the traditional view that because they create and maintain a means of payments, in their deposit liabilities, the commercial banks therefore occupy a unique position among the complex of financial institutions. Previously it was always held that because of this monetary function the banks were to be distinguished from institutions like building societies or the trustee savings banks whose liabilities, however liquid they may be, do not actually circulate as money. This approach was usually linked with a belief that the total stock of means of payment was an important economic quantity, control of which could influence the level of economic activity, in part directly, in part indirectly through its effect on interest rates.

The Radcliffe Committee disagreed radically with this analysis. They took up the position that money as hitherto defined (i.e. currency plus the deposits of commercial banks) is merely one of a range of highly liquid assets, the whole of which is relevant to the capacity and disposition of firms and individuals to spend. In the words of the Report:

> 'Though we do not regard the supply of money as an unimportant quantity, we view it as only part of the wider structure of liquidity in the economy. It is the whole liquidity position that is relevant to spending decisions . . .' (para. 389).

This 'wider structure of liquidity' was interpreted partly in terms of the total stock of liquid assets (i.e. money plus short-term assets), partly in terms of the ability of the firm or individual to raise money by borrowing or selling an asset. As a corollary to this revised view of the relative importance of money and other liquid assets, the Committee produced a modified assessment of the role of the commercial banks in the total money system. They regarded them primarily as lending institutions and only in the second place as creators of means of payment.

To most people the Radcliffe treatment of 'liquidity' seemed to confuse money as such with a range of assets which, while admittedly very liquid for the individual holder, nevertheless require to be converted into the actual medium of payment before an act of expenditure can be undertaken. However, some, including the present writer,[1] while rejecting certain aspects of the Committee's analysis have agreed with what they take to be the essential message of the Radcliffe doctrine of liquidity: that what in the traditional terminology is known as the velocity of circulation of money is highly flexible; that the role of near-money assets is to increase this flexibility; and that because of this the actual supply of means of payment is not the dominating element in the monetary situation that it was once held to be.

Nevertheless, however much we incline to demote bank deposits from their previous eminence among liquid assets, the fact remains that they are monetary assets of great importance, more liquid than any others except currency, unique in serving, with currency, as a

[1] My views on this part of the *Radcliffe Report* are set out in 'Liquidity and the Monetary Mechanism', *Oxford Economic Papers*, October 1960, pp. 274–93.

means of payment; and that it is important to know how their quantity is determined. The special question with which we are concerned here is whether or not there are any peculiarities in the deposit-creating activities of the Scottish banks. But before we look into this there is a prior question to be clarified: how is the volume of bank deposits determined in the British banking system as a whole? This question too has aroused controversy in the recent past, although now there is a measure of agreement on it.

Let us begin with a proposition about which there is no dispute. Most bank deposits are created by the action of the banking system in acquiring assets either through lending or by purchasing bills and securities.[1] When a bank does either of these things its action must lead to an increase of deposits somewhere in the banking system; on the other hand when it takes repayment of a loan, or sells a security, an equal amount of bank deposits will be extinguished somewhere in the system. The important question here is what factors limit the banking system in its acquisition of assets and hence its creation of deposits. The traditional answer was 'the cash position' and this view of the matter may be called the 'cash doctrine'. We have already glanced at it (in Chapter 7) when examining the monetary effects of the note issues, and we will restate it very briefly here. The primary proposition of the cash doctrine is that the creation of credit by the banking system is controlled by three things: the quantity of cash in the system (defining 'cash' as currency and bankers' balances at the central bank), the cash ratios maintained by the banks, and the public's demand for cash (in this case currency) to hold in circulation outside the banks. According to this doctrine the banks' operative ratio—the ratio that determines the credit effects of their lending and investing activities—is the cash ratio. And there is of course the corollary that given constancy in this ratio, and in the public's demand for cash, the authorities may control the superstructure of credit by varying the size of the cash base of the system.

This is the view of the credit-creating process which is enshrined in the Macmillan Report[2] and which most people held until the middle 1950s. At that time a number of commentators began to point out that a complex of developments in the structure of public debt and in the practices of the banking system had radically affected the nature of the 'cash base' and had caused a change in what were the significant controlling ratios. The position which most people (including

[1] For a fuller and more advanced exposition of the theory of credit creation see W. T. Newlyn, *Theory of Money* (Oxford, 1962), Chs. 2 and 3.
[2] *Macmillan Report*, paras. 73–87.

the Radcliffe Committee) now take is that because of the vast increase, both absolute and relative, in the volume of short-term government debt (we can equate this roughly with the Treasury bill issue) and because of the way in which this is taken up by the banking system and of the associated changes in the practices of the bank with regard to their liquid assets, the cash position in the older, narrower sense, has ceased to be the limiting factor governing the volume of bank deposits. The facts are that the banking system, and here we include in this the discount market, in effect underwrites the Treasury bill issue through the syndicated bid of the discount houses. This bid is backed by an informal mechanism whereby the commercial banks always supply the market with the necessary resources to do this. As part of this mechanism, the authorities in effect allow complete interchangeability between Treasury bills and cash; the English banks never allow any significant variation in their cash ratios, and the cash position is always made up automatically to produce 8 per cent. In these circumstances what was formerly known as the cash base has to be widened to include the volume of Treasury bills; while the operative ratio controlling the part *played by banks* in the credit-creating process is their *liquidity ratio*, i.e. the ratio which they maintain between all their liquid assets (cash, bills and loans to the discount market) and the total of their deposit liabilities.[1]

[1] This summary of the 'liquidity doctrine' is no more than a sketch: it omits some stages in the argument and many qualifications. We have ignored, for example, the place of interest rates in the mechanism, as well as the fact that the discount houses hold short-term bonds and commercial bills as well as Treasury bills. The latter introduce the complication that the commercial banks' loans to the money market, forming part of their liquid assets for liquidity ratio purposes, do not simply represent holding of Treasury bills at one remove. To the extent of about one-third they enable the discount houses to hold other assets, and these other assets, plus the banks' own holdings of commercial bills and certain export credits realizeable at the Bank of England, must be regarded as forming part of the total 'liquidity base' of the system. The whole doctrine is subject to the very big complication that the banking system holds only part of the Treasury bill issue; a significant fraction is held outside the banks and this fraction can vary, so affecting the liquidity base. Also, under modern conditions of debt management, purchases of longer-term securities by the banks, consequent upon an extension of the liquidity base, and possibly due to a shortage of suitable private borrowers, may lead to a reduction of that base, through funding. This again modifies the working out of the process of credit creation. It should be made clear that the 'truth' of the liquidity doctrine is not an ineluctable consequence of unalterable conditions: it depends in large measure on choices which the monetary authorities make between courses of action. They could choose a course of action which would make the true position coincide with that posited in the 'cash doctrine'.

Finally it must be emphasized that we are using the 'liquidity doctrine' for the

After this summary of the modern view as to how the banks, for their part, help to determine the level of bank deposits in present-day Britain, we can now turn to examine the position of the Scottish banks in the credit-creating mechanism. Just how do they contribute to the level of bank deposits in the British system? The fact that they form part of a unified money and banking system, and that the regional economy which they serve is completely integrated with the rest of the British economy—these facts mean that the role of the Scottish banks as creators of bank deposits is not to be conceived as beginning and ending with the quantity of bank deposits for which, at any one time, they themselves are liable. As we have seen the process by which deposits are created is one which involves the whole banking system: the actions of any individual bank in lending or buying securities normally create deposits in other banks. What this means for the Scottish system is that the primary determinant of the quantity of bank deposits in the Scottish banks is the level of deposits in the British banking system as a whole. Between the overall level of British bank deposits and Scottish deposits, at any given time, there will be a definite relationship governed by the numbers, wealth, banking habits, and business operations of the customers of the Scottish banks in relation to the same four properties of the customers of the remaining banks in the system. Through this 'real' relationship any alteration in the general level of bank deposits will tend to affect the level of Scottish bank deposits. But from what we have seen (in Chapter 4), and from what we know about the changes that are going on, this relationship is by no means static. It may be assumed to be constant only in the very short-run; all sorts of developments, industrial, financial and social, affect it, and can make themselves felt in a comparatively short period. Nevertheless at any given time the general trend of bank deposits in the country as a whole is always a major element determining the Scottish deposit total.

The obverse of this position is that the volume of bank deposits in Scottish banks is determined only to a minor degree by the credit-creating activities of the Scottish banks themselves. These activities are by no means unimportant, but their effects work themselves out in the system at large: they contribute to the overall quantity of

comparatively narrow purpose of defining the *banks'* part in the process of credit creation. The doctrine as we use it is only a part of a broader and more complex theory which takes account of a wider range of 'leakages', and which increasingly is becoming integrated with the theory of income determination. See R. S. Sayers, *Modern Banking*, 6th Edition (Oxford, 1964), Ch. 10; also W. T. Newlyn, op. cit., Ch. 3.

deposits. What is the precise effect on the volume of bank credit of the operations of the Scottish banks? Does it differ in any way from the corresponding activities of the English banks?

The answer to this question is that there is a difference in the credit effects of the Scottish banks' operations and that it follows from the different liquidity ratio of the Scottish banks. We saw in Chapter 8 that the cash of a Scottish bank can be divided into note cover on the one hand, and 'non-cover' cash on the other. The latter includes balances at the Bank of England and with Clearing bankers, and holdings of legal tender other than those required for note cover purposes. The size of the note cover fund, as we have seen, is determined by the circulation of Scottish bank notes. Over this the Scottish banks exert no positive control and it is in fact determined partly by the overall currency needs of the Scottish public, and partly by the extent to which these needs are satisfied by the use of Scottish notes rather than other kinds of circulating media. Thus as far as the banks are concerned the note cover fund is a purely passive element within liquid assets; consequently it plays no determining part in the operations of the Scottish banks. As it has no direct influence on the lending and investing operations of the banks it can have no influence on the credit-creating effects of those operations. In the credit-creating process the note cover fund is equivalent to currency in circulation with the public: it is part of the 'internal drain', and its effects on the creation of bank deposits are exerted from this direction.

Hence, when we analyse the credit-creating effects of the Scottish banks' operations we must exclude the note-cover element of cash entirely—and this is so regardless of whether the 'cash doctrine' or the 'liquidity doctrine' applies. In terms of credit effects the equivalent in Scottish banking of the English banks' 8 per cent cash reserve is the low ratio of non-cover cash—at present between 2 and 3 per cent of deposits.[1] If the cash ratio were the operative one in the British

---

[1] Even this is not precisely true. The non-cover cash of the Scottish banks contains one element, balances with London correspondents, which is part of the credit 'superstructure' and not of the 'cash base'. The appropriate step, when calculating the true equivalent, would be to include only a fraction of these balances in the Scottish operative reserves, the fraction being equal to the reserve ratio (whichever one is chosen) of the Clearing banks. But there is yet another adjustment that should be made. Account should be taken of the fact that *gross* deposits (on which reserve ratios are normally calculated) are higher in proportion to *true net* deposits in Scottish banking than in English banking. This works in the opposite direction to the previous qualifications. The two adjustments are not exactly self-cancelling, but one is not led into gross error by assuming that they are. We shall therefore ignore both qualifications and speak simply of the 'ratio of non-cover cash'.

system this ratio would determine the credit effects of the Scottish banks' operation. But we have seen that in the present day it is the banks' liquidity ratio which is the operative ratio, and the question we must now ask is this: what is the operative *liquidity* ratio of the Scottish banks? We have already answered this question in discussing the application of the concept of 'liquidity' to the Scottish banks.[1] As far as credit effects are concerned, liquid assets are to be defined as non-cover cash, bills and money at call, and the operative liquidity ratio of the Scottish banks as the ratio of the total of these assets to deposits. It is not suggested here that the Scottish banks are influenced by this as an overall ratio; but so long as the constituents are determined by positive decisions this ratio will perforce be the operative one for them in a system in which cash is not a limiting factor. That these assets will, separately, be the object of decisions in regard to their minimum levels we know both from statements by Scottish bankers,[2] and from their very function within total assets. Since the late 1950s such minima as the banks would themselves observe have been reinforced by the request of the Bank of England to the Scottish banks that they observe their 'usual' minimum liquidity ratios. In the case of some of the elements of the Scottish banks' non-cover cash the minima take the form of *absolute* rather than *proportionate* levels, in the short-run, and this causes some enhancement of the short-run effects of Scottish banking operations on the volume of credit.

From the figures of liquid assets in Table XVIII (pp. 110–11) it is clear that the aggregate liquidity ratio of the Scottish banks as we define it has varied over the years. If we look at the annual average values of this ratio it has been moderately stable in recent years at around 16–17 per cent. But it has been much lower than this: in 1951, for example, it was down to 10 per cent. We must also bear in mind that these are annual averages and that monthly figures are always below this level, normally by about 2 percentage points, in March, at the seasonal low-point of deposits. It is most unlikely that the Scottish banks would today be prepared to see their liquidity ratio fall as low as it was in the early 1950s. Perhaps something like the 13–14 per cent (annual average) of the war years would correspond to their present absolute minimum. Such a minimum however is likely to be raised by

[1] pp. 126–8.
[2] *Radcliffe Evidence*, QQ. 5027–38. The precise definition of the liquidity ratio implied in these statements has already been criticized: p. 126. However, the essential point is that the statements imply that the items which we include in liquid assets are subject to some more or less definite minimum.

2 or 3 per cent when the monetary outlook is uncertain; when short-term rates are reasonably remunerative, as they are at present; or when there is uncertainty about the long-term rate.

The fact that the operative liquidity ratio of the Scottish banks is lower than that of the English banks means that, relatively, the credit effects of Scottish banking operations are greater than those of English banking operations (this would be so to an even greater extent if the cash ratio was the operative one).[1] So if we take a simplified view of the credit-creating process, a given volume of liquid assets will support a greater volume of deposits in Scottish than in English banking. But the higher deposit-generating capacity of the Scottish banks has its effect on the overall level of bank deposits in the British system as a whole. Monetary conditions and the level of bank deposits in Scotland are determined by its place within the economy and financial system of Britain as a whole. The extra credit created by the Scottish banks' reserve practices spills over into the system at large raising the average level of deposits above what it would be if the Scottish banks merely copied English liquidity conventions.[2]

However, as if the above were not complex enough, there is one final complication to introduce into this analysis. It has been pointed out in recent writing that in some circumstances the liquidity ratio is not the relevant ratio for determining the role of the banks as creators of credit.[3] If the banks will not permit their holdings of gilt-edged to fall below some minimum proportion of deposits, then the definition of the credit-expanding capacity of the banking system must take account of this fact. If the securities ratio was maintained at, say, 10 per cent, this may have to be added to the 30 per cent liquidity ratio

---

[1] If and when the minimum liquidity ratios of the Clearing banks are lowered to (say) 25 per cent, as envisaged in the Mansion House speech of the Governor of the Bank of England on October 16, 1963, the disparity of operative ratios between the two systems will be reduced.

[2] We can interpret this in two ways. If the quantity of liquid assets in the system is determined independently of monetary considerations, e.g. by the needs of Government borrowing, the Scottish banks increase the credit superstructure which the banking system as a whole raise up upon the liquidity base. On the one hand, if the authorities have complete control over the amount and structure of debt, they may aim at producing a certain structure of interest rates. In this case the quantity of money (and, therefore, bank deposits) will be the dependent variable. The banking system will be supplied with the amount of short-term debt necessary to support this given amount of bank deposits. In this latter situation the effect of the Scottish banks' liquidity ratios is to reduce, slightly, the amount of liquid assets that must be provided.

[3] See W. Manning Dacey, 'Treasury Bills and the Money Supply', *Lloyds Bank Review*, January 1960, pp. 5-7.

199

to produce a total government debt ratio (ignoring commercial bills) of 40 per cent, to give the operative ratio of the banks in any process of credit expansion. This analysis is only valid if the monetary authorities meet an increased demand for bonds on the part of the banks by selling bonds 'off the shelf'. Under modern conditions, with the authorities operating continuously in the gilt-edged market, this is broadly true.[1] What is much less certain is that the banks, English and Scottish, have yet reached the end of the secular reduction in the size of their portfolios. That they would wish to maintain some minimum ratio of gilt-edged is indisputable, but what it is we cannot yet say.

One result of this argument, potentially if not yet actually, is to confer some importance on the size of the minimum securities ratio. If, for whatever reasons, the Scottish banks decide to maintain a higher minimum ratio of bonds to deposits than the English banks, as a matter of policy, then this might modify their influence on the volume of credit. It might in fact make up, wholly or in part, for the lowness of their liquidity ratios. If we assume, for example, that the Scottish will not wish to go below a 26 per cent investment ratio, and the English banks below 16 per cent (these were the 1962 ratios), then the addition of these to their respective liquidity ratios would produce overall operative ratios of (about) 42 per cent and 46 per cent respectively. But at the present time one can do no more than point to this as a possibility which may be realized when the attitudes of the banks to their ratios of investments and advances have assumed a clearer shape.

II. THE TECHNIQUES OF POLICY AND THE SCOTTISH BANKS

It remains to describe and discuss the actions of the monetary authorities in their pursuit of monetary policy as they impinge upon, and work through, the Scottish banks. Inevitably, we have touched on these matters in earlier chapters, but here we must take them all together and look at them from the central standpoint of policy. Monetary policy in this country today operates through four main instruments: interest rates; 'open-market' action; the special deposit mechanism; and directives or 'requests'. There is a fifth, very important weapon in controls over hire purchase contracts, but this does not involve the commercial banks directly, and we shall ignore it here. We shall take the four policy measures that impinge on the

[1] If the banks buy their bonds from the public with no compensating sales by the authorities the above analysis does not hold good.

banks as a framework for observing the relations of the Scottish banks to monetary policy.

Interest Rates

The first element of monetary policy, interest rates, will not detain us long. The practices of the Scottish banks in regard to their interest rates (as we saw in Chapter 11) present few significant differences from those of the English banks and none that are of major significance for policy. There are slight differences of level—deposit rates a shade lower, overdraft rates a shade higher—but the important thing from the point of view of policy action is that the Scottish rates, like those in England, move broadly in step with Bank Rate. One change of practice since the war has a certain significance for policy; this is the retention of the full normal margin between the Scottish overdraft rates and Bank Rate when the latter moves to a very high level. Previously it was the custom for this margin to narrow when Bank Rate rose to 6 per cent, and to disappear when it reached 7 per cent. Now, however, when Bank Rate is at the crisis level of 7 per cent, Scottish overdraft rates are $8\frac{1}{2}$ and 9 per cent, at which levels they must surely have an impact on some borrowers.

But there is a further aspect of interest policy which has some bearing on the Scottish banks. It will be recalled that the Radcliffe Report laid a good deal of stress on the so-called 'Roosa effect' of interest rate changes and the influence that this supposedly has on the lending activities of financial intermediaries. The mechanism of this is, briefly, that when interest rates are raised by the actions of monetary policy, the capital values of fixed interest securities are forced down and this inhibits lending by the institutions in one or other (perhaps both) of two ways. In the first place, the fall in the market value of their portfolios may make the institutions feel less liquid: this, to be effective, would have to result in their building up compensating reserves of cash or short-term assets. Secondly, and this is much more relevant to the banks, the fall in the market values of securities will deter financial institutions from selling them in order to acquire other assets.

During the last few years the sale of gilt-edged securities has been the major vehicle of expansion of bank advances, and a means of controlling it is of great importance to the authorities. But whether the Roosa effect can be relied upon to do this is doubtful. There are two important reasons for this. One is that the banks hold appreciable amounts of short-dated stocks the capital values of which decline least when interest rates rise; furthermore—and this perhaps is even

201

more important—they have considerable tranches of securities due to mature each year. The second reason is the frequently overlooked fact that capital gains and losses on the portfolios of the banks are treated as income for tax purposes, since the banks are classed as 'dealers' in these securities. The effect of this second factor is automatically to reduce all losses on the sale of gilt-edged by about a half.

One would expect the Scottish banks to be more vulnerable to the Roosa effect than the English banks, in that their investments have long formed a larger proportion of their total assets, and are of longer average maturity. However, we have seen that, proportionately, their holdings of short-dated stocks are similar to those of the English banks; this means that they normally have comparable amounts of securities maturing in any given year and so contributing to liquidity. In recent years the behaviour of the Scottish banks' investments and advances shows no signs of greater sensitivity to the influence of high interest rates. It must, however, be conceded that a really sharp use of interest rates for this purpose has not been tried. Indeed during recent phases of large-scale liquidation of securities by the banks their ability to do so has to an extent depended on official support of the gilt-edged market. If the Roosa effect were ever called into play on an appreciable scale the Scottish banks' portfolios would be bound to depreciate more than those of the English—indeed they did so in the mid-'fifties—and this could conceivably be pushed to the point where it affected their actions.

Open-Market Action
In the pure theory of monetary policy 'open-market policy' is the name given to the action taken by the authorities to influence the volume of bank credit by means of the purchase and sale of securities in the open-market. At the level of simple exposition it is usually presented as amounting to a straight swap of securities for cash between the authorities on the one hand and the public on the other, a swap which has the effect of contracting (by a sale of securities) or expanding (by a purchase) the cash base, particularly that part of it composed of the commercial banks' balances at the central bank. This has the further effect of producing a multiplied contraction, or expansion, of the superstructure of bank credit. But in Britain (as distinct from the United States) the reality of the matter has hardly ever coincided with this simplified account, and in recent decades the position has become even more complicated. To begin with, for the 'cash base' we must now substitute the 'liquidity base': it must

include, that is, all the liquid assets—Treasury bills, commercial bills, short-term bonds, guaranteed export credits—which in one way or another, directly or indirectly, make up the quantum of assets which the commercial banks are permitted to 'count' towards their liquidity ratios. Leaving aside for the moment special deposits, contraction and expansion of this base no longer takes place only through swaps of securities for cash, but also through alteration of the structure of public debt by means of funding operations. Pressure on the liquidity base now requires the authorities to take action which will restrict the quantity of Treasury bills carried by the banking system as a whole (i.e. including the discount market). The principal way of doing this is to reduce the volume of the Treasury bill issue as a whole, either by funding bills into longer-term securities, or by using a budget surplus to reduce the size of the floating debt; but pressure can also be exerted by raising short-term interest rates and so encouraging the purchase of Treasury bills by non-bank holders.[1]

Whatever means are used to restrict or relax the supply of Treasury bills to the banking system the important consideration for the authorities, as far as the commercial banks are concerned, is that they should maintain a liquidity ratio of some definite order.[2] This provides the necessary fulcrum against which the actions of the authorities can press. Hence the Bank of England's request to the Clearing

[1] Even this is a highly simplified picture of the way in which the authorities operate. For example it excludes one important type of open-market action, namely the almost daily action by the authorities to smooth out shortages and surpluses of money in the money market as they arise from the vast and continuous turnover of funds between the private and the public sectors. The purpose of these operations is, from the policy point of view, negative in that they aim to eliminate unwanted disturbances to interest rates. Another complication is that because of the continual maturing of long-term debt the authorities are faced with a constant need to issue funded debt, simply to maintain any given maturity structure of debt. This means that action to increase or relax pressure on the liquidity base comes down to an acceleration or deceleration in the rate of sale of long-term debt to the public. Yet another complication is the fact that the rate of sale of long-term securities to the public has an influence on the long-term rate of interest, and in recent years this has increasingly become an objective of the debt operations of the authorities.

[2] Contrary to what is often said an absolutely fixed ratio is not what is wanted. The ideal ratio is a ratio which can move, but which the banker will always try to restore to some definite level. If a ratio is prescribed by law (as are the minimum cash ratios in the us) then the authorities cannot take action to force the ratio down unless there is some means whereby the banks can put themselves within the law (e.g. the rediscount facilities of the Federal Reserve Banks). In this case the pressure has to be exerted by some other means, such as a limitation on the period of borrowing from the central bank.

banks, in 1955, that they should maintain a minimum liquidity ratio of 30 per cent (now reduced to 28 per cent), and the somewhat later request to other banks, including the Scottish banks, that they should observe their 'usual' minimum ratios.[1] We have seen that while the Scottish banks are not by tradition so 'ratio-conscious' as the English banks, they do have a strong interest in maintaining an adequate reserve of liquid assets, particularly money market assets. This means that there has always been some point at which a shortage of liquid assets would cause them to feel illiquid and to want to replenish their liquidity by reducing their non-liquid assets. But in the past this point has been much less clearly defined than in the English case. The recent official request that each bank individually should observe its usual minimum was not particularly helpful to banks which had never had any hard and fast rules about reserve ratios —of cash or liquid assets; but its effect may have been to cause the banks to make up their minds on what their 'usual minima' should be.

Would it help the operation of monetary policy if all vagueness about the Scottish banks' liquidity ratio was removed, and they were required to observe a quite definite minimum? The answer is no, and the reason for it bears on the apparent contrast between the positions of the English and Scottish banks in this matter. The fact is that the requirement of the Clearing banks that they observe a 30 per cent minimum (or whatever figure is eventually evolved) is in one sense ineffective: it does not determine precisely the actual ratio that they observe through time. If these banks cannot fall below this ratio of liquid assets without incurring some penalty (even if it is only official displeasure) they must normally—and quite apart from the seasonal factor—work above it.[2] Their objective will not be to maintain a fixed ratio, as for example they do in the case of their cash ratio; they will aim at some minimum level, rather higher than 30 per cent, towards which they will always attempt to get back, if they depart from it. Thus although the 30 per cent ratio obviously determines the broad level of liquid assets at which they work, it will not be the precise operative ratio. The behaviour of the Scottish banks is probably

[1] In February 1958 when the Radcliffe Committee took evidence from the Scottish banks there had been no request to these banks from the Bank of England about observing a minimum ratio: see *Radcliffe Evidence*, Q. 5027. According to a statement in *The Banker* of June 1960 (p. 376), the request to the Scottish and Northern Irish banks to observe their 'usual' minima had by then been made. It is now envisaged that the English banks' minimum may be gradually lowered to some figure under 30 per cent.

[2] See p. 203, note 2.

very similar to this, though as we have seen, at a much lower (true) ratio of liquid assets. They too will normally be *aiming* at some level of liquid assets, rather than established at this level; and the fact that their liquid assets are so near to minimum requirements means that in all probability the ultimate floor of their liquidity ratio is hardly less firm than in the English case.

Should the Scottish banks be required to observe a minimum liquidity ratio equal to that of the Clearing banks? The cash position is a complication which obstructs any attempt to impose a uniform liquidity ratio on the two groups of banks, but the Scottish banks could feasibly be required to raise their holdings of short assets to a minimum of (say) 22 per cent of deposits. But there would be little point in this. It would merely find a home for an extra slice of the floating debt; the amount involved would not be large—perhaps £70 million at the most; it would be a once-for-all operation; and it would have only a slight effect on the 'gearing' between the liquidity base and the volume of bank credit.

Special Deposits

In 1958, along with the relaxing of all restrictions on bank lending, the Bank of England announced a new control measure: the 'special deposits' mechanism. Under this innovation the Bank can call upon the Clearing banks and the Scottish banks to deposit funds with it in special Treasury accounts. These deposits, which carry interest calculated weekly at the average rate of the previous Treasury bill tender, are not to be included in liquid assets for the purpose of reckoning liquidity ratios. The purpose of this measure is to give the authorities a means of reducing the banks' liquidity without having to resort to the net funding of short-term debt: there are occasions when conditions in the gilt-edged market make funding difficult or when it would conflict with other objectives—for example a desire to keep long-term interest rates down.

The special deposits arrangement was originally recommended to the banking world as an instrument that would obviate future 'requests' to the banks to limit their advances; and it was described at the time as a temporary measure to be reconsidered when the Radcliffe Committee reported. In the event the Committee expressed a preference for the alternative device of the prescribed variable liquidity ratio. But the Bank of England preferred its own variant of the direct liquidity control. Not that originally it had much fondness at all for the principle of direct action on liquidity; but action was forced upon it and the first special deposit call went out in April 1960.

This was followed by a second in June of the same year, and a third in the sterling crisis in July 1961. The third call raised the prescribed percentage (of special deposits to gross deposits) to 3 per cent for the Clearing banks and $1\frac{1}{2}$ per cent for the Scottish banks; at each of the previous calls the Scottish percentage was half that of the English banks. On only one of the three occasions did the special deposit call appear to reduce the liquidity ratios of the banks, and in this case it merely reversed a previous increase. In general the calls seem to have been met partly by sales of gilt-edged, and partly out of concurrent increases in liquidity due to public finance. On the last occasion when a call was made the figures suggest that the authorities may indeed have taken steps to ensure that the call had no impact on bank liquidity, and that it should merely replace an equivalent volume of advances within the banks' assets. During 1963 special deposits were progressively released as part of the expansionary policy of that year.

The significant point about the position of the Scottish banks in relation to the use of special deposits, so far, is that the calls on them have been only one-half of those on the Clearing banks. It is usually assumed that the reason for this discrimination is the special needs of the Scottish economy; that the intention has been to put a lighter pressure on a region which, economically, is lagging behind certain other parts of the country. But there has actually been no clear official explanation of the policy. There is, indeed, a strong argument for this kind of discrimination, where it is technically possible, when anti-inflationary policies are being applied. A positive policy of encouraging expansion in the lagging regions has at last been firmly embraced in Britain. This being so it is natural to expect that a policy which encourages even greater expenditure in these regions at times when the whole economy is being given its head, must logically include a willingness to subject them to a lighter degree of restraint when the economy is being reined in. But having stated this as a principle one must promptly recognize that monetary policy allows comparatively little scope for discrimination between geographical areas. To begin with, it is impossible to insulate any particular region from the broader expenditure-reducing effects of a restrictive credit policy. Nor, in a country as financially unified as Britain, is it possible to apply *market* techniques of policy—interest rate changes and open-market operations—in a regionally discriminatory way. What can be done is to exempt particular areas from the application of 'control'-type measures when they are among the policy weapons in active use. If this is done certain investment schemes in these areas

206

may continue, when otherwise they might have been postponed. There are obvious possibilities of applying directives of various kinds in this way, and we shall look at these measures in the next section. But where Scotland and Northern Ireland are concerned, each with its own set of banks, it is also possible to discriminate in the special deposit calls.[1] Thus in July 1961 the Scottish banks were required to immobilize £12 million of resources, instead of the £24 million which the full 3 per cent call, as applied to the English banks, would have claimed. In theory this difference of £12 million[2] could be used to sustain bank lending in Scotland; and on this particular occasion this was the probable effect since the special deposit call was accompanied by a specific request to the banking system to reduce advances.

However, there is a justification for discrimination in the special deposit call on purely technical grounds which have nothing to do with the state of the Scottish economy. We have seen that the operative liquidity ratios of the Scottish banks are about one half those of the English banks. According to the theory of credit creation this means that a given change in the minimum liquidity ratio of the Scottish banks (which is what a special deposit call effectively causes) has approximately the same effect on the total credit volume as a change of twice the size in the English banks' liquidity ratios. In other words, if we assume that the purpose of the mechanism is to influence the volume of credit, the authorities have been making this discrimination in favour of the Scottish banks at no cost to themselves in terms of the technical effects of the special deposit mechanism. Indeed, one might argue that a real concession to the needs of the Scottish economy would reflect itself in an even wider difference between the Scottish and English banks in the special deposit calls. But as we have seen, there is some doubt as to how far the mechanism has really been used in this way: if, indeed, it is to be regarded simply

[1] The possibilities of regional discrimination are rather more complicated than the above account reveals. A fuller examination will be found in my article 'Credit Policy and the Regional Problem', *The Bankers' Magazine*, September 1960, pp. 151–8.

[2] There are of course regions of England and Wales whose economic problems are every bit as serious as those of Scotland. But since they are not served by separate banks any discrimination in bank lending in their favour would have to come as the result of an administrative arrangement *within* the Clearing banks themselves. In some respects these areas are better placed than either Scotland or Northern Ireland to obtain such treatment in that the possibilities of a redistribution of lending in their favour, within the total of Clearing banks' advances, are greater simply because of the larger scale of English bank lending and the wider area involved.

as 'ritualistic'[1] then the credit effects of any particular percentage call are irrelevant.

Directives

Besides changes in interest rates, open-market operations and special deposit calls, the British monetary authorities have, since the war, resorted to various 'requests'—in effect, directives—to the commercial banks to follow particular lines of action in their lending policy.[2] Before July 1955, these requests were broadly qualitative in form. The banks were asked to restrict credit to 'essential purposes' and to observe priorities which varied from time to time but have included the defence programme, the export drive and projects designed to increase productivity. They were also asked to limit or eschew specific types of lending such as loans for the finance of hire purchase, or for the speculative holding of stocks. Until 1958 the granting of bank loans for capital purposes was subject to the approval of the Capital Issues Committee which, until 1953, also controlled the terms of such loans.

In July 1955 there was a new departure in the series of 'requests'. This was a year of strong inflationary pressure. Bank advances had begun to rise in 1954 and this went on during the first half of 1955 in spite of the pressure exerted on bank liquidity by the action of the authorities and also by the increased appetite of the public for Treasury bills with the higher rates of interest then prevailing. This pressure on liquidity held down, and indeed caused some decline in, the total of bank deposits; but the banks were able to go on expanding advances by selling gilt-edged. The authorities took the view that even though bank deposits were falling the increases in advances were inflationary. In July the Chancellor (Mr R. A. Butler) made a request to the banks, through the Governor of the Bank of England, that they should make 'a positive and significant' reduction in their advances. This was the forerunner of other requests into which the

---

[1] Cf. R. S. Sayers: 'English Policy on Interest Rates, 1958–62', *Banca Nazionale del Lavoro Quarterly Review*, June 1962, p. 111. In the 6th edition of his *Modern Banking*, p. 125, Professor Sayers referring to the different treatment of the Scottish banks says, 'possibly it is based on recognition of the fact that the Scottish banks have rather more of the element of savings bank business, and have held rather higher proportion of government bonds'. I would not myself give much weight to these reasons; I think it more likely that the policy reflects a desire to give some visible evidence of favoured treatment to the Scottish economy as a whole.

[2] For a summary of direct control measures over capital issues and bank borrowing up to 1958, see *Radcliffe Memoranda*, vol. 1, pp. 103–4.

total quantity of bank advances entered as an explicit objective of official policy. In 1956, the banks were asked 'that the contraction of credit should be resolutely pursued'; while in 1957 they were 're-quired' to restrict their advances to the average level of the previous twelve months. Finally, and in spite of Heathcoat-Amory's hope when he introduced the special deposit device, that it would allow the authorities to dispense with requests for restriction of advances, Selwyn Lloyd issued a request to the banks to put a ceiling on their advances, along with a special deposits call, in his measures to deal with the 1961 crisis. The problem in 1961, as in 1955, was that the ability of the authorities to restrict bank liquidity, and so prevent a rise in deposits, did not prevent the banks from expanding advances at the expense of their holdings of gilt-edged securities. So far the authorities have shown no willingness to employ the special deposit mechanism positively against this substitution, and so they were forced in 1961 to revert to a quantitative request.

The Scottish banks have been subject to these requests along with the other banks in the country. But it appears that when they requested a reduction in advances, in July 1955, the authorities went to a much smaller degree of trouble in making their wishes known to the outside banks than to the Clearers. The Scottish bankers told the Radcliffe Committee that they were not consulted at all on this; it is not even clear how they were notified of the request. They were left to make their own interpretation of a 'positive and significant reduc-tion'—as indeed were the English banks.[1] The English bankers decided that the words required a 10 per cent reduction in advances; and with this decision in view the Committee of General Managers of the Scottish Banks decided that for them a $7\frac{1}{2}$ per cent cut was appropriate in view of the fact that Scottish bank advances had not been rising as rapidly as English advances. But, apparently, no word was vouchsafed as to what the authorities thought of this interpreta-tion; nor at the time was there any guidance about exemptions, such as export credits, from the squeeze.[2] In the event Scottish banks' advances (excluding loans to the nationalized industries) fell by 9·6 per cent between July 1955 and January 1956; as the total had risen only slightly in the first half of 1955 the fall over the year as a whole was quite marked—much more so than in England where the decline

---

[1] See *Radcliffe Evidence*, QQ. 4918–32. One interesting fact revealed in this evidence is that there was 'at least one case where a Scottish bank was called in question to explain what appeared to be a move contrary to what was expected of it'.

[2] Ibid., QQ. 4935–6.

in the latter part of the year merely cancelled out the earlier rise.

With the exception of Harold Macmillan's request for continued contraction of credit, in July 1956, the subsequent directives have been more specific than the first Butler request as to what was expected of the banks. In 1957 and 1961 the banks were asked to place a ceiling on the advances, in the one case at the average level of the previous year, and in the other at the level at which they then stood. In 1956, Mr Macmillan made his request in the presence of the Governor of the Bank of England and 'of leading representatives of the Clearing banks, Scottish banks and other banking institutions operating in the United Kingdom'. From that occasion forward it seems that the lines of communication between the authorities and all the banks—but especially the outside banks—have been improved. In the case of the Scottish banks this improvement has continued and has been reinforced by the plight of the Scottish economy and its need for special treatment. In connection with the regional application of monetary policy it is interesting to notice that the first move in the major relaxation of 1958 came in the form of an indication to the banks that they could begin to lend freely in areas of high unemployment.[1] We have also remarked[2] that the behaviour of Scottish bank advances in 1961–2 suggests that the Scottish banks were exempted from the 1961 requests.

Throughout the post-war period the distortion of the banks' assets structure, the legacy mainly of war finance, has created problems for monetary policy and has underlain the resort to directives to control the level of bank advances in times of inflationary pressure. What of the future? In particular, what difference has the tremendous liquidation of gilt-edged by the banks, since 1958, made to the prospects for monetary control? At mid-1964 the investments of the Clearing banks were 15 per cent of their deposits, while those of the Scottish banks were 26 per cent. With the parallel rise in their advances ratios to around 50 per cent bankers, English and Scottish, have declared that the question of safe limits now definitely arises. If this really is the case then it eases the operation of monetary policy: when the banks are down to their minimum level of securities, advances are controlled by deposits, and this increases their sensitivity to the various devices for controlling liquidity, including special deposits. From the investment ratios just quoted it looks as though the Scottish banks are further from this point than the English banks,

[1] The Northern Ireland banks were exempted from the restraints on advances throughout the credit restriction of 1955–8.
[2] p. 132.

and hence less amenable to control over their advances: but it depends which ratio is the important one for bankers. The Scottish advances ratio, calculated as a percentage of gross deposits, is practically the same as that of the English banks, and it is this ratio that bankers at present seem to be concerned about rather than the investment ratio. In both cases the advances ratio was around 50 per cent in mid-1964, and for the time being this figure may well be invested with a special and cautionary significance. (It may be that even at that time the Scottish banker regarded himself as still having some leeway. This is because the ratio on which he has his eye may be that of advances to deposits *plus* notes in circulation, and this, in mid-1964, stood at 45 per cent.) But how permanently will bankers, Scottish and English, regard a situation where one-half of their assets are in the form of advances as the furthest point to which they can extend themselves. Past events suggest that the power of particular ratios to impede movement by the banks towards more profitable asset patterns is not immutable. Bankers take time to get used to changes as large and rapid as those since 1958. But often as not, they do get used to them in the end, and the new position becomes transformed into a base for a further thrust forward. Indeed the agitation of the English banks in 1963 for a downward revision of their required minimum liquidity ratio suggests that this may already be the case. It is possible that both the Scottish and English banks would require some increase in the proprietors' interest before they allowed their advances to increase much; but this is not very difficult to arrange these days. However, while giving full weight to the view that a further rise in advances ratios at the expense of investments is far from ruled out, one must recognize that there is some ultimate limit to this process and the banks are very much nearer to it now than they were in 1958. Further increases in advances there may be, but they are likely to be more cautiously, even tentatively, undertaken than hitherto; and the problem of control that they are likely to present the authorities with, should be comparatively small.

CHAPTER 14

THE SUMMING UP

Looking back from the 1960s it is apparent that the comparatively static phase of British banking extending from the early 'twenties to the early 'fifties was exceptional. Scottish banking, which had consolidated itself so much earlier than English banking, had actually enjoyed a longer period, reaching back into the last century, during which change was slow. Today the pace of technological and economic change is much faster, and the rate of adaptive reaction forced on the banks has risen in equal measure.

The Scottish banks are subject to all the forces that press on British banking institutions. But at several points in this book we have seen them having to meet additional or variant pressures which stem either from their regional position or from their past history. These affect them in all areas of their activities. They are particularly important in conditioning the market environment within which they provide their services. The geographical spread of the Scottish population; the amount and types of banking services which that population wants and which in turn are strongly conditioned not only by the wealth and income of the country, but also by the past development of the Scottish branch network; all these forces native to the region have a strong influence on the character of banking within Scotland. On the specifically financial plane the regional position of the Scottish banks leaves them peculiarly exposed to loss of deposits when the ownership of Scottish business moves south or simply when Scots are induced to place money on deposit in a building society which has its account with an English bank. The high savings content of Scottish bank deposits which in the past has been, and probably yet remains, an element of stability may, with increasing competition for funds, prove a source of weakness. But in recent years the strongest drag on the growth of the Scottish banks' resources has been the state of the Scottish economy itself. For all the importance of their London business, and despite the geographical widening of their interests following their incursion into hire purchase finance, the fortunes of the Scottish banks remain basically tied to those of the Scottish economy with all its difficulties, past and present. Until these difficulties are overcome it is unlikely that the Scottish banks will be able to equal even the very modest rate of expansion which the English banks have enjoyed during the last decade.

As we survey the Scottish banks at this point in their history when so many of the original conditions under which they grew up have gone, when most of their characteristic elements have ceased to make them distinctive, and when the pace of change in all directions is quickening, we must ask ourselves two questions. The first is this: Does it now benefit Scotland to have its own group of banks? And the second: Is the Scottish banking system likely to survive as a separate system?

We have remarked on some undoubted disadvantages under which the Scottish banks labour and these must be reflected in the cost of the services, including the finance, with which they furnish the Scottish economy. The Scottish banks are—by English standards—a small-scale system and this presumably adds something to the real costs of the services they provide since there are economies of scale in banking. Added to this is the fact that the Scottish banks carry systems of branch offices, determined partly by historical, partly by geographical, factors—systems which because of the small size of many of the offices impose comparatively high operating costs. Some of the effects of these circumstances appear in the interest-rate structure of the Scottish banks: they charge higher rates to the average borrower than the English banks, and they pay lower rates on those of their deposits that bear interest. At first sight this fact strikes one as an important disadvantage of the system to the Scottish economy. But this view must immediately be qualified by recognition that the difference is small—a matter, in most cases, of $\frac{1}{2}$ per cent more on lending-rates and $\frac{1}{2}$ per cent less on deposit-rates. The total extra 'cost-plus-loss' of the wider spread must be under £4 million annually, but not all of this is a net burden on the Scottish economy. In part the wider spread of interest rates is the concomitant of lower charges for other services (as well as a higher level of service through the more widespread branch system) compared with the English system. It is of course true that those affected by the less favourable interest rate structure and those enjoying the lower charges are not always the same people. Where this is the case the effect is redistributive and, while it certainly complicates the picture, it does not constitute a burden on the Scottish economy as a whole. A more important point perhaps is the fact that, as far as borrowers are concerned, any extra 'burdens' that the higher lending rates impose are not equally distributed: the very largest firms escape it. However, giving all due weight to this point, the case is not strong since, with the 'gross regional product' of Scotland running somewhere in the region of £2,000 million per year, the sums involved are clearly negligible.

Looked at either as a deterrent to borrowing or simply as a 'burden' on industry the higher Scottish lending rates may be ignored. In comparing banking systems small differences in the cost of finance are much less important than differences in its availability, and here there are no grounds for supposing that the representative borrower from a Scottish bank is worse served than he would be in England. Indeed there is some evidence, which we reviewed in Chapter 10, that he is better served. The Scottish banks may be somewhat readier than the English banks to meet the needs of the small borrower, and to lend for longer periods to all borrowers. Where the Scottish banks do provide inferior facilities is in the range of larger business borrowers: here the smallness of scale of the system is a distinctly inhibiting influence. There is an indirect connection between the Scottish rate structure and the availability of bank finance. The low deposit rate in Scotland may be partly responsible for the poor performance of Scottish deposits in recent years. This sluggishness in the growth of bank resources has not hitherto affected the ability of the Scottish banks to lend, but it may do so in the future now that the liquidation of bond portfolios has brought the volume of lending into closer dependence on the volume of deposits.

Against the possible disadvantages of the separation of the Scottish banks must be set the advantages to Scotland of having institutions that are domiciled within the country. These advantages are more difficult to pin down but there is a strong presumption that they are there. One inheres in the simple fact that control over lending which in all banks, for loans above a certain amount, is centralized, operates closer to the ground in Scotland than in the much larger English system. It is reasonable to expect that this will make for a lending policy more closely geared to the various individual needs of the region. On the other hand the location of the ultimate direction of the Scottish banks away from the metropolitan hub of British finance carries dangers of provincialism and slowness in innovation from which they have not been entirely preserved.

But the continued separate existence of the Scottish banks must be placed in a wider setting of regional finance. Of all the regions of Britain, Scotland is the only one that can boast anything like a regional financial system. For besides the banks there is the important circle of Scottish insurance companies and the group, equally prominent in its own sphere, of Scottish investment trusts. With some other institutions of more recent growth—an issuing house, for example, and some finance companies—the whole adds up to a structure of localized financial institutions which is quite exceptional in Britain. Now it is, of course, questionable just what *financial* significance such localization carries. It has an undoubted occupational significance: the concentration of head offices of the banks and of other financial institutions in Edinburgh adds something to the strongly professional character of that city. But in a financial system as highly integrated as that of Britain one may legitimately doubt if such localization makes much difference to the financial facilities of the region. It is certainly impossible to demonstrate that Scotland receives a clear differential benefit from her native financial system; nevertheless, one may feel persuaded, on general grounds, that some advantage must accrue. So far as this is so it probably has its greatest effect at the longer end of the capital market rather than at the shorter end where the banks operate. But there is a close interconnection at the board level between the banks and the other Scottish financial institutions; and, indirectly, the existence of this locally-based system of banks helps to sustain the whole separate financial structure of the region.

Of course, one may also ask: Is it good for Britain as a whole that the Scottish banks should survive as separate entities? This raises somewhat different issues. It would certainly be disadvantageous to the country as a whole if the maintenance of separate banking institutions in Scotland retarded the progress of the Scottish economy; or if, without doing this, it brought benefits to Scotland at the expense of the rest of the country. I doubt if a serious case could be made out on either score. Such criticism as can be directed at the Scottish banks on the former of these two grounds, rests on faults of omission in lending policy which are by no means peculiar to them. But against any possible disadvantages of these kinds there must be set a clear advantage from the national point of view. This is the fact that the separation of the Scottish system increases the number of independent units within the British banking system. This is very important. The British banking system is extraordinarily concentrated. This has had the inevitable consequence of reducing to a handful the number of independent centres of decision within the system. In any industry this kind of situation is potentially harmful to innovation and development since it may seriously limit the diversity of thought and decision. It is particularly dangerous in banking

215

where the forces of conservatism are peculiarly strong. The Scottish banks add only three independent units to the British system, but where overall numbers are already so small this addition is not negligible. Furthermore the importance of this point has been demonstrated specifically in the Scottish case: it was a Scottish bank that led the way in the acquisition of a hire purchase finance company.

But will the Scottish banking system survive in its present, or indeed in any, form? One can only attempt an answer to this question for a comparatively short period ahead—say the next twenty years. Even within as short a period as this the possibilities are very wide, such is the state of flux in the economy at large and the financial system in particular. The most extreme possibility that one can contemplate is a complete merging of all the Scottish banks with English banks to form one consolidated system. This can be ruled out in the foreseeable future. The national susceptibilities of the Scots are still strong enough to deter any single bank from moving in this direction; such a move would have to be made by all in concert and, short of a catastrophic deterioration in the present competitive position of the banks, this is most unlikely. Competitive pressure on the Scottish banks will continue to increase and could become really acute if, for example, the trustee savings banks should obtain the coveted power to offer chequeing facilities. But serious though the threat could become, there are no grounds for thinking that it could not be met.

A predictable change in Scottish banking is a further consolidation of the system. At least one more union seems likely although the fact that one of the obvious candidates, the British Linen Bank, is owned by so powerful a bank as Barclays reduces its predictability. On purely economic grounds the Scottish system, reduced perhaps to four banks, might well be viable for a long time. Success in the committing of ever larger amounts of banking operations to the computer might affect things; but co-operation between the banks in the use of high-capacity machines could obviate any drastic consequences for the structure of the system.

But in attempting to discern the future patterns of Scottish banking it is a mistake to concentrate on development internal to the system. The most powerful forces for change may lie in quite a different direction. For the time being the British approach to the European Economic Community is in abeyance, but the internationalization of the capital markets of Western Europe and North America is developing steadily. Links are being forged between British institutions and those of the Continent and America, and the big English joint-stock banks have begun to participate in this movement. Once before when, in the decade following the First World War, a similar outgoing movement took place, some at least of the Scottish banks appeared to think that in order to reap the full advantages which this development offered they would do well to link themselves more closely with one or other of the London banks. The present trend of increasing interest in external finance may induce a similar reaction. But history never repeats itself exactly. Today the most dynamic element in British finance is the group of merchant banks. It may be by linking themselves with one or other of these resourceful institutions that the Scottish banks will find a way through to more expansive fields of action than commercial banking at present affords.

INDEX

References to the Scottish banks and the London Clearing banks or 'English banks' occur throughout this book. In this index references listed under these headings are restricted to those which present special points of interest and which are not listed under other indexed topics. References to journals and periodicals are to unsigned articles and editorial notes only. All other references to published work are made under authors' names.

For Product Safety Concerns and Information please contact our EU
representative GPSR@taylorandfrancis.com Taylor & Francis Verlag GmbH,
Kaufingerstraße 24, 80331 München, Germany

Printed and bound by CPI Group (UK) Ltd, Croydon, CR0 4YY
01/05/2025
01858397-0001